CITYSCAPES

Th

Other books by Anthony Burton published by André Deutsch

Remains of a Revolution (1975)

Josiah Wedgwood (1976)

The Miners (1976)

Back Door Britain (1977)

The Green Bag Travellers (with Pip Burton, 1978)

The Past at Work (1980)

The Past Afloat (1982)

The Rise and Fall of King Cotton (1984)

Wilderness Britain (1985)

Steaming Through Britain (1987)

CITYSCAPES

A TOUR AROUND THE GREAT BRITISH CITIES

Anthony Burton

**With photographs by
Helen McQuillan and John Brown**

ANDRE DEUTSCH

First published in 1990 by
André Deutsch Limited
105–106 Great Russell Street
London WC1B 3LJ

Text copyright © 1990 by Anthony Burton
Photographs copyright © 1990 by Helen McQuillan and John Brown
Cartography by Taurus Graphics, Abingdon, Oxon

British Library Cataloguing in Publication Data

Burton, Anthony
    Cityscapes: a tour around the Great British cities.
    1. Great Britain. Cities. Visitors' guides
    I. Title
    914.1'04858

    ISBN 0 233 98429 1
    ISBN 0 233 98430 5 pbk

    Printed in Hong Kong

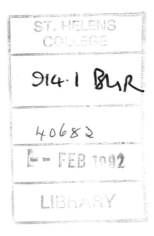

CONTENTS

General key to the maps for each city

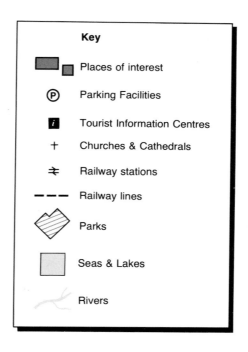

Key

Places of interest

Ⓟ Parking Facilities

i Tourist Information Centres

+ Churches & Cathedrals

⇌ Railway stations

– – – Railway lines

Parks

Seas & Lakes

Rivers

INTRODUCTION

'Woe to the bloody city! it is full of lies and robbery' – a biblical quotation which many would apply to the cities of today. Not me; I like cities, and as about one-third of the population lives in cities, one must assume that at least some of them agree. That is not to close one's eyes to the problems which produce the 'inner city crisis' headlines almost every week, but to affirm that cities remain centres of innovation, commercial dynamos and repositories of rich, historical treasures. I decided that it was time to reassess the great cities – not the capital, which is unique; and not the four-star attractions such as Bath or York; their appeal is obvious and they have long since settled down to the profitable task of marketing their wares. But other cities have their own appeal, and can range in size from places such as St David's, scarcely more than a village but centred on a cathedral, to the Victorian manufacturing towns whose growth eventually earned them their new status.

What I was looking for was, I suppose, diversity; those characteristics which differentiate one city from another. This is not an exercise in tourist promotion: cities depend on people living in them, not just pausing for a weekend, but the reasons for choosing to live there are often not so different from those for choosing to visit. There seem to be two trends working in opposite directions,

each of which has a potential for disaster or success. On the one hand there is commercial development based on the international, anonymous building which could be dropped as easily into Portsmouth as Leicester or, if it comes to that, Hong Kong. It is design which has no sense of place, and one sees it on every hand. The other extreme is a Disneyfication of the past in which every disused mill becomes a heritage centre and every cobbled alley is knee deep in film crews making commercials for wholemeal bread. I believe that there is another way which conserves the best of the old but is not frightened of the boldest of new ideas. This is what I was hoping to find on my city travels.

I had decided early on that I wanted to travel by train. Driving into a strange city can be a nightmare of one-way streets and hunting for parking places – scarcely the best introduction. The need to concentrate on the traffic means that you do not get any feel for a place or its surroundings until you switch off the ignition and climb out of the car. The railway offers its own perspectives and delivers you in or close to the heart of the city; besides, I enjoy train travel.

The other decision that I had taken was that I was going to look for the positive aspects of the cities. There has been no shortage of critics in recent years, but if there is to be hope for the future, as much emphasis must be placed on identifying what is good, seeing what can be used as the basis for renewal.

When I was discussing the proposal with my publishers, the Great British Cities Marketing Group was mentioned. These cities had combined to promote themselves; and while they were not the most obvious candidates for tourist prizes, they were claiming special qualities and character. The core of their promotion was short breaks based on rail travel, and they seemed to offer the ideal basis for this book. I accepted their hospitality, and am grateful for their help, but I tried not to let their generosity colour my judgement. The views of the eighteen cities are my own and not theirs. I am also grateful to Gold Star Holidays who provided me with free travel.

ACKNOWLEDGEMENTS

We gratefully acknowledge the assistance of Gold Star Holidays and the Great British Cities Marketing Group in helping Anthony Burton to research this book. For those who would like to follow in his footsteps, there is a brochure available offering Great British City Breaks in those cities featured in *Cityscapes*. To obtain a copy, please contact your local travel agent or write to Golden Rail, PO Box 12, York YO1 1YX.

PLYMOUTH

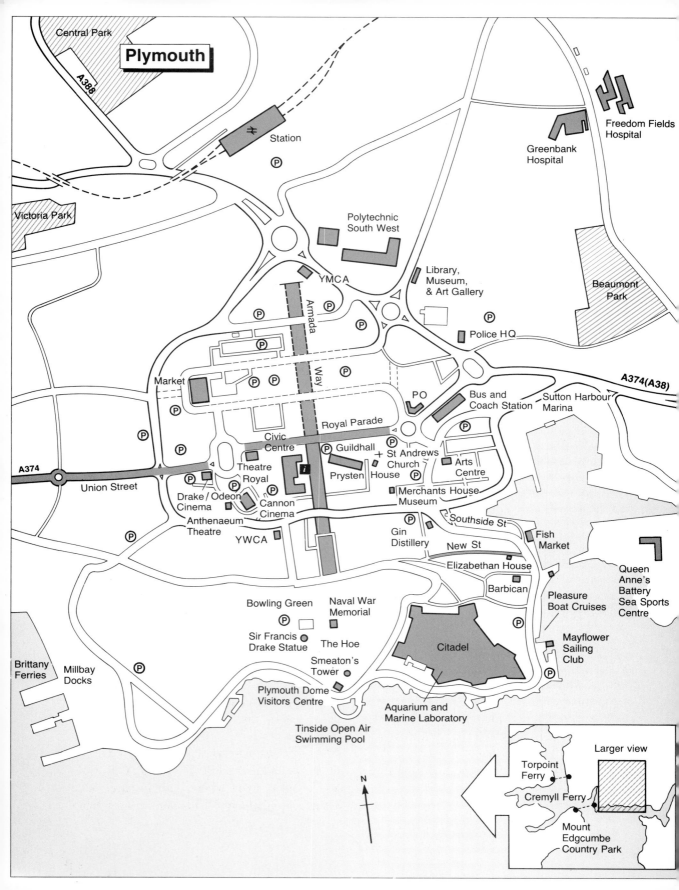

1
PLYMOUTH

The journey to Plymouth from my home in Bristol could hardly have been better. It was early April; a wet January had been followed by a glum February and a dreary March – and then, without so much as a preparatory clearing of the throat, spring arrived. The mist cleared in the heart of Somerset, in that flat land crossed by a network of ditches which began to flash in the sun.

Each mile added to the pleasant sensation of journeying to familiar delights, down a route which for generations of bucket-and-spade children meant West Country holidays, the route of the old Cornish Riviera Express. Everything reinforced the West Country message – from the almost vulgar richness of the red earth, fresh turned for sowing, to the spray-splashing breakers against the sea wall at Teignmouth. We turned inland to another world: dark, wooded, stony cuttings and the softly rounded hills which swell out below the stony heights of Dartmoor. Stone predominated – in little outcrops and quarries, in houses and walls, tiny bridges and high-riding viaducts. When the sea came back in a wide estuary, its mud clinging to the skeletal remains of old boats, one knew Plymouth was just ahead, even though nothing much was in view but the brick chimneys of a power station and the march of terraces up and down the city's hills.

The arrival was an anti-climax: an unremark-able station, and nothing outside except a large traffic island. But as I turned into the main road which runs due south there was a trans-formation – a wide avenue ending in the tall war memorial, the bloated barber-pole stripes of the old Eddystone lighthouse, or Smeaton's Tower, and beyond that the sea. The elements which had been collecting in the journey were all coming together. I tend to be more an alley person than a boulevardier, but if you are going to have a grand processional avenue let it be like this.

I dropped my bag at the hotel, the Grand, which lived up to its name, one of those monumental seaside hotels which seem always to have existed. Normally I find that the best way of getting to know a city is to meander with no pattern or purpose at all, and let the impressions evolve from the wanderings. But on this occasion I decided to do the opposite: I would see it all, spread out before me. I marched off to catch the Cremyll ferry. It may seem a perverse way to set about seeing a city, getting on a boat and leaving it, but the rush of spring sunshine was not without influence, and the idea of a boat trip across a sparkling sea was tempting.

The short boat trip takes you out of the county of Devon and into the Duchy of Cornwall, not far away from where a shopkeeper once inquired politely if I had come across from

Smeaton's Tower, the top of the old Eddystone lighthouse, on Plymouth Hoe

England. What I was going to see was a splendid example of an English country house, gardens and parkland unusually close to a major urban centre. Mount Edgcumbe House was originally built in the sixteenth century, but it took two centuries to create the park and gardens. The formality of flowerbeds dotted with statuary and little pavilions set off the false naturalism of the park, where everything is ordered to create casual beauty. The prophets of the picturesque decreed that the perfect landscape should contain a romantic ruin; if no suitable edifice existed, one had to be built. The folly on the hill is a perfect vantage point from which to view the entire city of Plymouth, and it is this view which made the short journey worthwhile. What I saw was not just a magnificent panorama, but a lesson in history.

The first glance takes in the wide bay of Plymouth Sound, biting deep into the land – the natural feature which called the port into being. Plymouth was then still exposed to southerly winds, so extra protection was provided by the massive breakwater with lights at either end and a guardian fort in the middle. Today the eye is led off through slalom pathways set by buoys, as complex as the flags on a ski slope. Around Drake's Island they go, then off in all directions – to the old harbour and the new, where the cross-channel ferries run, and some lead through the narrows between Cremyll and Devil's Point to direct ships of war to the naval dockyards at Devonport.

Plymouth is revealed as a city turned to the sea, but in a most complicated way. Much of the complexity can be seen from this little hill in Cornwall. The eye soon makes one distinction – between the military and the rest. Military buildings are in unrelieved granite of glistening grey; they begin with the old castle at the mouth of the Plym, continue in the rigid formality of the Citadel and again in the Royal William Victualling Yard and the vast complex at Devonport. In between is seaside Plymouth, where the terraces are prinked out in colour washes and the promenade sweeps up in a long curve to the east, like the bows of some great sailing ship.

Devonport is at once a part of Plymouth and separate from it. The dockyards grew up during the long rumblings of war with France which lasted from the 1680s to the defeat of Napoleon. Seeing it now, with its frigates and submarines lined up for repair and the busy passage of boats through the narrows, it is difficult to imagine that this was a series of mud flats until the first dock was built in 1695. From Mount Edgcumbe the modern docks are a distant prospect,

The naval dockyard entrance: the column marks the boundary between Plymouth and Devonport

but the old docks are very close. King Billy, the colourful figurehead on the point, stands outside a building known prosaically as No 1 Slip. It is a vast timber construction like a huge inverted ship and like the wooden ships it is beautiful but redundant. Privatisation has brought redundancies of both men and buildings, and a possible future for the old part of the dockyard is as a maritime museum. Whatever is done, there should be proper respect for the qualities of the old, which combine the massiveness of the huge stones of the graving docks and warehouses with the intricate details of individual buildings such as No 1 Slip. Devonport is an object lesson to anyone who doubts that it is possible to combine severe practicality with style and even beauty.

My viewing completed I returned to the ferry, said goodbye to the docks and set off to walk back to the city centre. Stonehouse, the area round the docks, is changing: the old is coming down and the new going up, producing some delightful incongruities. Survivors rub somewhat grubby elbows with the newcomers, so that fashionable Jaeger looks out over back-street pubs like the grandly named Lord High Admiral and the simpler Mechanics' Arms.

My way lay down Union Street, which has a bad reputation and has always had a bad reputation. I rather like it. There are unlikely juxtapositions, with Naval and Civilian Outfitters staring across at a second-hand car salesroom, and there are reminders of happier times. The Grand Theatre pub of 1847 has a fine Victorian tiled façade in shades of green and ochre, above which a pensive Ophelia stares at a preoccupied Hamlet. Sadly, the pub having been bought by Fosters Lager, a great banner of blue and gold advertises the Australian beer. Big companies sometimes make decisions which take no account of surroundings or atmosphere, so the vulgar sign ruins a splendid example of a small town pub.

Just across the road is the theatre which went with the pub – the New Palace – with a façade even grander than that of the pub: tiles again and art nouveau lettering which carries across to the Great Western Hotel next door. But the star attractions are the two ceramic scenes showing – what else in Plymouth? – the Spanish Armada setting sail at one side and being destroyed on the other. That is not the only nautical touch: the building boasts a turret for all the world like the top of the first Eddystone lighthouse. Shows have long since given way to discos at the New Palace, but the jaded grandeur is there. In any case, Union Street is not really the place for subtlety. The local pubs have done their best to turn it into Plymouth's answer to Las Vegas. Pubs are not just pubs, but fun pubs with fun names – Diamond Lil's Show Bar abuts Penny's Fun Bar. There is little room for sophistication in Union Street.

This all changes near the Octagon. The bombs of the Second World War blasted the heart of old Plymouth, so the city engineers decided to finish the job. What was left of the old was mostly bundled away so that a new centre could be built. New roads swept around the outside, and the middle was laid out as a grid of wide avenues, flanked by light and bright shops. The plan was devised by Sir Patrick Abercrombie and carried through by John Paton Watson, who wrote enthusiastically: 'Goodbye to the narrow and maze-like streets; broad ways and modern buildings will replace them.' And so they did and so it stayed until 1987, when the motor car was banished from the boulevards and pedestrian precincts were made – not without controversy.

Appropriately Shakespearean murals on the façade of the Grand Theatre pub

Some decried the vandalising of Abercrombie's city scheme, the overlaying of its simplicity with suburban details and the reduction of bustling city streets to provincial complacency. The opposition claims that Abercrombie's scheme was dull and bland and that the new offers people the chance to enjoy shopping without the stench of petrol and the roar of traffic. During my visit work was still in progress, so the water gardens had no water

9

and the flower beds no flowers, but some things seemed to work well. The children's play area in what was once the middle of a busy street was not just 'good design' – a phrase which can mean no more than that it photographs well for glossy magazines – but was fun as well. The children playing on the wooden animals were having a tremendous time. The animals certainly looked more interesting than the ubiquitous rocking motor cars found in the duller shopping precincts. The essential nature of the wide streets is not changed; it is just that people now walk where cars once drove and I found decidedly pleasant the freedom to walk where I pleased.

Inevitably, when a central area is planned en bloc, the overwhelming impression is of uniformity which, unless the planner is a Nash or a Wren, can lead to dullness. Plymouth has enough in the way of odd, quirky features to preserve it from that charge. Sometimes it is a happy conjunction which catches the eye: just off the Royal Parade, a concrete galleon floats out of the façade of the Drake Cinema; but what drew my attention was an odd little group of buildings: a lonely tower, a bank labelled intriguingly 'The Bank', a dull office block and the back end of a theatre. Individually they might not have registered, but together they represented a bizarre mixture. The clock tower was Derry's clock and once had a far more appropriate setting: it formed a centrepiece for the Royal Hotel and the Theatre Royal. The buildings were victims of the war and only the tower survived. Somehow it never quite fitted into the new arrangement, so that what was once a conventional piece of city ornamentation has now become slightly odd. The Bank is even odder – the name does not represent financial hubris, it is not a claim to be the only financial institute in the city. What was once a classic city bank is now an unusual pub – a fitting companion

for the lonely, lost tower. The theatre which has turned its back on the tower is also one of Plymouth's successes, largely because the designers had the sense to make the ground floor into an accessible, open café, popular with shoppers. The office block makes an anonymous backdrop to show off the rest.

The main street which cuts through the centre of the Abercrombie grid is Armada Way (one *does* begin to wish for more imagination in names in Plymouth). It leads to the Hoe via the Civic Centre, which is neither better nor worse than most of its kind, but even here there is another surprising building. Barclays Bank (1952) is the standard Fifties' mixture of regular block design with tall windows and a hint of neo-classical in the decoration. But this one comes with additions – the inevitable Elizabethan sea dog peers out over a bollard at one corner, and a duffel-coated sailor looks sternly from another. In between are Epstein-like figures representing industry. Power holds a stiff zig-zag of lightning in one hand, and a bizarre figure draped like a Grecian god grips a miner's lamp and pick. A walk around the shopping centre of Plymouth is never dull! And this is not the Plymouth that visitors come to see. I saved that for another day as I headed back for the Hoe where Drake's statue peers out across the waves and looks onto the bowling green where games are still regarded more seriously than passing distractions like wars and Armadas.

To turn from new Plymouth to the old is to enter a different world. The new is laid out in a ruthlessly precise pattern, the latter is all odd angles and changing views. This is the world of 'narrow and maze-like streets' which post-war planners turned their backs on and which survived almost by accident.

Then the mood changed, and bold, broad patterns were out and the old and 'characterful' were in. The Barbican was rediscovered, re-developed and is now where the tourists head, especially Americans, for the whole complex grew up around the harbour where the Pilgrim Fathers set sail. The obvious danger is that such an area can be attacked by Disneyism, a disease fatal in old historic town centres. The most obvious first signs are in shops and restaurants: the shops sell only souvenirs or antiques and the restaurants are all Le Vieux Moulin or Giuseppi's, with a likely meal coming out on the wrong side of £15 a head without

This sculpted family watches over the traffic on Armada Way

drinks. A more ominous symptom is the appearance of 'Ye Olde', and when the last resident is replaced by a council employee trying to look sensible wearing Elizabethan costume and horn-rimmed glasses there is no known cure. There are some disturbing signs, but the Barbican has not yet reached the critical stage.

The Mayflower Steps, where the emigrants left England to join the Mayflower

The harbour is the place to start, not because of the Pilgrim Fathers but because it was the heart of the old city. The first impression is of the round-the-bay boat owners shouting their attractions, but this is still a working harbour, with a restrained Customs House and fishing boats riding at their moorings near a fish dock which looks like a small railway station. Here was a real test of the Barbican. How many places do we know where harbours land fresh fish which appears only in the most expensive local restaurants?

Not here: the owners of Platters Café buy their fish from the market opposite their front door. Platters is a chippie, but one where they cook whatever the sea disgorges, so that among the familiar cod and chips and haddock and chips are sea bass and monk fish and John Dory. The place is crowded right through the day and, fortified by their fish, I continued my exploration.

At the harbour the new and old worlds compete for attention: across the water alloy masts with clanking gear and twanging stays mark the new leisure industry which is inevitably taking more and more of the space, as the old working boats diminish in number. The days of prosperous trading are often marked only by fading letters on old buildings. The London and South Western Railway offices still announce that they will carry parcels to all parts – but they won't. And there is a nostalgic whiff of old-style civic pride in a plaque on the quay announcing that the city was provided with iron pipes for its water supply in 1826. It is a long time since sea captains brought in exotic spices from the Indies and treasure from the Spanish Main to fill the stone warehouses. Now many of the old buildings hold antique stalls little better than bric-à-brac stalls at a parish jumble sale. Yet that is not important, for what matters is the integrity of the buildings themselves, and this is the true delight of the Barbican. Plymouth has, it seems, realised that quality is something worth preserving. Building use can change; what matters is the essential structure.

New Street epitomises the special qualities of the Barbican, with its mixture of timber-framed houses and stone warehouses. It is one of the happier paradoxes of the language that premises announcing themselves 'Ye Olde' often turn out to be knee deep in plastic, while a street proclaiming itself 'New' received its name 400 years ago. That was when everyone wanted to be at the heart of one of the most exciting ports in the country. The grandest and richest – the Drakes and the Hawkinses – might keep their distance from the hurly-burly of the new quays, but the captains and merchants wanted to be where the action was. Houses were crammed together in this little street which climbs up the steep hill. What the houses lacked in width they made up for in style and decoration. They lean towards one another across the cobbles like neighbours chatting over the fence. Not much space means not much light, so windows were made as large as possible, not just across the front of a building but projecting as bay windows to bring a little extra illumination. No 32 is now a museum, the Elizabethan House, and a very fine museum it is too. A ship's mast runs from top to bottom and around it spiral the wooden treads of the staircase. Restorers discovered that when a tread was worn the owners hammered a new one on top, so that some were four layers deep. It has been furnished in period, so that it is possible to believe a sea captain might still walk through the door. I was not too surprised to be told that the place was haunted – by a benign ghost which rocks the cradle in the main bedroom.

The Prysten House, a name a mere century old, belonged originally to a merchant and was known as Yogges House. It is very different from the New Street houses, dating back to 1498, built of robust stone and ranged around a courtyard. The Merchant's House nearby is on the grand scale – jettied out over the street, its oak-framed windows contrasting with the rough stone of the walls. It was the home of one William Parker, who made a fortune as a privateer on the Spanish Main and was at one time Mayor of Plymouth. The Prysten House is still used by the church and is open to the public, as is the Merchant's House which is a

museum showing different aspects of city life, based on the tinker-tailor-soldier-sailor list. One room is a reconstructed chemist's shop, which looks like a necromancer's laboratory or an alchemist's store. Neither Prysten nor Merchant can match the Elizabethan House in catching the atmosphere of the past.

New Street could have become twee if it had not retained the character of a trading street. Among the half-timbered houses are the sturdy stone warehouses, whose attraction lies in the contrast between rough, rubble walls and patterns of loading bays and gantries. The higher you go the better it gets, until it ends in a rounded corner which waggons could slide past. Quite suddenly the gritty world of commerce and trade gives way to breezy rows of B & B villas.

New Street is by no means the only one full of interest in the Barbican. Across the water is Looe Street, where restoration was first begun and which is now home to the busy little Arts Centre. And there are odd things to be found in unlikely spots: the Elizabethan garden at the back of New Street boasts an old doorway above which a two-masted merchantman of curious design was carved by someone who may have been a fine mason but was no sailor.

Happily, the Barbican is not just a tourist attraction: people still live and work there, even if the infants' school on Castle Dyke Lane is reduced to a single Italianate tower. And work and tourism are by no means incompatible, particularly if the work is the manufacture of one of Plymouth's notable products – gin. The 200-year-old distillery with its beautiful copper stills runs conducted tours, but the tourists spend more time looking at the audio-visual show than at the distillery itself, which is viewed at a distance through a plate-glass window. As a veteran of distillery visits in Scotland I found this frustrating – it was as if the contrived displays were more real than messy old actuality. It seemed to sum up the dilemma that such areas face: do you lay on 'attractions' or do you let the place speak for itself and visitors make discoveries with a minimum of fuss? It is perhaps worth saying that left to itself the Barbican had degenerated into a slum and its regeneration is almost miraculous.

Not everyone looks for the same thing in an ancient city. There will always be those who want the colouring added, and that they can find in Plymouth. Others take a more puritanical approach, not perhaps inappropriate for the city of the Pilgrim Fathers. Can you mix the new needs of an area which must survive on tourism with the qualities of a workaday seaport? You can if the new has a robust quality which matches the old. I ended my visit with what is perhaps a vindication of the theory that the mixture can succeed. The artist R. O. Lenkiewicz has an enormous mural outside his studio which attracts a lot of attention but how many people visit his gallery? He set out to chronicle the life of Plymouth in a series of big, vibrant canvases which fill every wall of the old warehouse. Art critics may argue among themselves about the quality of his work, but no one can mistake the energy caught and held. The art belongs to Plymouth, just as much as the old warehouse in which it stands, and as long as the city can hold its parts together as firmly as here, it will continue to be a living city and not degenerate into a museum piece.

PORTSMOUTH

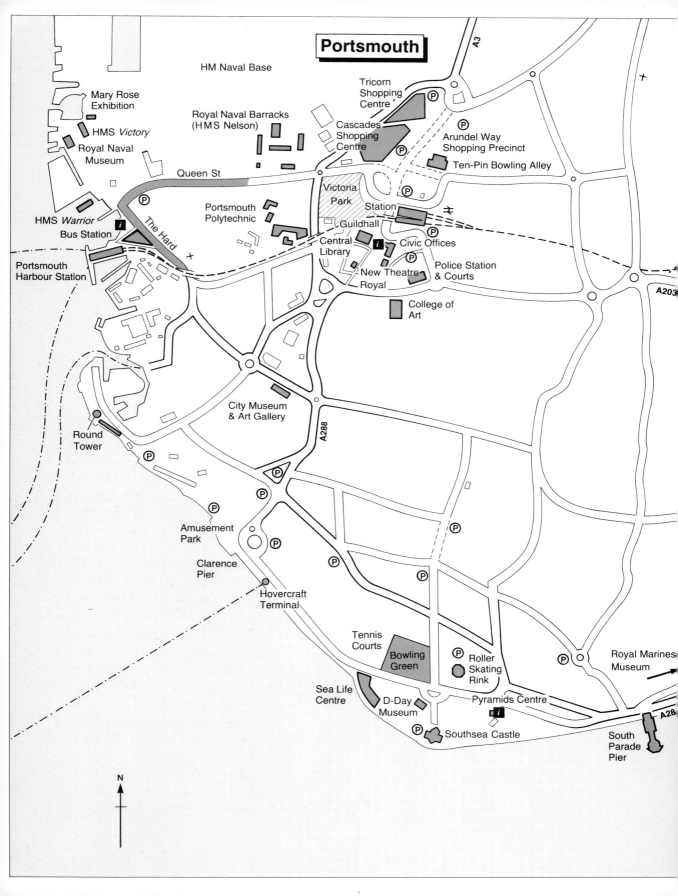

2

PORTSMOUTH

I thought I knew something about Portsmouth: I had been there briefly to catch the ferry for Europe and I had visited the special world of the dockyard to film HMS *Victory*. I had a quite definite view, anyhow, of what to expect – a rough and ready sort of place, Plymouth's Union Street on a grand scale, the sailors' Pompey. Of one thing I was reasonably certain: the two Ps would have very different characters, as different as south-west England from the south-east. My journey reinforced my prejudices.

The rail route from Bristol starts by following the lovely Avon valley, where the river carves a deep groove through the rounded hills, very much a West Country scene. Then out on to the rolling heaving landscape of the Wiltshire Downs and Salisbury Plain, taking you on to Hampshire. The changes soon begin. The River Wylye carves no deep channel, but wanders idly through the meadows. The grand view and the dramatic panorama give way to a more intimate landscape. Changes multiply: areas become more built up; the sea appears, not as crashing breakers but as a multitude of creeks and inlets, each ending in a coppice-like bundle of dinghy masts. And then the run into Portsmouth itself: I had expected a roughness at the edges, but this was overdoing it. Gas-holders sat like stranded whales on a beach of rubble – all that remained of the old works. They

were followed by the wire-topped walls of the prison, and then came a glimpse of one of those housing estates where the only bright spots are the plastic panels in primary colours, which are supposed to give a feeling of fun and gaiety but fail. That was it; the brakes were on and we were slowing for the station.

The station was a distinct improvement and will be better, for it was halfway through a face-lift. It is a classic station: simple and dignified brick buildings at the front and a train shed which relies on good proportions and on iron and glass with few fripperies. All that was needed was a touch of colour to the ironwork to set off the rich, local red brick of the main buildings. That is what it was getting: back to the livery of red and cream which it wore when it was part of the London, Brighton and South Coast Railway.

Heartened, I walked out into the city and my spirits rose. There are places where you need only sniff the air to say: this seems all right. Portsmouth is such a place. It is alive and is a city which has successfully combined the old and the new. There has been a tendency in recent years for architectural battle-lines to be drawn, with modernists on one side – thrusting, dynamic and unsentimental – and traditionalists on the other – tweed clad, complacent and firmly middle class or royal. I have come down on the side of the traditionalists, but I would argue that this is

17

a response to the deadly dullness of so many modern buildings.

The first thing that struck my eye as I came out of the station was a tall office block of dark glass, built on a curved plan which gave it a satisfying sense of elegance and rightness, of being the only possible solution for that building in that place. From that view I was led on to the main square where the modern buildings do not have the quality of Zurich

The Guildhall being watched over by Queen Victoria

House, but join with the old to make a city centrepiece that works.

The idea of the town hall as a sort of second division palace with its own square was developed in Italy and resulted in the grandeur of the Palazzo Vecchio in Florence and the Palazzo Publico in Siena, for example. Portsmouth may not match those, but by British standards it does extremely well. Town halls in other cities may be grand, but they look out not onto an open square but onto an overgrown traffic island. Portsmouth has a genuine square, surrounded by civic buildings of very different aspect. The dominant note is Victorian. The Guildhall is one of those sumptuous confections in startling white stone which leave you in no doubt that whatever its function its intention was to impress by grandeur. The message is simple: a city that can afford such displays of elaboration, such a wealth of steps and columns, porticos and turrets and such a feast of carving must be wealthy and important. The approach should also be made in the grand manner – up the main steps and under the lion-flanked portico to the massive main doors – but when I returned for a concert in the evening I had to go in by the side door, very infra dig. The concert hall had none of the splendour one might expect from the exterior; the stage was topped by a vulgar frieze. Sea horses were ridden by naked ladies who looked like pin-ups from a strip cartoon of the Fifties. The hall does, however, satisfy the more important criteria of comfort and good acoustics.

The Guildhall forms one side of the square, and the other three are made up of modern buildings, the Library and the civic centre. The offices have the mirror-glass cladding which pleases even those who seldom have a good word to say for modern architecture, because even if you dislike the new, you can still admire the old in the reflection. Here,

the new is perfectly decent and on a scale which complements rather than overwhelms the old. Queen Victoria has *her* face firmly turned to her own age as she peers down, a dumpy figure on a dumpy pedestal in the centre of the square. This is a case of a group of buildings, none outstanding, which work together to create a satisfying space, and it seems an appropriate place to pause and think about the character of Portsmouth.

The city stands on Portsea Island, but grew outwards from the tip until it filled the land. Tall buildings require no excuse: they answer the same problem which produced the skyscrapers of Manhattan. When you run out of land space, the only way to go is up. In the north are densely packed suburban streets; the west shelves off into the sea; the real interest lies in the south and east of the island. It is easy to see why this is so, because on the east a narrow but deep water inlet provides access to a wide sheltered bay. It is as natural a spot as can be imagined for the establishment of a port, and in the event the Royal Navy came to dominate the area and set the tone for much of the city's life. It is the centuries-old naval tradition which draws visitors to Portsmouth, attracted by three warships from very different ages. It would be absurd to consider leaving them out of a description of the city, so I thought I would start my wanderings with them. It is easy to see those ships, fine as they are, in isolation. I hoped that giving them a context might lead to some conclusion about the role of the navy in shaping the life and style of the city.

The easiest approach was to cut across Victoria Park and head down Queen Street. It was an appropriate choice and had a good deal to say about the special relationship between the city and the navy. The entrance to the park is behind a large and impressive war memorial – not a surprising place for a memorial, but

19

the park was a different matter. It has all the usual features of the urban park – walks and flowerbeds and lawns – but also phalanxes of memorials to individual ships, such as HMS *Victoria* sunk during the Boer War; a pagoda-like structure records the dead of a long-forgotten war in North China; even individuals, provided they reached the rank of admiral, have their monuments. The effect is like a combination of park and graveyard,

War memorials in Victoria Park

which scarcely makes for jollity and relaxation. If you read the inscriptions, you find that many were set there not by the navy but by the townspeople.

I walked on down Queen Street, which I half expected to be Portsmouth's equivalent to Union Street in Plymouth. On one side is the naval base and on the other some unadorned pubs and the occasional tattoo parlour, but there was little sense of fun or excitement, nothing to compare with Union Street. The

street ends at the Hard in a great mingling of features, a jumble of past and present. It is even more remarkable if you come from the east. There is something eerie about looking over the tops of double-deckers in the bus station to see the masts, spars and rigging of a square-rigged ship and yet more masts and spars behind the high walls of the naval base.

The Hard is a street facing the sea, a pleasing enough place, though it tends to be dominated by its transport connections. Portsmouth Harbour station certainly has a maritime feel; it runs out over the sea and if they stop running trains it would make a good entertainment pier. The bus station is in front of it, and the railway is carried away on a viaduct, the arches of which have been taken over by little shops. There is a small kiosk at the gate of the base, now a tourist information centre but once the naval police station, and through the gates one gets a glimpse of the majesty of HMS *Victory*. The scene is dominated by a recent arrival, HMS *Warrior*, moored in full public gaze across from the Hard. In the background is a steady passage of ships – ferries of all kinds from the modest ones leaving for the Isle of Wight to the cross-channel vessels heading for France. I went off to see the ships.

Victory is an overwhelming presence in the dockyard, but if you want to get a sense of development and change it is better to take the ships in chronological order. Look in first at the Royal Naval Museum. At first glance it appears to be an elegant museum which fits its setting. The buildings certainly are elegant, but they were built in the eighteenth century as nothing more than dockyard warehouses, proving again that a good building remains just that, no matter what its use.

The first of the ships, the *Mary Rose*, was a four-masted carrack, carrying square sails on her fore and main mast and triangular or lateen sails on the other two. She was built locally around 1510 and was at war against the French off Brest in 1512. In sea trials she outsailed the rest of the fleet and was described in a letter to King Henry VIII as 'the flower I trow of all ships that ever sailed'. She carried some armament but her main function as a fighting ship was to get soldiers on board, where they could fight the enemy with long bows or even hand-to-hand. This idea of a floating fortress is expressed in the tall structures in the stern and the bows, the castles, and the name of the forecastle, which lingered on and is still used as the shorter fo'c'sle for an area in the bows of a ship. Disaster came when the French invasion fleet appeared in 1545. The engagement was watched from the shore by the king, and the loss of the *Mary Rose* was through the incompetence of the English. In an attempt to give her more fire-power she had been heavily laden with cannon and ordnance. She was low in the water, her gun ports were open and the end was inevitable. Waves flooded through the openings and the great ship heeled over and sank – of the estimated 700 men on board less than 40 survived. That summary is not the whole story.

In company with millions of others on 11 October 1982, I abandoned work to watch television. I am not sure what I expected. In the long build-up to the recovery of the wreck, we had seen underwater film of the divers at work, but what emerged from the water was a metal cradle holding a lump of soggy wood. Whatever it looked like, it did not look like a ship; it lacked any sense of scale. The visit to the ship hall changed all that: through a thin haze of water, which is constantly sprayed to treat the hull, the remains of the old ship rose, as mysterious as the *Flying Dutchman* and heart-stoppingly magnificent. Its sheer size is

stunning but the amount of detail which has survived intact is its most remarkable feature. It is like a cross-section in a textbook except that it is real. From deck to keel the ship is revealed: the sweeping lines of the hull as it pulls in towards the stern post; the sheer walls of the stern castle as imposing as any castle on land; above all, the magnificent workmanship of her Tudor builders. In some ways I find the *Mary Rose*, even in her ruin, to be the most interesting and moving of the three great ships. As remarkable as the ship itself are the artefacts found with her: the machines of war, from ornate cannon to long bows and arrows; more mundane articles, from a backgammon board to a surgeon's syringe, which points out the inadvisability of being ill in those days. There are also parts of her rigging and navigation instruments. How curious to see a set of dividers we would still use today to measure distances on a chart.

The *Victory* has been in Portsmouth so long that she needs little description. She will forever be associated with Nelson and Trafalgar, though by then the ship was quite elderly, for she was launched in 1765, forty years before the battle. *Victory* had a long career which included the glory of Trafalgar and abandonment as a rotting hulk. Seeing the great ship today, refitted and restored, it is hard to believe that she so nearly didn't survive at all.

Tours are conducted by naval ratings. There have been suggestions that the job should go to professional full-time guides, but the point about her is that she has been a Royal Navy ship for over two centuries and still is, so it should be the navy who carry on the work. *Victory* is in every way a fine craft even if, like the Forth Bridge, the work of preservation never ceases. She also represents the end of an age when vast wooden ships carrying acres of canvas fought by firing cannon broadsides. In 1987 a survivor from the following age of naval power arrived at Portsmouth.

HMS *Warrior* is moored just outside the naval dockyard. I first made acquaintance with her when she featured in the television series The Past Afloat in 1981. She had been brought to Hartlepool from her sad berth at Milford Haven, where even the proud name had been replaced by Oil Fuel Hulk C77. The revolutionary warship had become a jetty.

What is so special about *Warrior*? Well, she was Britain's first ironclad battleship with rifled guns firing shells in place of the old cannon, and a steam engine to supplement her sail-power. Oddly it was easier to see the essential features when I visited her in her ruined days. The armour plating which made the ship special was exposed: the iron hull was encased in an eighteen-inch jacket of teak, and beyond that were four-and-a-half-inch-thick iron plates. I didn't believe that restoration would go to the present lengths. All thoughts of oil jetties have long since been forgotten, and you now visit a ship as she was in her prime at her commissioning in April 1861. Everything is there, from the slowly-turning cranks of the steam engine to the china for the captain's table. It is an astonishing transformation. The *Warrior* deserves her place with her neighbours from an earlier age.

This long discussion of ships is not riding a hobby-horse, but I have to stop myself from going on about vessels whose stories could fill the book. They have a direct relevance to the city of Portsmouth, because it was around the vessels of the Royal Navy that the city was built. The beauty of the craftsmanship in the *Mary Rose* is the craftsmanship of Portsmouth men of four centuries ago: a tradition which carries into the present day. It was around

the business of building and repairing ships that everything else grew: the dockyards, the complex of defensive forts and walls which kept them secure, and the homes of those who worked there. You can rarely leave the navy behind in this city, but it does come as a shock to turn a street corner and be confronted by dozens of parked cars and one parked frigate.

The emphasis on the ships can result in overlooking the shipyards which produced them and kept them afloat. The naval dockyards are fascinating; they are not open to visitors to wander around at will, but given the current cutbacks they soon may be, so this is perhaps an opportune moment to consider them. It is an irony which has not escaped the local populace that the government whose popularity recovered following the Falklands campaign is now presiding over cuts which make it doubtful if such a campaign could now be fought at all, let alone won. But my personal interest was in rather more distant history.

I was taken on a conducted tour by members of Portsmouth Royal Dockyard Historical Society starting, at my request, at the block mills. To reach them you walk past HMS *Victory*, and one glance at the rigging will tell you why it was necessary to have somewhere to make blocks – the pulleys through which the ropes for handling spars and sails must pass. They come simple and complex, large and small, but can be divided into simple components and individual blocks can be placed in specific categories. Originally they were made by hand, but in the 1790s a young Frenchman proposed a new idea which was accepted – remarkably, because England and France were not the best of friends. A whole range of machines was introduced in what we should now call a mass production factory. The Frenchman was Marc Brunel, whose son Isambard was born a few hundred yards away in Britain Street. One or two of these machines survive, but the buildings are echoing shells which offer splendid views over the yard.

Right in front is the Great Basin, which was new when Peter the Great visited, and leading from it are the eighteenth-century dry docks. Dominating the view, as ever, is the *Victory*. There are ship museums and boat museums, but less seems to be known about the men who built and maintained the vessels. The block mills are an ideal setting to commemorate a trade so essential to the city. We walked around the old buildings from the great length of the Double Ropehouse to the majestic Commissioner's House, built for the dockyard administrator and to house royal visitors, and ended up at a bizarre building. It began life as a water tank – with so much timber about, fire was not so much a risk as a certainty. It was an enormous structure on a cast-iron frame and could hold over 800 tons of water. In time the frame was filled in to create walls and the tank removed; the building now houses a huge jumble of things nautical. One day they may form the basis of a new museum.

The dockyard is like a town within a town and I continued the military theme with an exploration of the old city and the waterfront. It began at the round tower on the Point which was fortified in the fifteenth century and much changed over the years, so that what we have now is largely Victorian. The tower itself was not so exciting, but it gave me my first real views of the old town. Why everyone has not been shouting its praises for years I cannot imagine. It is jammed with splendid buildings, though few are more attractive or have a better view than the house next to the old fort. It has fine bay windows facing over

The elegance of the old city

the sea and a look-out tower topped by a ship's weather vane. I thought how wonderful it would be to live there and have my study in the tower, but decided that I might never work again, just sit watching the sea. It is not merely that individual buildings are good, but that there are streets of them and they are always tied into the fabric of the town. I caught a glimpse of masts and rigging over the rooftops, and a warship slid past the end of the street.

From the Point one can walk along the old curtain wall defences and come out to another aspect: naval Portsmouth disappears, to be replaced by a jolly seaside town. In a way, that is a delusion, for Southsea first developed as a residential suburb, occupied by naval officers and their families in the early nineteenth century. The military had it to themselves long before that. Henry VIII decreed that 'a ryghte goodlie and warlyke castill' should be built and there it stands today – Southsea Castle. There was nothing new in a king ordering such defences, but it is unlikely that one had previously decreed that it be

The Artillery Officers' Mess now houses the Royal Marines Museum

designed as a gun battery. There have been many alterations to the basic plan, but the square, uncompromising keep remains largely unaltered: outside all harsh angles, inside the rolling curves of vaulted ceilings. It is now a small but interesting museum.

Portsmouth may come to be thought of as the Bayeux of the twentieth century. There have been two Norman invasions: the one of 1066 and that going the other way, in 1944. Lord Dulverton commissioned the Overlord embroidery to tell the story of the D-Day landings. It is immense, bigger than its older relation in France. The young artist, Sandra Lawrence, took great pains to ensure authenticity; she also showed vivid imagination. No camera could have captured the scene she depicts of the great armada stretching to the horizon under the protective wings of the RAF. It is touching to know that Bayeux was among the first French towns to be liberated from the Nazis. The tapestry is on such a grand scale that it required and got a new museum in Southsea, a low rotunda which also has more conventional displays telling the story of those times.

There is one other aspect of military life remembered in the area: that of the Royal Marines. Their museum occupies the sumptuous Artillery Officers' Mess of 1868, in what seems a very private museum. It is like a family showing off its history, all personal and low key but bristling with pride. The mess has its new function, but what is to happen to the barracks outside? It is the same problem that touches the old dockyard buildings, though it is not hard to envisage some shrewd property development. For this is Southsea, which may once have been a military stronghold but is now fresh air and funfairs.

Old military buildings can be put to good use. Portsmouth is by no means just about the navy, and the military past slides into a more peaceful role. Is there anything to tell you that the City Art Gallery began life in 1880 as the Clarence Barracks? Yes, and the place puzzled me until I discovered its origins. Seen from the road, the building is a bit ornate but nothing special. At the back it is a riot, like a cross between a Scottish baronial castle and a French château. It is not turning its back on the world but facing the old parade ground.

It is so easy to become so obsessed with the naval past in Portsmouth that you lose sight of everything else, but this city has a separate life of its own. It has its offices and houses, churches and pubs, theatre and cathedral – but so do other cities, so perhaps the emphasis has to remain on what sets Portsmouth apart. But it would be a pity to finish without recording a few more impressions. For a start it is a city where one can look at new buildings without feeling a sense of shame. The Portsmouth Building Society's offices show that a building

The City Art Gallery was once the Clarence Barracks

can be simple without being dull, by providing something other than a four-square elevation. And you do not need elaborate decoration on the façade if you have mirror cladding and twiddly older buildings around. But among the new developments room has been found for restoration of the old. The New Theatre Royal was begun in 1884 by C. J. Phipps and remodelled by Frank Matcham in 1900. It was in a sorry state when restoration began in 1980, but already the outside is quite magnificent, with a glazed balcony striding over the pavement on elegant cast-iron legs.

Inside slow, careful work goes on to bring the theatre back to life.

It seemed a suitably optimistic note on which to end a visit. Portsmouth is, in some ways, like Plymouth – it is hunting desperately for a new way forward as the old dependence on the navy is threatened by government cuts and privatisation. It is unthinkable that a naval history which goes back to the Normans will ever be forgotten, but as more and bigger buildings become redundant it will be a test of ingenuity to keep a hold on the past while ensuring prosperity in the future.

SOUTHAMPTON

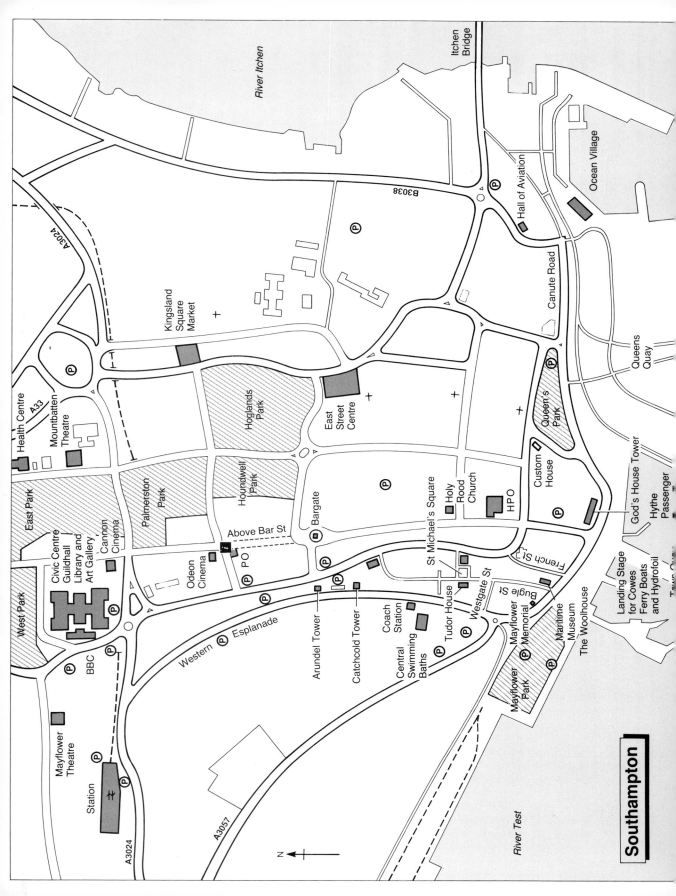

Southampton

3
SOUTHAMPTON

First impressions of Southampton were a little confusing. The journey from Portsmouth looks as though it ought to be simple backtracking, but the rails have been pushed inland by a series of creeks and inlets and the need to find a crossing point over the Itchen. So the train sidles up to the city tentatively and seems not quite to make it all the way. I emerged to a nondescript suburb which could have belonged to almost any town or city in the country.

Railway travel is a bit of a lottery: sometimes you arrive at the front door, on other occasions you are shunted round to the tradesmen's entrance. Southampton is very much coming in by the back door. But only a short walk reveals one of the city's claims to fame: its wide acres of civic greenery. Suddenly there is a feeling of airy spaciousness. Where Portsmouth had to cram what it could where it could on the island, Southampton has all the space it could need, ample room for expansion. So the civic centre looks out not on an enclosed square but on a wide green, dotted with broad-limbed horse-chestnut trees and magnolias, which were bright with blossom. Above these the civic centre tower rose like a white pencil against a blue sky.

My first thoughts were of getting to the hotel. The trouble with my sort of travel is that I keep collecting paper, so the farther I go the heavier I become. The hotel was modern but showed a rare touch of whimsy

– yellow plastic ducks for my bath. I resisted their blandishments and walked back through the sunbathers and loungers in the park to the civic centre.

The buildings are unusual in that they date from the 1930s and represent Britain's first civic centre where a group of buildings were pulled together in one plan. Between 1932 and 1939 the Municipal Offices, the Law Courts, the Guildhall, the Library and Art Gallery had all been completed. It is restrained, apart from the soaring campanile, and a little prim and proper. Inside, the municipal offices are Kafkaesque, with a signposting system of bewildering complexity. One section, however, cannot be accused of dullness, quite the contrary: the Art Gallery. The building is remarkable, centred on a beautiful vaulted main hall, bathed in a soft golden light from its north-facing windows, and around it are grouped eight side galleries. Paintings are hung by theme rather than style, which makes a refreshing change from most galleries, which follow the convention of the ancients through medieval to the romantics, and then come to an embarrassed halt somewhere around the first part of the twentieth century. From the start, Southampton had a policy of collecting British art from the eighteenth century to the present day – and they continue to buy contemporary works. They now have a collection

Sculptural detail from the 1930s civic centre

All three of the southern cities suffered intense bombing in the Second World War which inevitably meant large-scale redevelopment. In Southampton the scheme is decent but uninspired – a definite pattern based on the broad main street. Bargate provides the key: there can be no mistaking what it is, the medieval gateway that once pierced the city walls. To emphasise the point, the street to the north of the gate is Above Bar Street. I lingered, watching the pavement artists, but the end results – an alarmingly livid Mona Lisa, and a startlingly orange sunset – did not seem worth the effort.

The Bargate is impossible to date. The central arch is basically twelfth century, though modified by Southampton Tramways in the 1920s. It proved cheaper to vandalise a medieval building than to modify a tram. The modern solution to traffic problems shows lateral thinking at its best: change the road. A new roadway was constructed either side of the gate, leaving it isolated but at least free from the hammers and chisels of the transport department. The front and back are fifteenth century as is the chamber above the gate, which was used as the Guildhall until the new building was completed in the 1930s. Bargate shows two faces to the world: a grimly defensive one staring out from the city walls, but cosily domestic when it faces its citizenry.

The museum provides a vantage point from which to view the pattern of the city. You can see the line of the city walls and it is still possible to walk all the way around them. So I did. The wall is seen most clearly on its western side and very impressive it is too. Walking along Bargate Street you can keep the wall in view until you reach a massive stone tower at the corner. This is named after Sir John Arundel, who constructed the wall in Richard III's time on a natural cliff above

large enough to change the displays at regular intervals, and they bring in touring exhibitions as well. The gallery goes out of its way to bring the public in – especially the children. There are workshops for schools in term time and holiday activities which include cake sculpture and making Caribbean carnival costumes, as well as the more conventional arts. Small wonder that many look on it with a special affection: the London gallery owner Arthur Jeffress left them a choice from his collection. The success comes from the combination of a fine building and an adventurous and exciting policy.

The greenness is really quite remarkable. The West Park is only a small part; four others lead down in procession towards the sea, so you could well believe yourself to be in one of the garden cities built in the early part of the century. Elsewhere the effect is very different.

the River Test. The view is no longer over a peaceful river valley but across what would be a typical landscape of office blocks and car parks, were it not for the distant view of a forest of cranes at the docks. There is also what appears to be a disembowelled building, its lurid intestines bursting out through the walls. It has a far from sinister purpose: this is the swimming pool, and the tube which loops in and out of the wall is the giant slide. What a wonderful idea to slide in and out of the building before the final almighty splash into the pool. Apart from the medieval remains, it is the only building of real interest – and certainly the only one with a sense of fun.

When I turned south along the wall above the Western Esplanade, another tower appeared. I like to think that Catchcold Tower earned its name from generations of medieval soldiers standing guard while the wind drove sleet and snow into their faces. A flight of steps leads down to the esplanade; having viewed the walls from the top, I now looked at them from the bottom and discovered the Arcades. Having just left Portsmouth, I was struck by the different orientation of the defences: there everything faced out to sea, across to the old enemy France. Here the most imposing show of strength is on the landward side. These walls are much earlier, Norman structures – but why should Normans have felt the need for protection from their fellow countrymen? On the other hand, the defeated Saxons were not too happy and might have been expected to rebel at any time. The Arcades originally looked out over the quays on the Test, and were not only unfortified but were not arcades either, just a row of merchants' houses. The merchants appreciated having direct access to trade – until 1338, when the French raided the town. The authorities decided that safety was more important than commerce, and the houses were incorporated into the new defensive wall – you can still see traces of blocked-in doorways. Arches were built to carry a walkway on top, and the arcade took the form we see today.

On the way, I had passed the Castle Vaults. There was no entrance, but it is difficult for anyone with even a tinge of romanticism to ignore a castle, so I marched back up the steps I had just marched down. Southampton was providing me with plenty of exercise. The castle site is well within the city walls, but precious little can be seen apart from the excavated twelfth-century hall with sections of barrel vaulting like packhorse bridges and the royal loo. A latrine tower also stands on the walls close by, a medieval public lavatory. The actual site turned out to be occupied by an unlovely block of flats, but there were compensations, for I was now close to the heart of the old city. At its centre is St Michael's Square, with a church which dates back in part to the early years of the Conquest and was the only one of Southampton's old churches to survive the blitz. Its greatest treasure is the carved font of black marble from Tournai in Belgium.

Southampton suffers a schizophrenia more profound than most cities. To the east are the wide shopping streets and formal parks, having no relationship to the past, an environment planned to provide a pleasant setting for shoppers and office workers. This it does very ably; what it does not do is to arouse any curiosity, a need to see around the next corner, because it is unlikely that the next corner will offer anything different. The old town is full of streets, inconveniently narrow by modern standards, which are liable to finish up as dead ends against the wall and the cliff. But it demands exploration – not just of the streets, but of individual buildings.

The most obviously important building

is Tudor House, which is so ornate, so perfectly preserved, that you might take it for a 1920s' exercise in mock Tudor, but its slightly fake-looking exterior is the result of misguided 'restoration' in the early years of this century. There is nothing the least mock about the house, which was built by Sir John Dawtry in the late fifteenth century. It is a complex building which swallowed up earlier houses and then connected everything by

The medieval merchant's house in French Street, proclaiming its business with barrel sign

passageways and a gallery. Inside, everything creaks in a satisfactory manner. It is now a museum with Tudor reconstructions and things of Southampton, but leavened by some real oddities as well. One object which I took to be an ornate oven from a Victorian kitchen turned out to be a Carboton Garage Stove. If it were mine I would not let it sit unadmired out in the garage.

Different ages have different notions about restoration. Victorians and Edwardians tended towards a mental idealisation of an age. Where Pugin, say, borrowed his motifs from the gothic, the restorers of the genuine old churches tended to bring them to the same condition as a new Pugin. It was not a circle, but a spiral of rising 'gothicisation'. Similarly, the Tudor house is more Tudor now than it ever was five centuries ago.

The medieval merchant's house at 58 French Street has also been restored, but today's restorers are more concerned to strip away additions than add embellishments. The building announces its function through a barrel suspended from a roof purlin extended to provide a convenient bracket. The advantage of the modern approach is that the basic form of the structure is easy to read. The main living quarters extend out over an arcade; this provided a convenient dry area for potential customers for the shop which once occupied the ground floor. Behind the timber façade – like all shops of all kinds, it presents a handsome face to the road – the main structure extends back in three distinct bays. Something of the original use survives in that the ground floor still houses a shop, and the rest of the building has been restored as decidedly spartan living quarters. Perhaps the search for 'purity' had gone too far: everything brought down to a minimum, so while forms are clearly visible, there is no sense of a living presence – no clutter, no mess, no

humanity. It is particularly disappointing that the vaulted cellars, such impressive features of Southampton's medieval houses, are not open to the public. I paid £1 to go around the house and came out a touch disgruntled.

Individual buildings may be viewed for nothing or at quite considerable expense; the streets are still free for all. Bugle Street is splendid, though my first thought that it might be associated with the defences – calls to arms and that sort of thing – turned out to be wrong. It was originally Bull Street, though how a bull became a bugle is a mystery. Its days of importance as one of the main roads of the medieval town have slid away, leaving it a modest role as a mixture of houses and offices – but what a mixture. Every conceivable style is on show: shaped gables next to the angular symmetry of a Regency town house which rubs elbows with the complex timber forms and jetties of

Westgate and the Tudor Merchants' Hall

the medieval, while the modern age has added a cosy touch with neo-vernacular buildings, all jolly red tiles and subdued brick.

Just around the corner is Westgate Street: no misnomers here, it really does lead to the West Gate. There are connections with Portsmouth, for it was here that Walter Taylor began developing block-making machinery in the eighteenth century, starting a process which culminated in Brunel's block mills. Up against the wall is the Tudor Merchants' Hall, a name which scores one out of three: it is not Tudor, it was not a merchants' hall, but it was a hall – a medieval cloth hall, though the ground floor was an open arcade used as a fish market, which could not have improved the aroma of the cloth. It has been a busy little building; it originally stood in St Michael's Square but was sold to Alderman Edward Exton in 1634 for just over £13. He moved it down the road and filled in the arcade.

Bugle Street brings you down to the southern defences and the first real glimpse of the Southampton that faces out to sea. I felt it would soon be time to get away from the medieval aspects and come closer to our own age, but I paid one last visit to the archaeology museum housed in God's House Tower. It seemed an odd name for what was clearly a military installation. God's House was the hospital of St Julian's Church, and the artillery tower borrowed its name. It is a good museum in an entirely appropriate setting, but other matters were now beginning to absorb me.

For a city which grew and prospered as a seaport, the signs of that long history are disappointingly few. The only indications are the ornate but isolated dock offices. To find out what Southampton was in its greatest days, in that period before the Second World War when the Queens ruled the Atlantic, I found myself pushed back into the medieval past.

The Woolhouse dates from the fourteenth century when Britain's prosperity was built on wool – how often fragments of that story were to appear in my travels. The wool trade was in the hands of the Church and the wool came from the flocks grazed by the monks of Beaulieu. In time the trade declined and the old buildings saw many uses from grain store to prison – French prisoners have left their initials carved in the beams. Now it is a maritime museum and a very good one, with an enthusiastic and knowledgeable staff. So many museum attendants are bored men and women whose sole role is to stop the customers fingering or appropriating the exhibits. Here they positively want to talk to you, which gives it a value far beyond its size.

The museum starts off by showing you a large model of the docks in 1938 when they were at their grandest. Here are models of the great ships, and the most splendid of them has the most splendid of models: the *Queen Mary* is over twenty feet long, perfect in every detail. I love models like this for their intricacy and because they represent a past short-lived but glorious. The great age of the transatlantic steamer came with the monstrous ships driven by steam turbines. It began with the *Mauretania* of 1907 but barely notched up its half century before the jet airliner brought it to a halt.

The cruise ships continue, but they do not have the glamour of the great liners of the past. The Ocean Terminal has gone and the brief age of glamour went with it. That glamour was always spurious because there was none for the black gangs shovelling coal in the bowels of the ship and precious little about the pale green American matrons, swathed in blankets on the boat-deck weakly sipping beef tea. Among the models is one of the MV *Britannic* in which I crossed the

The maritime museum is the medieval Woolhouse

Atlantic in the 1950s. There was something undeniably boring about getting up each morning to the same grey, lumpy sea and a list of entertainments which would not raise an eyebrow in a Trappist monastery. But the romantic image survives the remembered reality, and I spent a happy hour or two looking and chatting.

Surely Southampton deserves something more than this? The museum staff do wonders with what they have, but there is no denying that it is dreadfully cramped. That the story of twentieth-century transatlantic shipping should be told in a medieval warehouse scarcely seems right. But if they do find

bigger and better exhibits for a bigger and better museum, I hope they find people who will make it as friendly and pleasant as the Woolhouse is today.

The story of the docks is one of land reclamation, using what had been a muddy home for waders and gulls. They divide neatly between Eastern and Western. The former are the earlier, closer to the city centre, but all modern activity is at the Western docks, well out of sight beyond the old city walls. They date back only to the 1920s when 400 acres of glistening mud were marked as the site of the new complex. The docks were opened in 1933, but a decade later the liners had been replaced by the troop ships and landing craft of the D-Day invasion fleet.

Southampton was fortunate in the post-war years, when other great ports were seeing their trade slip inexorably away. It was ideally situated for the new container ships. There were no dock gates to impede progress, and by one of those happy accidents the port has twice the usual number of tides, making for a quick turnaround. The trade may lack the glamour of the Queens but, together with the car ferries, it keeps the port working. What it does not do is leave any obvious mark on the town – apart from the convoys of container lorries trundling up and down the A33.

The Eastern docks are a different story. In the 1830s the London and Southampton Railway built their station in an area known unpromisingly as The Marsh. At the same time the new dock company began work on their first installation. A new Southampton was being born to set beside the old. The main road past the old station site is Canute Road – and a very appropriate name it is, for the Victorian engineers succeeded where the king failed. They turned back the sea and changed the shoreline.

The station where it all began is now a car park; the grandiose, ebullient station hotel houses offices and the BBC. What looks like the old waiting-room is Jeeves Club. Only a sign saying 'Private road to station' now sends out a clear message. The whole area is in a state of flux: renovation is going ahead at a great rate. The London Hotel, all tile, terracotta and engraved glass is being done up. The early nineteenth-century terraces of Oxford Street, with their bulbous bow windows at first-floor level, have already been done – but they still look out on the Sailors' Union and the Sally Army. You can shop for bouquets of flowers or ropes and blocks, but the bouquets are winning and the

chandlery will no doubt soon have its window full of yellow wellies. You can see the changes at their most dramatic from the site of the original dock.

The dock of 1842 has a new name now – Ocean Village. Dinghies and yachts ride at their moorings in the new 450-berth marina which has managed to find space for the occasional traditional craft, including a Thames barge. The area was a mixture of completed houses and scruffy building sites when I was there. The attractions were obvious: your luxury house comes complete with a guaranteed berth in the marina. This is very much an up-market development – the old working port pressed into service to meet the demands of a new leisure industry. The houses are once again inoffensive neo-vernacular, with an attempt to create a St Tropez atmosphere in the bright pantiled roofs. When I thumbed through the brochure, there were more pictures of boats than houses – not much doubt what the selling line is. The sold notices were sprouting everywhere; apparently there is no shortage of customers with £200,000 plus.

Ocean Village is a self-centred enclave, distancing itself from the city. There is a quayside pavilion of shops which echoed emptily, but it is early days and no doubt things will change when the scheme is complete. It must all be a bit chicken and eggy: you cannot sell the goods until the people move in, and people are reluctant to move in until there are facilities. I wandered about, less than happy with the fussy pavilion in its garish blue and red livery, and eventually found myself out on the river front. What a pleasure to be reminded of the graceful simplicity of the Itchen Bridge, and there was a welcome touch of workaday reality in the Vosper Thornycroft yard across the water. I have always enjoyed the thought that people still make things in cities, apart from

The Hall of Aviation, with its glass extension round the tail of the Sandringham flying boat

money. Southampton has a proud engineering history, not just connected with the sea: it has taken to the air as well.

The Hall of Aviation across from Ocean Village has one exhibit so big that a sort of overgrown greenhouse is needed to get in the bit that sticks out beyond the main building. This is the Sandringham flying boat, which in pre-jet days whisked the sahibs and memsahibs away to red patches on the world

37

map. Flying was not a furious dash across the sky. Imperial Airways were happy to take you to Singapore provided you could afford the fare and spare eight days for the journey. There are memories here of great events, of the Schneider Trophy races out of which grew the design for the Spitfire. The museum does for aviation what a new museum should do for the story of the port of Southampton.

The more I walked round Southampton the less certain I felt about where it was heading. There are so many elements pulling in different directions: the development of Ocean Village on the one hand, a new-found enthusiasm for their important and extensive medieval remains on the other. Fifty years ago, before the bombs and the jetliner, it must have had a recognisable character: a city which did as it had done for centuries, turned to face the sea. Southampton is still a successful port, but the exigencies of the modern container trade have pushed the shipping away from the city. Bold signs may still announce Messrs May and Wade, Export Grocers and Shipping Contractors, but such sights are getting rarer. One is left with the divisions: the medieval walled city on one side, and the broad streets and shopping precincts on the other, though few shopping areas come surrounded by inviting greenery.

All three of the south coast seaports had been faced with a similar dilemma: how to rebuild an identity after the devastations of war. Each had an answer yet each seemed now to be trying to grasp what remained of the ancient roots before the new city grew into something alien. The pleasures given by Plymouth's Barbican, Portsmouth's old town and Southampton's walled city are of a similar nature and provide standards against which the new can be tested. The greatest pleasure in old Southampton was to find that work was still going on, that new houses were being built behind the wall. The archaeological and medieval remains were being seen not as part of a scheme to be set under glass, preserved yet sterile, but as a link in a story of continuous change. There is concern to keep the city centre a living place, and without that sort of commitment it is difficult for any city to survive.

However, Southampton is nothing if not forward looking. An underground system is to be built and geothermal energy will be tapped by drilling into the rocks below Western Esplanade. The idea is to release water at 76°C to heat shops and offices. The notion of getting a central heating system from beneath the medieval walls suits Southampton.

COVENTRY

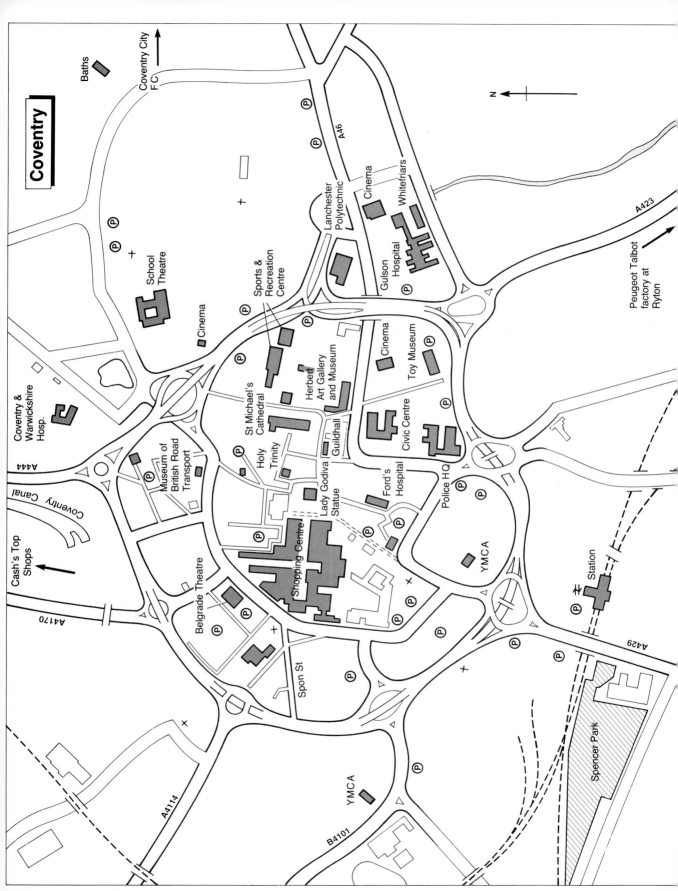

4
COVENTRY

A curious and pleasant feature of railway travel is that it often seems an overture to the main work; not merely because it is a necessary prelude but because it provides a glimpse of the themes to be developed later. Travelling to the Midlands is a notion which most people find unexciting. There is something dull about the middle of anything: the middle way, the middle of the road – a suggestion of compromise and blandness.

The journey soon dispelled that notion. The gently swelling Malvern Hills on one side, the steep scarp of the Cotswolds on the other – and in between our route was up the broad Severn valley. The farther north one travels, the more waterways provide the connecting links which hold everything together. The Avon arrives to swell the Severn, and soon there are glimpses of the narrow, shining lines of canals which the railway crosses in many places and runs alongside for much of the way. After one has made the seemingly inevitable change of trains at Birmingham, the canal joins the rails in threading through the concrete forest of Spaghetti Junction. It could be a symbol of what can happen in our cities: the old made subservient and all but obliterated by the demands of road traffic. Something of this feeling recurred when I got to Coventry, which might be expected, since Coventry is the city of the motor car. But it was an important place long before

that – in the fourteenth century it was the fourth largest town in England, and set about building a surrounding wall when other towns were deciding that such walls were obsolete.

There is little hint of Coventry's true character in its flowery, leafy suburbs. They do not last – a few whiffs of blossom then one crosses the modern barrier which has replaced the old encircling walls, the inner ring road. The city centre is remarkably compact, scarcely more than half a mile in diameter, which makes exploration on foot easy as long as one stays inside the charmed ring. It is easy only in the sense that you never have to walk far, but it is certainly not easy to grasp patterns of development.

Fifty years ago there would have been no problem. At the heart was the medieval city of guilds and merchants, with later development outside the crowded centre. That overall pattern still holds, but the heart has been changed, for it suffered some of the fiercest air raids of the Second World War. And where in Southampton or Plymouth's Barbican the post-war planners kept to the recognisable lines laid down in the past, the Coventry planners took a different decision. They determined to re-think the city in terms of the needs of the late twentieth century. What was done after the war no longer looks strange or even particularly modern, but at the time it seemed revolutionary. The fact that it now seems

The new cathedral

unremarkable is a measure of the planners' success, and they have received the most sincere form of flattery – their ideas have been widely imitated.

In spite of the changes, one could look at the Coventry skyline and believe that some things have remained the same. It is still dominated by three great spires, yet they are not what they were. All three were once majestic symbols of piety – Christchurch, Holy Trinity and St Michael. Worshippers still use Holy Trinity but Christchurch is a shop selling ceramics and the cathedral church of St Michael, begun in the twelfth century, was destroyed by bombs in the twentieth. It survives as a reminder of Coventry's wartime agony. Equally symbolic is the new cathedral built next to the old. There is no better place than here to start an exploration of Coventry.

The site of the cathedral goes back to the foundation of a monastery in the years just before the Norman conquest. Little remains of that foundation, but the 300-foot spire of the cathedral still rises over a recognisably great church. Open to the sky, it is like a vast, elaborate skeleton. Where so many old churches have suffered at the hands of insensitive restorers, St Michael had all its extraneous trimmings blown away on 14 November 1940. The delicate tracery of the windows stands in pure relief against the light, and the old cross remains gaunt and charred on the altar. All cities have their war memorials, but none is more moving than this.

When the time came to rebuild, the decision was taken not to restore the old, nor even to build in the accepted style of English church architecture, but to build a church unashamedly of its age. A competition for a new design was held in 1951 and the winning architect was Sir Basil Spence. He was in an unenviable position: if he opted for tradition he would have been flayed by the critics; if he chose out-and-out modernism he would probably have displeased the public. His solution evokes a feeling of the past in its interior – with the proportions and rhythms of the great naves of the perpendicular churches – but could not have been built in an earlier age.

You enter through the tall sandstone pillars of the porch, past Epstein's St Michael and the Devil, which seems to lack conviction. The real power of the building is in its echoing nave. John Piper's window shouts with energy, but far more satisfying are the tall windows which line the nave, so placed that they become visible only when you turn back at the altar. The great set-piece was the most controversial of all the cathedral's works – the 75-foot-high tapestry by Graham Sutherland. The overpowering intensity of colour affects everyone, whether or not they like what they see. It is meant to impress, to haul you up short and make you think. This is a cathedral not an art gallery, and must convey the essence of religious feeling. The feeling recurs in details such as Elizabeth Frink's eagle lectern and Basil Spence's wrought-iron crown of thorns at the entrance to the Gethsemane chapel. There is much to admire inside, but the exterior is less happy. In spite of the richness of its sandstone, it contrives to look featureless and bland. The flèche, or open spire, evokes memories of old RKO movies, but whatever one's view of the new cathedral, it has had a profound effect on the city landscape. The new sits next to the old on equal terms, neither a wan pastiche nor a brash intruder.

From here I faced a choice of ways: to continue in pursuit of the new or to go to find the old. I chose the old, largely because the new was already on display in the shape of a modern hotel and the bus station. A special medal should be struck for any architect who can make a bus station interesting, let alone appealing.

The ancient street scene centred on the medieval Guildhall

Old Coventry lay up cobbled pathways and enclosed, twisted streets, which seem always to offer excitements – come-hither streets whose lure I find irresistible. On this occasion there was no false promise, but the reality of St Mary's, the Guildhall built in the 1340s for the newly formed Merchants' Guild and enlarged around 1400 for the Trinity Guild. A few paces from the swirl of traffic and the twentieth-century cityscape of hotels and bus stations you step through an archway into a medieval world. Inside, a staircase leads to the Guildhall itself, of a grandeur that would satisfy the demands of a Hollywood epic. It has everything: a stained-glass window, a tapestry showing Henry VII and his queen kneeling before the Virgin and the apostles, and a minstrel gallery. Over it all is a magnificent roof from which angels look down, mouths open in perpetual but silent song. It is a hall which proclaims the power and prosperity of the medieval city, yet there is little on the outside to suggest this splendour. St Mary's is a celebration of wealth by and for the wealthy, a medieval version of the gentleman's club.

If public wealth was a feature of Coventry's medieval life, so too was public piety. The churches which still dominate the skyline tell their own stories of the city's history. The oddest is perhaps Christchurch. It dates back to the Greyfriars Monastery, when the city was a great religious centre, with the Whitefriars' Carmelite settlement, part of which still stands, and a Benedictine priory. The Greyfriars boasted this grand tower and steeple which survived the destruction of the monastery by Henry VIII. It stood in isolation until the 1830s when a church was tacked on to the end. Then came the bombers and the church disappeared again, but the spire survived. The old life did not return, hence its use as a ceramics shop.

The medieval parish church of the Holy Trinity is one of the few survivors, though it has not escaped restorers and rebuilders, some of whom have enhanced the original building, while others have fussed away, obscuring the original patterns. The most famous church, apart from the cathedral, is not the grandest. It has no tall spire nor is it specially distinguished architecturally, but it has the distinction of adding a new phrase to the English language. In the Civil War royalist troops were imprisoned in the church and no one was allowed near them: they had been sent to Coventry.

In a city which has suffered so much, each relic of the past seems to have special significance. No one wanders around York or Chester exclaiming at the sight of an old building. Here each comes as a delightful surprise.

There are two sets of almshouses: Bond's Hospital is by far the grander; built mostly in the early sixteenth century, it looks out over a wide courtyard. It is undeniably fine, but I found the more modest Ford's Hospital totally enchanting. It was a victim of the war, but what could be saved was saved and patched and repaired with materials from the ruins of other ancient casualties. The street frontage on Greyfriars Lane offers a satisfying complexity of angles and planes: the timbers of the frame, darkened by age, stand out against the plaster and fill in the shapes of oriels, gables and the single-arched entrance. But it is the courtyard and surrounding houses beyond the arch which are the real gems. Ford's seems a marvellous place to grow old: part of the life of the city, but a centre of peace.

Inscriptions on the walls tell that the little community was established in 1529 by William Ford for five men and one woman who were given five pence a week each. Later the numbers were raised to six couples who received seven pence halfpenny, 'And in the room of the sixth poor man and his wife, there shall be one honest poor woman of the said City taken into the Beadhouse, who shall be between forty and fifty years of age, to superintend these five poor men and their wives, as necessity shall require.' Feminists will not be surprised to learn that if a wife died the

The courtyard of Ford's Hospital

weekly allowance remained unchanged, but if the husband was the first to go the widow's allowance was halved.

The case for rebuilding Ford's Hospital must have been unanswerable, but the city faced real problems in the immediate post-war years. They were surrounded by acres of devastation, which urgently needed to be rebuilt into an entire city centre. Among the ruins much of quality still stood, but what do you do with a lonely little medieval building? Do you incorporate it as a self-conscious note of quaintness? Do you knock it down? Coventry decided there was another solution. They rounded up their stray old buildings and herded them together – dismantling and re-erecting in what can only be called a new medieval street, Spon Street. Some started life here, others were brought from different parts of the city. It is inevitably a compromise: the street will never have that special compound of cohesion and diversity which comes only through centuries of development. Yet I can think of no better solution, for the buildings have not only survived but are back to use, and simple explanatory plaques show their original plans.

Anyone hunting the old Coventry soon realises the importance of the containing walls, within which the ancient buildings jostled for space. There are remnants of these and their gateways – though the finest remaining gateway is not a city gate at all, but a fourteenth-century monastic gatehouse which now houses a toy museum. This is a delightful anachronism: what was built as an entrance to a world of austere piety is now devoted to games and frivolities. But such remnants have little visual impact, for they are dwarfed by the new barrier of the ring road. Old streets are brought to a halt at its edge and pedestrians have to search out underpasses much as their forebears had to find their way to a city gate.

Central Coventry remains an enclosed city, with new and old meeting at its heart.

Broadgate has a statue to the city's most famous resident, Lady Godiva, who rode naked through the streets to save the citizens from unfair taxation. That the event is unlikely to have occurred has in no way affected the story's popularity. She rides on, looking rather more like a twentieth-century pin-up than a medieval lady.

A somewhat demure Lady Godiva

It is difficult now to see the shopping centre as in any way remarkable. The plans were drawn up in the war years, showing a brave faith in its outcome and a sound understanding of the need for a new approach to the devastated city. That the old pattern of streets had to go was accepted; the new idea was for a series of squares which could be brightened with trees, flowers, sculpture and fountains, where people could shop or chat or stroll at their leisure, untroubled by traffic. Around these squares would be grouped not just shops but public buildings such as the Library, a new hotel and a market.

Nothing like it had been tried in Britain before, and responses were inevitably somewhat mixed. The optimists dreamed of a Continental atmosphere of pavement cafés and bright, chattering crowds, forgetting that the British climate was unlikely to permit it. Others mourned the passing of the old style of shopping streets – but they had yet to experience the tremendous increase in road traffic which was to clog so many city centres. It is now possible to look at it more objectively. Sir Nikolaus Pevsner had a typically wry comment when he described the scheme in 1966: 'It is a boon for shoppers right in the centre to be away from the cars, and the architecture as such can largely be overlooked.'

It is still a boon, and the architecture is still best ignored. Nevertheless, it has become a brightly attractive area: the saplings have grown and flourished; the open areas have the bright cheerfulness the planners intended. So many later schemes have been cramped, poky affairs, but the Coventry precinct gave the designers scope to provide different levels and a satisfying complexity of plan. Now that everywhere has, it seems, a shopping precinct, it is possible to measure the original against its successors, and it comes out of the test extraordinarily well. Individual buildings may be characterless, as they are in most later schemes, but the overall effect is bright and cheerful, helped by such amenities as the Belgrade Theatre. I visited the theatre when it was new, at a time when new theatres were rarities. It was wonderfully exciting and some of the excitement lingers; as at Plymouth, it draws local shoppers in for a coffee or a meal, and is very much part of city life.

Not all the new buildings fall within the central area. The Herbert Art Gallery is a bright, cheery place, outside which is the statue of the sculptress Elizabeth Frink whose bird lectern graces the cathedral. And Coventry has one

The sport and recreation centre: look hard enough and you see it as an elephant

new curiosity – its sport and recreation centre at the edge by the ring road. Seen in profile, it looks like an elephant, trunk and all. This is no accident but a deliberate evocation of Coventry's insignia – the elephant and castle.

My wanderings had finally brought me to the ring road, and it is as well to remember that there is life beyond the traffic. Indeed, on a previous visit, my transport had come to a halt on, as it were, the wrong side of the tracks: I had come by water and journey's end was at the canal basin. It was then a sorry place, where rubbish stirred and slid over empty quays under dilapidated warehouses. The whole area was overlooked by tower blocks, which are still there, but the old warehouses have been restored. True, their wooden canopies and covered hoists no longer serve any purpose, for the days have long gone when boats came here loaded with cargo; but the buildings have been given a new role. The old stores are now workshops and offices and the conversion has taken away none of their robust character.

It required no great insight to realise that these were buildings of quality, but the point was taken that part of that quality is tied to the working life of the canals they serve. The memories of that life have been preserved in simple ways – stone setts on the quays, among which plain iron mooring rings have been embedded for the pleasure boats which have taken over from the narrow boats. How easy and cheap it would have been to tarmac it all and stick in a few posts for boats to moor; how reassuring that the temptation was resisted. However, the scheme is not yet complete and it remains to be seen whether the special atmosphere of the basin can be preserved.

The canals were to eighteenth-century England what the motorways are to our age: the principal routes of trade and commerce. Just as today's factory owners look for sites close to main roads, so a canal-side site was then considered the best place to set up shop. There was no room left inside the old city limits by the time the Industrial Revolution arrived, so the canal formed a natural line for development. A stroll down the towpath reveals just how important it was.

Coventry's medieval prosperity had been built on wool and cloth, but the industry peaked in the Middle Ages and went into steady and irreversible decline. Two new-comers brought prosperity in the eighteenth century: ribbon-making and watch-making. The results are still there – even if not easily recognised. Ribbon-making did, how-ever, produce one of the industrial world's odder set of buildings. Joseph Cash set up his workshops near the canal in 1857, when there was still reluctance to leave the ways of the cottage and the hand loom for the world of powered machines and factories. Cash tried to

unite the two worlds: he built rows of houses, quite conventional except that few terraces have a factory occupying the top storey – a great continuous workshop stretching the length of the terrace. When the factory bell was rung each morning, the workers had only to climb stairs to pop up like pantomime demons from trapdoors ready for the day's work. The firm is still in business; all over the country children go to school with Cash's name tapes sewn into their clothes.

Watch-making was once important in the city. It involves intricate work with mechanical parts, and the skills that went into it were carried over to other trades, including the manufacture of sewing machines. In 1868 a young gentleman called Roly Turner rode a French boneshaker bicycle to his uncle's Coventry Sewing Machine Company and sug-gested there might be a market for these contraptions. The Coventry Sewing Machine Company became Coventry Machinists, and bicycle manufacture became an important industry. It was a natural progression to motor cycles and on to motor cars, on which much of the city's modern prosperity has been built. The Museum of British Road Transport in Hales Street tells this story in an impressive and entertaining display, but I went to see the real thing.

Peugeot Talbot is one of the new names on the Coventry scene, but the French connection is continuing the story begun by Mr Turner and his Velocipede, and the works are part of the continuing story of change. The Ryton factory, on the outskirts of the city, built aircraft during the war and switched to the motor car when peace came. It was part of the Rootes empire, turning out Hillman Imps and Sunbeam Talbots, and acquiring quite a reputation in the world of rallying. In 1967 the group succumbed to a bid from across the Atlantic and became part of the Chrysler Corporation. Then came the oil crisis and profitable car companies plunged into deficit. In 1979 Chrysler stepped out and Peugeot stepped in. What I was about to see was the assembly of a multitude of parts from France and Britain into a complete motor car.

The image of modern car manufacture is of a world of computers and robots – efficient, impersonal, never taking holidays, never asking for pay rises – perfect employees. Do they produce better cars? I have no idea. Do they make for work satisfaction and a contented community? There I do have a few. Assembly-line work is something those of us on the outside regard with horror, an activity satirised by Chaplin in *Modern Times*, but it is work and can offer some rewards beyond the pay cheque.

Peugeot Talbot have not gone as far as some companies down the automation road, though there are some remarkably advanced machines at work. They have concentrated to a great extent on people: informing the work force of changes, involving them in those changes and making individuals responsible for the quality of their work. I have to admit I would hate to work in the great echoing shed with its never-ending procession of bits and pieces which come together to make a car. The work struck me as noisy and dully repetitive, but there seemed to be a recognition of human needs among the machines. I had to admit that it is all very impressive. Even the official statistics sound grand – assembly in one thirty-four-acre building, for example. I have known smaller farms. The Peugeot 309 has 3400 separate welds; organising that in a system of continuously moving conveyors was more than my brain could comprehend. At the end I got the test drive – over bumps, around corners, up hill and down dale. It was

comforting to know that each and every car gets this attention.

When I set out on these tours I made a simple rule: I would only go to see places I could walk to in the city centre. At Coventry I had broken the rule, since it seemed nonsensical to ignore its most famous industry. Having left the confines, I saw no point in being too fussy about other places. I was delighted to find something which could scarcely be more different from motor car assembly – organic gardening. I am no gardener; I once struggled ineffectually with an allotment but abandoned it when the rabbits had a midnight feast of everything above ground level. I now stick to window-boxes but if anyone could convince me to take up gardening again it would be the zealots of the National Centre for Organic Gardening at Ryton-on-Dunsmore.

Most of us are aware of organic gardening as a movement which turned away from artificial herbicides, pesticides and chemical fertilisers. Its popular image is of a bearded chap in plastic sandals – no leather, you see – standing watch over a batch of misshapen carrots. I was not prepared for the sensible, practical and, above all, scientific approach. The emphasis is not on what not to do, but on the positive things you can do. Never have I known such enthusiasm expended on the subject of compost. It is unlikely that I shall ever put the theories to the test, but they are undeniably attractive in the abstract. I love the notion that the right native wild plants will attract the nice beasties which will gobble up the nasties busy consuming your best veg. Judging by the food in the restaurant the system produces healthy, tasty fruit and vegetables while protecting the environment. A city which boasts an organic gardening centre next to a car factory cannot be accused of lack of variety.

LEICESTER

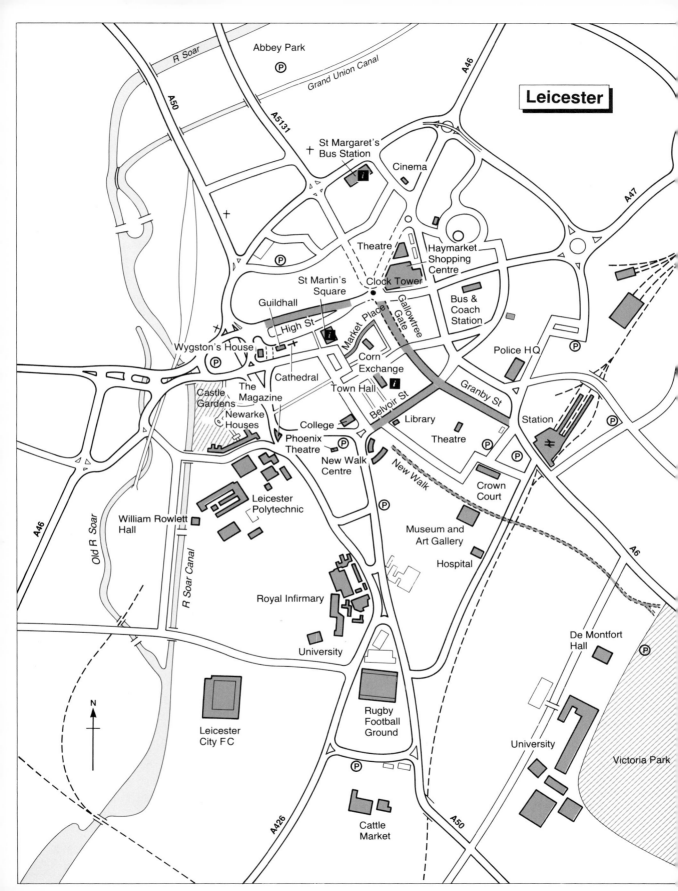

5
LEICESTER

It takes less than an hour to travel from Coventry to Leicester and nothing dramatic turns up along the way, though near Nuneaton I caught a glimpse of what seemed to be a Romanesque church but was revealed as an ornate water-pumping station. There was also a reminder of the organic gardeners of Ryton at Hinckley Station, where a desolate patch of grassland announced itself to be a 'Nature Garden'. I have had one of those for years.

I spent the journey feeling slightly worried. I knew most of the cities on the tour reasonably well, but it had been many years since I was last in Leicester. What I remembered and what I had read did not encourage me to expect a great deal. I was wondering not so much whether there would be anything good to say about the city but whether there would be much of anything to report. Arrival brought immediate encouragement.

Leicester once boasted two railways and two stations. The old Grand Central Railway and its station were abandoned in the 1960s, leaving the Midland Railway's London Road station in solitary splendour. It really is rather splendid, though quite modern by railway standards. It was built in 1892 to an exuberant, florid design by Charles Trubshaw. The façade is red brick and terracotta of a hue reminiscent of an Edwardian gentleman overdoing the port. Everything speaks of those days: the front is dominated by the *porte-cochère*, the

huge porch under which carriages could be driven; arrivals and departures were marked in ornate terracotta lettering. (Somewhat perversely, British Rail now insists that taxis and cars go in the out and out the in.) In its grand flourishes, its arches and turrets, it exudes a confidence of purpose rare these days. Perhaps the years before the First World War were the last age when anyone could look to the future with confidence, even if that confidence was hopelessly misplaced.

Still, there it was, a lovely introduction to the city and, as I was to discover, an appropriate one. All cities have their keynotes. In Coventry it had been post-war reconstruction. In Leicester it was to be *fin de siècle* ebullience. Before that could become clear, the city centre had to be reached – and if there is a more attractive way from railway station to city centre than New Walk, I do not know it.

The walk was new in 1785 when it was laid out as a tree-shaded promenade out of town and into the fields. The nineteenth century was a time of rapid expansion – New Walk remained a leafy path but one increasingly hemmed in by buildings. You can see the different periods clearly, though it is sad to note how as you get nearer the centre and move forward in time as well as distance the standards of buildings deteriorate.

At the station end, the early nineteenth-

The elegance of New Walk

century houses have the effortless rightness of style and proportion which is the hallmark of the period, and the delicate iron verandahs are mouthwatering. Regency terraces of red brick, precise and formal, give way to the grey brick Italianate terraces of the mid-nineteenth century, notably heavier in style. Yet everything contrives to hold together, largely because the language of architecture remained the same, even if the earlier builders used it more eloquently. When the twentieth century breaks in, it appears as a crude intrusion, with little regard for what was already there. It is difficult not to sound old fogeyish in such a situation. We all know the past was by no means always good nor is the new always bad, but it is bad here and you cannot get away from the fact. Fortunately, New Walk as a whole retains its identity. It is still as its designers intended it to be, a place where people can wander untroubled by traffic, and it remains a visual delight.

Halfway down, it opens into Museum Square. This is a pleasant area, dominated by the Museum. Its portico of vast columns is suited to a civic role, but must have been quite forbidding when the building was a nonconformist school. Inside is a most curious collection. No doubt there was once a logical reason to explain it all, but it is hard to see the pattern now. It is certainly reasonable for a provincial art gallery to put together a collection of English paintings, but how did they acquire a set of German expressionist works? One cannot imagine a greater contrast, even weirder against a background of recorded birdsong from the environmental galleries. The Museum and Art Gallery will irritate those who need to see precision, order and logic. Those who believe that 'variety is the spice of life' will find this museum well spiced.

By the time I reached the end of New Walk, Leicester had won me over. It is such a simple concept to have a promenade leading from the heart of the city that one wonders why more cities do not have something similar.

The city centre was before me, but there was the familiar dilemma: where do you start? what order do you follow? Some cities have clear patterns which are easy to follow. This is not true of Leicester, which makes it an intriguing place to stroll, because you are never sure what to expect next. The best thing is just to wander, and on this occasion my wanderings brought me to the market. Leicester claims that it has one of the biggest in Europe, and as a devotee of markets I decided to explore.

The only sad thing about it is its cover – overgrown egg boxes on posts – though the good news is that it is to be replaced. This is still essentially an open market, and part of the square is still open to the elements. The Corn Exchange is quite a remarkable building, with two flights of stairs leading up to a platform at first-floor level. It is quite difficult to avoid the feeling that at the top you should turn back to the square and deliver an oration. Not that many would pay attention, for they are all absorbed with the business of trading and a would-be orator would have to override the shouted patter of the stallholders.

This is not one of your new-style, genteel markets, but the real rumbustious thing. It was a favourite occupation on Wednesday lunchtimes for schoolboys to go down to the market and listen to the sales pitches, delivered with speed, conviction, wit and enthusiasm. The stallholders were entertainers who knew that once they had collected a crowd they had collected their customers. A good deal of that spirit is still found in Leicester. If you believed half you were told, you would come away convinced that it was an institution run by benevolent individuals whose sole aim was to give away their goods or certainly make them almost free. But these are no con artists; they are playing a game and we know it is a game. We get our bargains and they, despite protestations of certain ruin, get their profits. If you do not want to buy anything, you get a free show from characters who would make most stand-up comedians sound dull and slow-witted. As I said before, I like markets, and I liked Leicester's very much indeed.

St Martin's Square is a new development approached under an art nouveauish archway. It is new, but looks as though it has been there for ever, largely because the old has been mixed in, including some lovely, ornately carved shopfronts. One shop in particular – Pauline's – has a doorway overlooked by two demons leering evilly. Pauline sells clothes, but I should not be surprised to hear that she can also boil a mean cauldron. A solitary offshoot of the market was selling records from a stall, so I mooched about to the accompaniment of

Miles Davis – quite enough to put me in a good mood. This is an area which encourages my sort of aimless wanderings, for it is full of odd corners and twists and turns which lead you off to see what is around the next corner. It was such an excursion that brought me to old Leicester.

At first the cathedral seems to promise little of interest. From the outside it looks what it was until 1927: a big Victorian parish church, although inside there is ample evidence of the earlier foundation, including splendid thirteenth-century arcades of shapely solidarity. The inside is not especially exciting, but outside there are superb examples of a specialist craft. Slate is found locally, and the churchyard is crammed with beautiful carved headstones. The inscriptions have a quiet dignity: I noted that Joseph Smith died in 1826 after twenty-five years as macebearer having 'discharged the duties of that office with zeal and fidelity'. The carver displayed the same virtues.

From here, it is a short walk to the Guildhall. Originally built for the Corpus Christi Guild in 1343, it was later taken over by the corporation and used until 1876, when the new Town Hall was built. Approached through its courtyard, it has the charming intimacy of an ancient inn or manor house, with all the features which make buildings of that period so attractive. The shapes are complex, and the upper storeys jetty out so that no surfaces ever seem to meet at a conventional angle. But what really gives life to the courtyard is the rich mixture of materials: stone and plaster contrast with old, weathered timbers; the gables carry deep-hued roofing tiles above the wide bands of the windows.

The inside may not have the imposing grandeur of Coventry's St Mary's, but it is a lesson in the medieval art of timber-frame construction: the main frame of the walls

The nineteenth-century cathedral spire rises above an eighteenth-century terrace

with the spaces between the principal timbers occupied by smaller posts or studs and those spaces filled in to create the wall. Towering over everything and giving shape and unity to the hall are the crucks, pairs of curved timbers which meet in an arch to support the roof. It is not perhaps beautiful in any conventional sense, but it is wonderfully satisfying. The other rooms also have special pleasures. There is a massive chair fit for Gargantua, carved in the piece from an oak stump blown down in 1890. It stands over six feet high at the top of a grotesquely carved back, and the semi-circular seat is almost five feet across. It was used by the lord of the manor when he collected rents, and no doubt was designed to impress. It is wonderfully ugly.

The library, on the other hand, is wonderfully beautiful. It was moved to a wing of the building in 1632, but was assembled a good deal earlier; it was already mentioned as a public library in 1587. Does anyone now read these volumes in their old leather bindings encrusted with the patina of age? Nearby is the recorder's bedroom, a tiny space which was probably never used by any recorder. One wing of the old building was converted in the last century to make room for the police and their cells, which are as cheerless as one would expect.

In Coventry, I had found a spattering of medieval houses around the Guildhall, and the same was true here. The oldest is Wygston's House, dating back to the fifteenth century. The centre is original, but the house was extended and one of the wings given a fashionable Georgian front. Its appeal is similar to that of the Guildhall, but it is also home to a costume museum. The new use has not been allowed to obscure the old building; I have at best a mild interest in costume, but could still enjoy the building for its own sake. The museum had one exhibit that did stop me in my tracks: a reconstruction of a draper's shop where (as in the emporium on the hill in Mr Edwards' *Under Milk Wood* dream) 'the change hums on wires'. The reconstructed Edwardian draper's did not seem out of place in a medieval merchant's house.

I had been picking at Leicester in a haphazard manner, so it seemed time to get to the old heart and core of the city – the castle and Newarke. The way is marked by the tall slender spire of St Mary de Castro – just as well since pedestrians have to tangle with the complex of underpasses and tunnels which mark the new road system. There is, in fact, no castle left, just the motte or mound on which it stood and some fragments in the castle gardens, where there is also a statue to Richard III who rode out from Leicester to lose his crown and his life on Bosworth Field. The hall remains, heavily disguised as the court house. Perhaps the additions and alterations will be swept away one day and the hall revealed for what it is; one of the finest Norman great halls in the country.

The area was once enclosed, and there were two gatehouses: the Turret Gateway, which was virtually destroyed in the election riots of 1832, and the timbered fifteenth-century gatehouse which now leads to the Newarke or new work, an extension to the walled castle built about 1330. It is now home to the Royal Leicester Regimental Museum. The Newarke area has a number of special buildings. The Trinity Hospital almshouses were there from the beginning, though they have been greatly changed over the years. A chantry house was established later by William Wygston; it survived as part of a growing complex of secular building which made Newarke a rich man's enclave from the sixteenth to the nineteenth century. The Newarke Museum occupies the Wygston house, which was supposed to have been home to William's brother Thomas, and its grand seventeenth-century neighbour.

So far I had seen a prosperous town of merchants and nobility. The museum introduces the other Leicester, the city which grew up with the Industrial Revolution, when it became a major centre for hosiery manufacture. This was not quite the traumatic experience that other forms of industrialisation represented. For a long time the only new machine was the stocking frame, which could still be used in the home. Inevitably, the time came when machinery was moved into the factory, and other mills were established to spin the cotton thread for the knitters. This period transformed the old market town and I decided to investigate.

I woke to a bright sunny day made for a stroll to the edge of the city to find that other side of history. But, having decided to move forward from the medieval town to the eighteenth and nineteenth centuries, I found myself first going back in time.

The obvious starting place for exploration of the industrial past has to be the water, for rivers were the main transport routes and the source of power through the

The Pex textile mill by the Soar Navigation

waterwheel. Once again I was finding parallels with Coventry, for the canal age came here as well. The River Soar was canalised and what is now the Leicester arm of the Grand Union was constructed to join the river to the main canal system of the Midlands. These facts provide a clue as to why Leicester is here in the first place. Navigation above this point had to wait for the canal, so for centuries the city was the end of the line for trading boats. It was so in medieval times and a good deal earlier as well. Roman generals always had a good eye for a place of strategic importance, so it was no surprise to find extensive evidence of the Roman settlement on the way to West Bridge.

Jewry Wall is a massive chunk of building which survived because it was partly incorporated into the adjoining medieval church. Built of stone and tile and pierced by arches, it stands beside the excavated remains of a bathhouse. This is the spot where old and new achieve a fine, if all too rare, harmony. The museum carries echoes of its older neighbour in its rough barrel vaulting, but the use of wide areas of glass could only be twentieth century. You can see the Roman relics and the displays inside while keeping touch with the buildings outside. So often museum exhibits exist in a sort of timeless limbo; here they relate directly to the world outside the museum doors.

That interlude over, I made my way to the river and a very different scene, where all the elements I have enjoyed for many years came together. It is a world of locks and weirs, an unfussy place where appearance is dictated by function. It is also a world of contrasts – the spiky outlines of lock beams and the gear which moves paddles and sluices standing against the changing, wavering reflections of the water. A lot of people have misconceptions about the early industrial world. There were horrors – maltreatment of people, particularly children –

but they rarely show in the buildings. Later industrial areas could be dark, gloomy, smoke besmirched, but the early mills were different. The Donisthorpe factory is a classic example, standing by the river's edge. Only the stumpy chimney added in the nineteenth century gives it away, otherwise you could take it for a large if plain Georgian manor. A little cupola rises above the pediment, decorative but practical; it houses the flood warning bell. That is topped by a gleaming weathervane in the form of a ram. It looks rather lonely, for many of the surrounding buildings have been cleared away.

It will be interesting to see what happens to this area, where there is still a thriving working life. I like the atmosphere: the subtle differences between the natural river and the man-made canal; the rush of water over weirs and the swirl and eddy around the reeds which rise up beneath the old factory walls. Can it be kept? Should it be kept? Or should we begin to think about the day when industry leaves the Soar and plan a new use? It is not hard to envisage expensive residential schemes, with perhaps the Donisthorpe factory as luxury flats. I hope the working world of the riverside will never disappear completely, partly because it provides healthy realism in the environment, a reminder of the old bases of the prosperity some are enjoying. It also ensures that such areas do not become simply privileged enclaves. For the present, the riverside-canalside walk is exhilarating and packed with interest.

I walked along the towpath to Abbey Park. There was once an abbey, but you need a vivid imagination to get the faintest impression of what it was like. As a historical site the place has little to offer, but it is everything a city park should be, with almost everything it should have. There is a miniature railway and a bowling green, a bandstand and a lake complete with ducks for feeding. Abbey Park

Railway excursionists puff across the façade of the former Thomas Cook building

has a bonus – the river flows through its heart. One thing I did not see, which surely no self-respecting municipal park should be without, was a floral clock. Perhaps I missed it, because this is a big park. I would not like to think Leicester had been remiss over such an essential feature.

My objective lay beyond the park: the Industrial Museum. I was being self-indulgent in walking so far out from the centre to visit one site. But the museum is rather special – though a bald description might not make it appear so. The main collections are of knitting machines and vehicles, and they are housed in the

former abbey sewage works. They are mainly of interest to specialists, though most people take a macabre delight in the old horsedrawn hearse. But a sewage works? It would be more accurate, if not more appealing, to describe it as a sewage-pumping works. The work was done by four huge steam engines, and no word but huge is suitable. These are beam engines built in 1891. Each has an overhead iron beam twenty-nine feet long. Power is supplied to a piston moving in a cylinder, much as a car's power is supplied today, with the difference that each engine has two cylinders, the largest of which is four feet across. The pistons push one end of the beam up and down, so that the pumps hung off the other end of the beam go up and down as well.

That is only a part of the story. You might expect a sewage works on the edge of town to be a purely practical place, but that makes no allowance for the pride of the civic improvers of a century ago. Their machines were grand and did a vital job: they deserved a dignified setting. So the engine house was lined with richly-coloured tiles and the main columns which support the building and act as a frame for the steam giants were cast in iron with complex foliated capitals. Very few people came here apart from workmen when the machines were still working, but anyone who did would have found a mixture of shining metal, polished brass and gleaming wood in a setting that would grace a town hall. Perhaps it is a little florid, but it was worth the long hot walk to get there and it provided the right background for the commercial heart of the modern city.

Back in the centre, I headed for one of Leicester's landmarks – the clock tower at the crossing points of the major streets. No one could mistake this for anything but a Victorian exercise in gothic extravaganza. It was built to commemorate four worthy city benefactors, but it contrives to look totally frivolous, which is no bad thing. As I was to discover, frivolity is a feature of the centre.

There is something endearingly daft about the buildings of Leicester. At first glance, all you see is the standard shopfronts of any city centre, though a few buildings do stand out. The elegant County Rooms were designed as hotel and ballroom for racegoers in the 1790s. The decoration is classical, with cavorting Greek maidens to lend inspiration to punters. Civic pride is manifest in the Town Hall, Victorian but cool and restrained in the

Queen Anne style which became popular in the early twentieth century – though not always executed as stylishly as this. It looks out not on the grand square of more Italianate contemporaries but on a friendly green with a handsome fountain.

Restraint is less marked in the banks. I always thought that the crown for the city with the most elaborate banks went to Halifax but I am now not so sure. Leicester has some corkers! At the corner of Belvoir Street and Granby Street, the Yorkshire Bank is riotously baroque with a superabundance of carving. Bas-relief figures sport in a purposeless way around the window arches and peer down at mythical beasts which lurk between pillars. Eight, not nine, muses sit in niches. Even this building is outfaced by the Midland Bank farther down Granby Street. The outside is striking, but the inside is extraordinary. The main hall is an echoing chamber open to a timber roof which would grace the finest

The turkey struts – above the Turkey Café

guildhall, while the light passes through pale, stylish art nouveau windows. It is a true temple of Mammon. After those, one begins to take a livelier interest in the streets. I soon found the secret: look up.

Much of Leicester was rebuilt in the Edwardian era and nobody seems to have decided the style. Above shopfronts are Dutch gables and plain gables, hipped roofs and cupolas, turrets and towers and balconies. Styles are French and Italian, English and gothic and sometimes original inventions, dreamed up from every architectural device. Decoration runs riot: the most striking example has to be the Turkey Café in Granby Street, where a stylised multi-coloured turkey struts above what can best be described as Moghul arches, the effect enhanced by the decoration being picked out in coloured tiles.

Other buildings have particular stories. The Singer building of 1902–4 has a surprisingly modern appearance with its preponderance of glass in the façade and in the vaulted arch in the centre. But the decoration makes plain that it dates from the heyday of Empire, with the Union Jack rising above a menagerie of animals selected from the red bits of the map: elephant, kangaroo, polar bear, camel, tiger, ostrich. Some edifices in the High Street have special historical significance. The Co-op was an early arrival – the first branch started in 1860; the Arcadia Electric Theatre, the city's first cinema of 1910, is still recognisable and still good fun, but my favourite is the Thomas Cook building in Gallowtree Gate. The name 'Gate' has nothing to do with gateways but goes back to the Danelaw town – it is simply a Danish street. Bronze relief panels show important events in the Cook story. Working backwards, there is his jubilee year of 1891, represented by a train steaming across the just completed Forth Bridge. In the next, a paddle-steamer chugs past the Pyramids; an excursion train speeds to the Great Exhibition in the Crystal Palace and then, at the very beginning of his package tour business, a special train which left Leicester in 1841 with 570 passengers in open wagons heading for a temperance meeting in Loughborough.

That brought me back to the railways, where I began. But Leicester had not quite finished with its surprises. As I walked back to the aptly named Grand Hotel, a lady sitting in a shop doorway rose and solemnly removed all her clothes. And I had been worried that there might be nothing to say about Leicester.

NOTTINGHAM

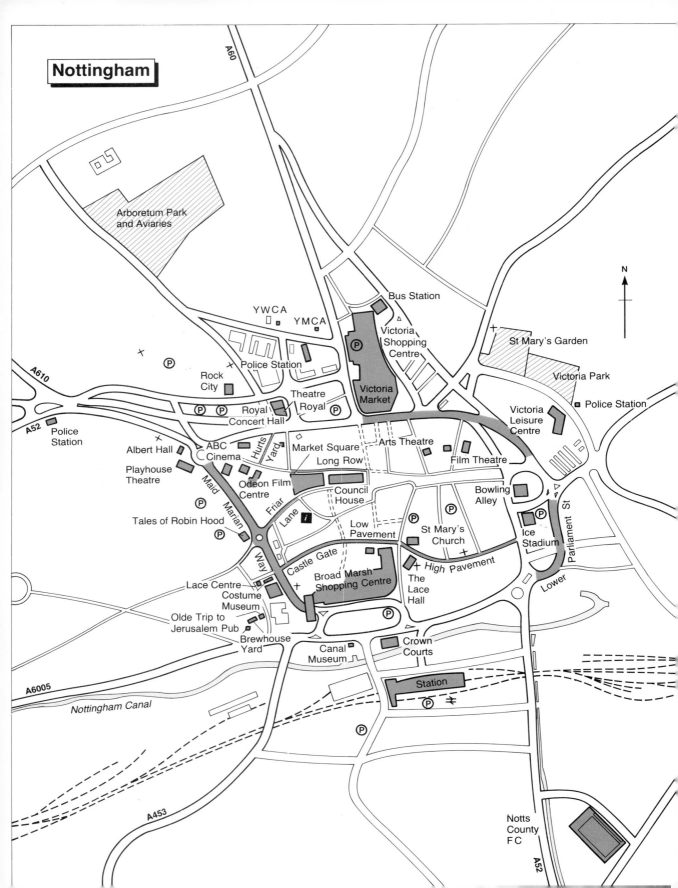

Nottingham

N

Arboretum Park and Aviaries

A60

A610

A52

Police Station

YWCA
YMCA

Bus Station

Victoria Shopping Centre

St Mary's Garden

Victoria Park

Police Station

Rock City

Police Station

Theatre Royal

Royal Concert Hall

Victoria Market

Victoria Leisure Centre

Albert Hall

ABC Cinema

Hurts Yard

Market Square
Long Row

Arts Theatre

Film Theatre

Playhouse Theatre

Odeon Film Centre

Friar Lane

Council House

Bowling Alley

Tales of Robin Hood

Maid Marian Way

Low Pavement

St Mary's Church

Ice Stadium

Parliament St

Castle Gate

Broad Marsh Shopping Centre

High Pavement

The Lace Hall

Lower

Lace Centre
Costume Museum

Olde Trip to Jerusalem Pub

Brewhouse Yard

Canal Museum

Crown Courts

A6005

Nottingham Canal

Station

A453

Notts County FC

A52

6
NOTTINGHAM

My trip around the Midlands was being conducted in a series of short hops – shorter than ever in the move from Leicester to Nottingham. The stations are similar, not surprisingly since both were built at much the same time by the same company. So I began with an expectation that the cities might be similar, and realised that I had always paired them mentally because of a similarity in their industrial past. The stocking frame which had been such an important factor in Leicester's growth was developed in Nottingham. True, the latter can boast its own industrial product – lace – but lace is such a flimsy, fragile thing that it somehow seems less important than a sensible pair of socks.

I was to find that my experience of the two cities and my reactions could scarcely be more different, even if there are superficial similarities and even though the themes of one were to recur in the other. But, just as in music, say Britten's Variations on a Theme of Purcell, what one hears is unmistakably Britten, so themes I had first met in Leicester appeared now as unmistakably Nottingham's own.

The similarities are soon plain: both cities developed at river crossings, and both were established as important centres, as Danish boroughs or burhs, long before the Norman conquest. Under the Normans they grew into thriving markets, protected by the lords in their castles. By then patterns had been established which were still recognisable even after the boom years of the Industrial Revolution. So if overall patterns were so similar, why are the effects so different? The main answer lies in geography, the physical landscape in which the two cities are set. This is not immediately obvious at Nottingham station, but it soon becomes clear if you set off in the right direction.

The importance to Nottingham of the River Trent does not need stressing. It is one of the great navigable rivers of England which provided, and still provides, access to the sea. And yet it remains oddly peripheral. Coming out of the station, you turn right for the city centre but left to reach the river. It is worth going the 'wrong' way, if only to see Trent Bridge, which is not only a handsome structure in brightly painted iron but has also given its name to a handsome cricket ground. As I was to spend the weekend in the city, I promised myself an afternoon of cricket – a decision which produced an instantaneous darkening of the sky with rain clouds. The bridge also separates two rivals: Notts County on one bank, Nottingham Forest by the cricket ground on the other.

The river is wide and free-flowing but misleading, for the bridge marks what is almost the limit of navigation. But what nature failed to supply, man has provided: immediately upstream of the bridge is the entrance lock to the Nottingham Canal, which passes close to the heart of the city. You can walk into the city along the towpath but it is easier and quicker to walk back to join the canal just beyond the station. You realise at once the importance that water traffic once held in the development of the region but holds no longer. A tall, dull warehouse block rises above the water, its rows of windows soiled and broken, its loading doors creaking on their hinges. Nearer is a smaller wharf development housing the Canal Museum, which has a lot more to say about the city than its name might suggest. But before visiting it, I went for a walk down the towpath to see the canal world, as it were, from the working end.

This little section gave me as much pleasure as the waterway in Leicester. The black and white beams of a lock gate could be glimpsed under the road bridge, and I would have wagered a good sum that such a conjunction would have encouraged someone to open a pub for thirsty boatmen at this natural stopping point. I would have won the bet. Before getting to the bridge, I came on a side turn where the towpath had to be carried over on one of those bridges which are as pleasing in their simplicity as the elaborate ironwork of the Trent Bridge. Most canal bridges are anonymous, but a cast-iron pillar informs passers-by that it was the work of Samuel Parr and C. Woodward, overseers, and T. Godfrey, assistant overseer, and was finished in 1869.

The group of which the museum is part is the most interesting. There is a small wharf with a hand crane, behind which is a complex of buildings. A large warehouse straddles a short arm of the canal, and a pair of boats can be seen under the arch. This was a common design, because it meant that the vessels could be floated in underneath the building to load and unload in the dry. These were the familiar

narrow boats of the Midlands' canals: the one with a swan-neck metal tiller was the motor boat, while the other, with the heavy, curved wooden tiller, was the butty, an unpowered craft towed behind the motor. Writing on the wall by the warehouse announces that this was once the Fellows, Morton and Clayton wharf. In their day FMC were among the largest operators, running a fleet of over two hundred boats on the canals. So this was an important point on an important trading route which played a large part in Nottingham's development, even if it is now reduced to an insignificant backwater.

The museum tells the story of both of Nottingham's waterways, the canal and the Trent. It explains why town centre and river crossing are so far apart: the Trent floods, viciously on occasions. From the first, settlers moved to the high ground and you can see how steeply the streets climb from this point. But I was not quite ready to explore them.

The museum occupies only a part of the site: the rest has been turned into a home-brew pub, and pub and beer have been named after

A stonemason who obviously could not spell

the three boating gentlemen, Fellows, Morton and Clayton – full marks to those responsible for showing an awareness of history. The adjoining restaurant is called 'Joshers' which must bewilder some customers. There is a simple explanation: one of the original trio was Joshua Fellows, whose boatmen were always known as joshers.

Across the road from the pub is a small park, above which a sandstone bluff is topped by a large but not at this distance imposing building. It was a view familiar to millions who remember the old cigarette packets of Players of Nottingham: this is the castle on the hill. Its entrance is through the gatehouse at the corner of Castle Road and Friar Lane, and it seemed a good idea to head resolutely for that point. The gateway is a solid, imposing stone affair, but inside there is none of the hoped-for castle presence, just green lawns and tumbling brooks forming a pretty little park. There is, however, the inevitable statue of Robin Hood. Was he real or was he legend; did he have anything to do with Nottingham and its sheriff? Those are arguments for experts, but nothing will ever persuade the town that Robin Hood and his merry men were not outlaws dedicated to helping the poor against King John and the sheriff. Equally, nothing anyone can say to people of my generation will convince us that Robin Hood was not a dead ringer for Errol Flynn.

There is little here, apart from the statue, to stir memories of those days. Yet the legends had a firm base in reality, which becomes obvious when you climb to the top of the hill to see the city spread out below. This was the site of the old Norman fortress, the centre of power for a French community. From here the sheriff ruled over the royal hunting forest of Sherwood and over the town and trade of Nottingham. The ancient burh begun by the Danes and developed by the Anglo-Saxons was close to but separate from the castle. You can see that settlement on its own hill, clearly marked by the spire of St Mary's Church. The Norman sheriff controlled both communities, punishing law-breakers and collecting taxes – not a brief likely to gain popularity. Legends grew of the sheriff as oppressor and Robin as champion of the poor. They were fuelled by the stories surrounding Richard I and his brother John, neither of whom could possibly have been alive at the time of any historically plausible Robin Hood.

The Norman castle fell at the end of the Civil War, and the site was taken over at the Restoration by the Duke of Newcastle. His taste ran to Venetian palaces not medieval keeps, so a new, unwarlike building rose to top Castle Hill. It too suffered when it was attacked by election reform rioters in the 1830s, but was rebuilt as a municipal Art Gallery and Museum in 1878. This may be interesting, but it is no comfort to small children, heads full of wicked lords and men in Lincoln green. A small boy viewed the edifice with undisguised disgust. 'What's this?' he demanded. 'It's the castle,' replied his father. 'No, it's not,' said the son, and burst into tears. Errol Flynn would not have thought much of it either. But if Nottingham Castle is no medieval fortress it has a museum and gallery which show real imagination and flair.

Nottingham's collections are not outstanding in the widest view, but they are exciting in a way many grander and greater collections are not. The city succeeds in some areas by an emphasis on the local: there is some superb engraved glassware, but I really enjoyed the pots. The medieval pottery is especially vivid: an old man strokes down his long beard to form the jug handle, an idea elaborated in a jug of 1250 where two friends stroke his beard instead. There is a sense of fun: a transfer

Nottingham Castle gateway

printed jug of the 1820s shows pedestrians with steam engines strapped to their legs and is entitled 'Symptoms of walking made easy'. Best of all are the lively Nottingham bear jugs, ceramic reminders of the bear-baiting of the markets and fairs.

No one would pretend that the pictures rival the National Gallery, but the gallery has done everything to make its collection interesting to even the most casual of visitors. A regular gallery visitor knows the shell-shocked expression which comes over the faces of visitors presented with acres of High Art. Here notes bring the pictures to life and succeed in conveying real enthusiasm. One note forces you to attend to the painting of a dead tree. It explains how the artist loved it and points up the energy of the long brush strokes which convey the shape and essence of decay. The artificiality of a stylised Venus is emphasised in a down-to-earth way. Local artists are also on display, modern experimenters next to polite water colourists. I have seldom visited a gallery where so much effort has been put into bringing to life the painted oblongs on the wall. Among them was a painting with a vision I tried to keep in my head during my stay – a seventeenth-century view of the castle on its hill and the ancient borough on another, with the first tentative links being forged between the two communities.

The area at the foot of Castle Hill is full of contrasts. The land to the west was grabbed by wealthy Victorians who appreciated the wide views across the Trent and built some astonishing villas, many reminiscent of cartoonist Charles Addams' house for his family of ghouls. To the south, old buildings shoulder up to the sandstone cliffs. Here you can find Brewhouse Yard and one of the most ancient recipients of the brew, the Olde Trip to Jerusalem, a pub which runs counter to one of my pet theories that anywhere with 'olde' in the title probably isn't. The Trip dates back to the time of the Crusades, hence its name. It is a place mercifully free of gimmicks which still offers good beer in decent surroundings. And the buildings of Brewhouse Yard give a clue to the siting of so many beery establishments close together. The present group of restored seventeenth-century houses are altogether respectable, serving as a museum of local history.

They tell stories of the less attractive past,

including a section devoted to the wretched children who were sent up Victorian chimneys, their services offered by this jolly jingle:

Ladies and gentlemen wishing him to employ
A Brass Plate they may see on the cap of each
   boy;
His name on the front he thought proper to fix,
To prevent imposition and slippery tricks;
Tho' honest his calling, yet as in others you'll
   find
He may have his opponents to roguery inclin'd.
This notice he gives that his friends they may
   know
For certain they're employing their servant
   J. Lowe.

This is perhaps the sort of Victorian morality we are all being encouraged to emulate.

One can explore a complex of caves carved out of the sandstone at the back of the houses – ideal spots to keep a few barrels of ale in prime condition, as the owners of the Trip long ago discovered. Nottingham's rock is riddled with such holes, as though the whole city stands on a giant honeycomb. The most famous must be Mortimer's Hole, down which Edward III's men crept in 1330 to discover Queen Isabella in the arms of Roger Mortimer.

A series of roads leads from the castle to Nottingham's other centre – the Saxon borough. Castle Gate boasts a superb mixture of seventeenth- and eighteenth-century houses and is now home to a museum of costume and textiles, reflecting the city's importance in this field. Both ends of the street are fine, but in between is Nottingham's disaster: Maid Marian Way, a dual carriageway which slices right across the old street pattern in the most brutal way imaginable. A local told me years ago that the city was still trying to make amends for the crimes of the 1960s, but there is little to do here – what has gone can never be replaced. The one thing to be

Reflections on the Royal Concert Hall

said with complete confidence is that when you have confronted this horror you have seen the worst of Nottingham. It is of course easy to criticise one's own age, and it is perhaps worth remembering that offensive though the road is, it is nowhere near as bad as the courtyards of the nineteenth century, which contained some of Britain's vilest slums. And, as we shall see, the city has made amends with some modern buildings of quality.

You do not have to travel far to see that quality. At the northern end of Maid Marian Way there is a decent, restrained office block with sufficient variation in line and angle to give interest to the façade. On the other side of the Way post-modernism puts in an appearance in a building using new materials but incorporating motifs from the past. It is perhaps fussy in some of its details, but, compared with some of the office towers down this road, Barclay House is easily digestible.

Nottingham has what I regard as one really successful modern building down in Theatre Square. The old Theatre Royal is one of those classical parochial theatres that one finds throughout the country, acceptable but scarcely exciting. The new Royal Concert Hall could have picked up and modernised the same theme, but the architects went for bold use of a potentially interesting corner site. The building rises on bright blue pillars as a giant glass wedge, but jettied out like a twentieth-century version of a Tudor house. The glass gives a constantly changing image of the rest of the neighbourhood, interestingly distorted by the complex curves of the new building. I can think of many structures which use mirror glass to add interest to what would otherwise be dull and bland – a tacit admission that the designer finds the old environment more visually exciting. This is not the case here: the Royal Concert Hall would be a pleasure

to see even if the glass reflected nothing but a cloudless sky or a blank wall.

Continuing my walk around the outer edge, I came to the Victoria Shopping Centre. The new generation of these complexes have at least aimed for style and light and avoided the claustrophobic oppressiveness of their predecessors. The pastel shades may not be to everyone's taste and in the end it is just a shopping precinct with a hat on, but it is not stodgy and has one glorious piece of fun – the Emett clock and fountain. Hang around and wait for it to strike, for metal birds and butterflies circle the skeletal clock tower in an animated fantasy.

It was time to return to the main pattern of Nottingham, a whole series of streets converging on the old Market Square. The more interesting are in the south, leading up from Broad Marsh Shopping Centre, an earlier version of the Victoria Centre and predictably duller. On Saturdays these streets burst with life; you could hardly move for people, not just shoppers but street entertainers, pavement artists and janglers of boxes collecting for everything from crippled cats to striking seamen. In the square an all-girl kazoo band performed complex manoeuvres with the precision of The Brigade of Guards. An admiring crowd applauded as they marched and counter-marched in front of the town hall steps. Although this looks like a town hall and functions as one, it is officially called the Council House. Regardless of its title, it is a building in the great Victorian town hall tradition, a gargantuan cross between a Greek temple and St Paul's Cathedral.

Market square was once home to the famous Goose Fair, which dates back to when fairs were for buying and selling, with a bit of fun on the side. Gradually the business side dropped away and the funfair became bigger, noisier, more crowded – and more fun. It was always likely to outgrow the centre and was duly moved to the outskirts, which seems a pity. Cities probably need a few days of mayhem to prevent their becoming too serious and too absorbed with money-making. No doubt the local shopkeepers, traders and office workers had a legitimate grievance, as they do in every city where a fair is traditional. But no one went bankrupt on fair days and the offices were not seriously disrupted by a bit of rowdy fun.

Although the fair has moved out, much of old Nottingham has survived. If you look above the bland shopfronts, you can see old patterns – older indeed than those in Leicester. There is a grand arcade in Long Row and some of the survivors reach down to ground level. The Bell Inn has not changed much and there are interesting details among respectable commercial buildings. The old *Express* offices wanted to proclaim their respectability to the world: no page three stuff here, for who would dare to suggest such a thing when every day was passed under the collective gaze of Victoria and Albert, Gladstone and Disraeli. There is even a glimpse of a more distant age in the Georgian shopping street of Hurts Yard.

The market originally occupied the no-man's-land between Saxon and Norman Nottingham,

The heart of the Lace Market area

so I set off towards the former. It is a spectacular and visually exciting area, best approached via Low Pavement which leads on to High Pavement. No street could be more aptly named: it stands on the edge of a cliff, and the scene must have been even more remarkable when Nottingham was served by both a low-level and a high-level railway. The latter is remembered now only in a series of tall arches striding boldly into space. Little remains of the ancient foundations of this area, apart from the just discernible grid of the streets. But there is still plenty which echoes the city's great claim to fame, the manufacture of lace.

The first signs of industry are an echo of Coventry and the ribbon-makers, and are common to most houses used by hand-workers – long rows of windows on the upper floors like Cash's top shops. Here workers laboured at their knitting frames, making stockings like their contemporaries in Leicester. But by the end of the eighteenth century there were too many hosiers and too few customers, so the Nottingham men began to look for alternatives. The machines which made stockings duplicated the action of knitting needles. Why not adapt the technique to duplicate another handicraft, lace-making? In 1786 the first machine was set to work and a new industry was born. The old town centred on St Mary's Church was once highly fashionable, but gradually the smart houses were taken over as workshops; warehouses and offices were built to serve the factories which clustered round the edge of the area. The old town laid out by the Danes received a new name: the Lace Market.

The story is told in a new museum housed in an imaginatively adapted Unitarian chapel. It is worth a visit even if you have no interest in lace, to see how an old building can be given a new life and retain its original quality. That quality includes stained-glass windows

*Albert Hall tower and the spire
of the Catholic cathedral*

designed by Edward Burne-Jones and made by the William Morris Company. There is delicious irony in the fact that a chapel closely associated with the archpriest of medievalism and a return to simple handicrafts should now contain an exhibition centred on the machinery of the Industrial Revolution. I enjoyed the whole experience enormously, but especially the lecture on the big lace-making machines by a former operative. He knew the machines intimately and had a real enthusiasm for sharing information. His explanation was clear if complicated, but one would not expect a machine which could make lace to be simple.

The Lace Market turned out to be the sort of city area I most enjoy. There is something special about a live, working environment where houses, shops and restaurants inter-mingle with warehouses and factories yet contrive to come together with rightness and unity. There are some intriguing conjunctions

73

– the houses on Short Hill, for example. A beautiful Georgian house has a big Venetian window above a graceful door and fanlight, but there is an addition above the parapet with a row of long windows. The old house had been converted to a warehouse and the windows gave light to an area where lace could be inspected. The fine houses do not just front the street: doorways lead through to little paved courtyards, quiet, dignified retreats from the busy roads and pavements.

The old pattern was broken by the Victorian merchants and manufacturers who built new streets such as Broadway, which twists and turns to reach into every available building plot. Here they built their new warehouses, designed to impress and still impressive today. T. C. Hine, whose work included one of the first warehouses in Stoney Street, described his building as 'a noble symbol of the community and its important trade'. So it is, and so are many others. They hem in the old church of St Mary and it is worth keeping an eye open for details. One of my favourites has carvings representing trade and industry – a squarerigger enters harbour on one side while a train crosses a viaduct past a mill on the other. Beyond the warehouses you glimpse the tall chimneys of the mills. There are still factories making Nottingham lace today, thriving again after the slump of the Twenties

and Thirties. Judging by the notices around the district there are plenty of vacancies for those who can claim to be competent overlockers or cross-stitchers, though I confess to only a vague idea of what such jobs might be. Almost lost in this wealth of good Victorian architecture is the old County Hall of George III's time.

The Lace Market has changed and is changing. The ancient borough became a fashionable suburb, then a working area and now it is becoming fashionable again, for the very best of reasons. Although use changed, all who built brought quality to this corner of Nottingham. It is as apparent in the Victorian warehouses as in Georgian courts and terraces. It seemed a happy note on which to leave the city, but I had one last call to make, for walking round cities is a thirsty business. I visited the New Market Hotel at the edge of the Lace Market district in Lower Parliament Street. I cannot remember when I last visited a pub where absolutely everyone was drinking pints of beer – not lager, not shorts, just beer, and most of them were enjoying that fast disappearing commodity, a pint of mild. It was a friendly place with a pleasant atmosphere, though the regulars were too engrossed in card games for idle chatter. The whole bar was full of railway memorabilia, a reminder that it was time to pick up my bags and move on.

Britannia presides over the entrance to the Devonport naval dockyards.

Plymouth from the ramparts of the Citadel.

The magnificently restored HMS Warrior dominates Portsmouth's waterfront.

The Tournai marble font in St Michael's, Southampton.

Leicester Cathedral at dusk.

Above: *Coventry's medieval cathedral survives in effigy within the ruins of the building itself, destroyed by wartime bombs.*

Opposite: *Edward Burne-Jones' great window dwarfs the machinery on show at Nottingham's Lace Hall.*

The Man of Steel makes a suitably heroic symbol of Stoke's industrial past.

Not a prematurely autumnal tree, but sculpture in Hanley Park.

Birmingham's industrial pioneers, James Watt, Matthew Boulton and William Murdock in perpetual conference.

A workshop in Birmingham's Jewellery Quarter.

Newcastle's Tyne Bridge seen from Stephenson's high level bridge.

STOKE-ON-TRENT

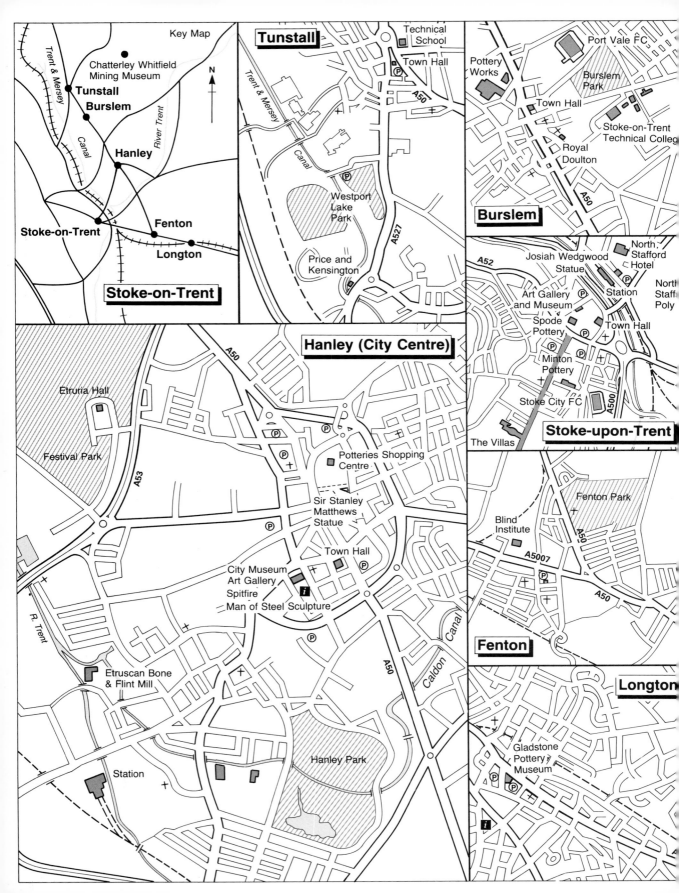

Key Map

Chatterley Whitfield Mining Museum

N

Trent & Mersey

Tunstall
Burslem

Canal

River Trent

Hanley

Stoke-on-Trent

Fenton

Longton

Stoke-on-Trent

Tunstall

Technical School

Town Hall

Trent & Mersey

Canal

A50

Westport Lake Park

A527

Price and Kensington

Burslem

Pottery Works

Port Vale FC

Burslem Park

Town Hall

Stoke-on-Trent Technical College

Royal Doulton

A50

Stoke-upon-Trent

A52

Josiah Wedgwood Statue

North Stafford Hotel

Art Gallery and Museum

Station

North Staff Poly

Spode Pottery

Town Hall

Minton Pottery

Stoke City FC

A500

The Villas

Hanley (City Centre)

A50

Etruria Hall

Festival Park

A53

Potteries Shopping Centre

Sir Stanley Matthews Statue

Town Hall

City Museum Art Gallery
Spitfire
Man of Steel Sculpture

i

R. Trent

Etruscan Bone & Flint Mill

Station

Hanley Park

A50

Caldon Canal

Fenton

Fenton Park

Blind Institute

A5007

A50

Longton

Gladstone Pottery Museum

i

7

STOKE-ON-TRENT

It was a slow but pleasant journey from Nottingham through the most English of landscapes and one which is increasingly under pressure. From the window I could see green fields, polka-dotted with early dandelions and divided by hedgerows. There was no arable land, only pasture, no lurid yellow of rape fields and no wide acres created by grubbing out the old divisions of the land. Then the Potteries appeared, quite suddenly it seemed, at Longton. Scarcely had the first houses come into view than I caught sight of the tall, shapely bottle ovens which were once the dominant features of the area.

I remember extolling the beauties of a set of these kilns at the Elektra Porcelain Works in Longton in a book I wrote in the early seventies, *Remains of a Revolution*. I was rung up by the local paper. Was I, the reporter asked, particularly fond of those kilns? I confessed that I was. 'In that case,' he replied, 'you'll be sorry to hear they were knocked down this morning. Any comment?' None he could print. Stoke had been careless with its past, and just woke up in time to realise what it was losing.

Longton was followed by Stoke Station. Our little diesel looked insignificant in the setting of one of my favourite stations. The old North Staffordshire Railway Company had a penchant for Jacobean styles and in 1848, when they came to build this important

station, they decided on a whole Jacobean enclave. The building is a passable imitation of a manor house, with shaped gables and a huge bay window which looks out across the square to another mansion – the North Stafford Hotel. It was once possible to go by tunnel from the station to the hotel, but I had to cross the street, which gave me the opportunity to pay my respects to one of the area's most interesting and influential sons, Josiah Wedgwood. He stands in the square, carefully inspecting a vase. I later found out that if I had used the underground route it would have brought me into the hotel basement right by the resplendently tiled gents, which announces its identity in a single ceramic message: LAVATORY. What my walk to the hotel did not give me was so much as a glimpse of the city centre, but then there really isn't one.

Stoke-on-Trent is unlike any other city in Britain, for it is a string of small towns once separate but now grown together without losing their identities. These are Arnold Bennett's five towns, except that there are six of them. The five which he thinly disguised are Tunstall, Burslem, Hanley, Stoke and Longton. The one he missed out was Fenton, because 'the phrase "Six Towns" is not so grand as the sound of the phrase "Five Towns".' He was right: 'Anna of the Six Towns' does not have the right ring to it, though it seems a little hard on Fenton. Bennett wanted, he said, a 'broad sounding phrase' for the district, and again it was a wise choice.

The local accent is unique, hovering uncertainly between the north and Midlands. I asked a local which region he felt he belonged to. 'Neither,' he replied firmly. 'We're the Potteries.' The people of the Potteries are very much themselves, with little need to stress traditions which are still part of their everyday lives. But how does a visitor make sense of such a place, fit it into a pattern, make a cohesive whole? Take it a bit at a time, town by town, and hope that as well as individual character a pattern may emerge which runs through them all.

An unusual portrait head of Josiah Wedgwood

For the purposes of this trip, Stoke was just one city among many. I already knew something of its character and individuality, but I wanted to grasp what made it into a city. I could find that out only by going back in time to see how it developed. Its origins were very different from those of Nottingham, where there was an obvious starting point in the strategic importance of the river crossing, guarded by its high sandstone bluff. Stoke may also be on Trent, but here the river is reduced to little more than a large stream – you could cross it half a dozen times and not know it was there.

The area has the answer on view. You never have to travel far before a vista opens up, often with views of hills and lakes which are mostly grassed over spoil heaps and flashes, the ponds which form when the earth sinks into an abandoned mine deep below the surface. Surrounding these are row upon row of terraced houses, not grand but trim and, most importantly, affordable. This is an area where work space and living space are closely related. Without exception, the terraces are built of brick and the uniformity of the colouring gives a strong hint that the material is local. The more you look around the more you realise that everything is brick apart from the few buildings which need to stand on their dignity: the religious and secular centres, the churches and town halls, are of stone. The land dictated what Stoke would be, for the coal beneath the ground fed the furnaces in which the clay was burned to make bricks and pots. There was also a third element – iron ore – but the traces of the iron and steel industry, once so important, are disappearing from the landscape.

The area, then, was a natural for potters. Pots were made here long before there was a city, before there was even a string of towns. They were made when the six towns were six hamlets. The eighteenth century brought great changes and no one did more to bring about those changes than the gentleman I could see outside my bedroom window – Josiah Wedgwood. If you want to get a glimpse of how the Potteries developed, the place to go is Etruria, now a nebulous area roughly halfway between Hanley and Newcastle-under-Lyme. The main road runs past what was the site of a garden festival, and you can gather all sorts of clues about what happened here. Some things are just hints, like the grand house looking out over the old festival site, or a pub called the Duke of Bridgewater, and an odd little domed building by the road bridge over the canal. The canal is a major clue, as is a handsome building by the locks with the evocative name the Etruscan Bone and Flint Mill – inevitably associated with bone china. How does it tie in with the statue outside the station? We have to go back to the middle of the eighteenth century and the days of small villages and local craftsmen.

Early Staffordshire pottery was not generally in vogue in the age of the Georges, when delicacy and refinement were the rage. Staffordshire clay is mainly heavy and dark, and the pots made from it lacked sophistication. The easiest way to make a plate 'interesting' was to smother it in heavy glaze. In the City Museum and Art Gallery in Hanley – which anyone with an interest in pottery should visit – there are many examples of this early ware. I admire its robust qualities, the freedom and liveliness of the decoration, the rich tones produced in often unpredictable kilns. Toft ware is famous for its vivid forms and lively details. It is slip decorated – the decoration is applied by running liquid clay over the pot much as you would ice a cake. It might appeal to twentieth-century taste, but it did not meet fashionable requirements then, when what was most admired was the fine china: porcelain from the Far East or the great manufacturers of Europe.

Wedgwood realised that he needed to lighten the colour of the basic earthenware, so that it did not need a heavy glaze to disguise its hue. His cream ware (which made his fortune) was no startling innovation, just a new way of using existing techniques. Wedgwood also realised the need for good design, careful marketing and the provision of reliable, cheap transport. In short, he turned a craft into an industry. His basic ware did not use only local clays but ball clay from the south-west of England. Into this was incorporated ground flint which whitened the finished earthenware – hence the need for grinding mills like the Etruscan Bone and Flint Mill.

Overland transport was cumbersome, unreliable and expensive, but his raw ingredients were not available locally. He could have set up his works elsewhere, but there was a resource in the Stoke area which was difficult to find elsewhere – a skilled workforce. In 1761, the gentleman of the pub sign, Francis Egerton, third Duke of Bridgewater, had built a broad canal from his coal mines at Worsley into the heart of Manchester. A canal which linked the Potteries to the two navigable rivers of Trent and Mersey would solve Wedgwood's transport problems. His flints could be brought up the east coast then down the Humber and Trent to the canal; the clays from the south-west could reach him via the Mersey. His delicate pots could be sent by smooth waterway rather than rutted track. He became the chief promoter for the new canal, begun in 1766 and opened in 1777.

The little round house by the bridge is all that remains of the great Etruria Works he built – the name was the result of a misconception. Wedgwood believed that the pottery of Greece and Rome which he so much admired was Etruscan. It was not. Nevertheless, Etruria

was the centre of great developments which revolutionised the world of the potter. It was a factory in the modern sense, with specialist craftsmen contributing their individual skills to the finished product – previously, one potter did the lot. It was the centre of a working community, for Wedgwood built a

Etruria Hall, later extended, was built for Josiah Wedgwood as his family home

village to house his workforce and he looked out on it from that grand mansion on the hill, Etruria Hall.

A pattern developed throughout the area and survives today. There may be a blank space where Wedgwood's factory stood, but that is because the company have long since moved to Barlaston. There is, however, a second blank space. Pots may still be made in this area, but the Shelton Bar steelworks which once straddled the canal are long gone, and the spoil heaps are all that remain of the collieries which surrounded Wedgwood's fine house. Visitors can still see something of this other world over at Tunstall, where the former Chatterley Whitfield Colliery has become a museum, complete with underground visits. I was lucky enough to join the museum's first curator, Jonathan Bryant, on his exploration of his new underground domain. It was just as it had been when the last miner walked out at the end of the last shift. The Coal Board officials kept promising to tidy things up and Jonathan kept saying, 'No, no, leave it. I want to keep the muck.' He was right: a mining museum should give a glimpse of the reality of the work, not some glamorised image. Not that anyone would want too much of the reality – I told a miner that I was still blowing coal dust out of my nose days after spending just one shift underground. 'It's the dust that doesn't come down,' he drily remarked. 'That's what you have to worry about.'

I found that the world of the Potteries is not limited to museums. The industry is alive and well, and the great names are still here – Doulton, Minton, Spode, Wedgwood and the rest – but they represent only a part of the story.

The Potteries can be divided into regions: earthenware to the north, cheap china to the south and the aristocrats in Stoke. Different companies have different specialities. Twyfords made their money and reputation manufacturing lavatories, and countless small concerns turn out anything from novelty teapots to canteen crockery. I chanced upon one of these: Price and Kensington by the canal at Longport. What caught my eye was the top of a bottle oven poking above the roofs, so I stuck my head around the door and was invited in. I went through a room with teapots in every conceivable form, and was tempted by a cheery penguin with a beak spout. Potbanks are an incomprehensible maze at first glance, a complex of interconnected rooms and courtyards, in the outermost of which is the oven, as shapely and beautiful as all of its kind, even if its working life is done. The nearest you can get now to seeing these kilns in their glory is a museum, so I headed back to Longton and the Gladstone

Pottery.

As with Chatterley Whitfield I first came here before it was a museum. It was an eerie place like an earthbound *Marie Celeste*. Everything had been left where it was – teapots were half formed, cups were handleless, plates stacked ready for decoration. It looked as if work could restart the next day: but it wouldn't, or not in the old ways. I went back regularly to see the slow changes of museum development: on my wall at home is a plate fired in the last bottle oven firing of 1978.

The kilns are the great attraction. They were purely functional devices: at their hearts were coal-fired furnaces around which were stacked the pots and plates of pliable clay in fireproof containers called saggars. The whole was contained within the 'bottles', which were no more than combinations of covers and chimneys. But bald facts can give no hint of the majesty of the old ovens: sinuous and graceful from the outside, magical when you walk inside and the light streams down from the round opening high above. There was a time when it looked as if no bottle ovens would be saved. It is all right for visitors to romanticise, but when all the ovens were lit they sent up a foul, reeking smoke which sat over the Potteries as a black, impenetrable cloud. They say that Stoke never got bombed in the Second World War because when the pilots saw the smoke they assumed that the city was already on fire from end to end. Locals were glad to see the end of the kilns. But now that work has ended, the beauty remains. I could not have gone back to Stoke if some bottle ovens had not been saved.

Gladstone was not one of the great potworks. It was an everyday place producing everyday ware, but it was as complex as the finest. You can follow the progression from the mixing of

Bottle ovens at Gladstone Pottery

the clay in a lovely machine powered by a shiny steam engine through the stages of shaping and forming to the last and most delicate stage – applying the decoration. Craftsmen and women still demonstrate their trades and displays show the ware of Staffordshire, including a marvellous collection of lavatories – why not, since the flush toilet probably did more for public health than a hospital full of doctors? But for all its virtues, Gladstone is a museum not a working pottery. You can see these in plenty in the area and I enjoyed wandering around Longton to get a feel of one of the pottery towns.

One thing you see is the effect of Wedgwood's Etruria factory on others which followed. Aynsley China was built in the Wedgwood style, with a big central entrance for wagons leading into an enclosed works. The front has a big Venetian window, also borrowed from Wedgwood. After that I went on to one of the potteries which welcomes visitors, one of the great names of the trade – Minton. Others have similar stories to tell and use similar techniques, but the joy is that no two potteries are quite the same. Minton have traditions of which they are as jealously proud as any of the other famous names.

The Minton factory has a long pedigree. It began when Thomas Minton arrived back in Stoke in 1789, having learned engraving techniques in London. He began by making copper plates for manufacturers in the area, but soon decided to make pots to take his own engraved designs. By 1793 he had established a small factory in Stoke, little different from many others.

The decisive change came when his son Herbert joined the business. The company had moved from earthenware to bone china – the bones, like Wedgwood's flints, being ground in local mills. But what distinguished Minton's ware was the intensity of colour he achieved, the richness of decoration and gilding and, above all, the artistry of the modelling and painting. Minton brought over potters and artists from France and soon established a French colony in the town. Innovations continued, notably Minton's long battle to find a modern method of producing floor tiles in a style once ubiquitous in the great medieval cathedrals and guildhalls. He succeeded just in time for the gothic revival and some of the most famous buildings of the age were graced with Minton floor tiles, as far apart as the Palace of Westminster and the Capitol in Washington. The church at Hartshill is a local showpiece. Minton became a member of the Royal Doulton group in 1968 but their identity has never been submerged, and their success is still based on the very highest quality, without cost cutting. The best can never be cheap.

What struck me forcibly about Minton was how labour-intensive the work is even today – and how wasteful. Many manufacturers talk about quality control, but few have the exacting standards you find here or anything like the loss from accidents. Anything can go wrong at any time. The new generation of furnaces may be infinitely more reliable than the beautiful old bottle ovens, but plates still come out cracked, glazes are marked with tiny dust particles – and there's another broken crock for the rubbish tip.

No one can mistake the sheer skill on display: even the seemingly simplest job is the result of long practice and requires a steady hand and a keen eye. There are techniques which have scarcely changed since the first Thomas Minton set up shop. Etched copper plates, things of beauty in themselves, are still used for the finest decoration, but the artistry lies with the painters. Minton Ware is still synonymous with richness. Gilders brush on the gold in perfect patterns or build it up layer upon layer to produce an embossed pattern. Artists decorate plates by hand. If you want your family or your possessions immortalised, Minton will paint them on plates and saucers, cups and tureens. A personal dinner service was being prepared for an oil sheikh – and you would need to be an oil sheikh to pay for it.

The Minton works is about continuity – of tradition, of skills and above all of people. Look at a Minton wage book of a century ago and compare it with one today and you find the same names. That continuity is encouraged. We could dismiss it as archaic paternalism, but there are few complaints among the workforce. In retrospect, what was most surprising about the Potteries was how a way of life which scarcely exists in the rest of England still thrives here. The terraces which roll away from the works are occupied by the workers, and they stare in bewilderment at the idea of long-distance commuting. They walk. The main streets are liberally dotted

with plain, ordinary pubs which are taken up with shrieks of delight by middle-class trendies in other parts but here are what they always were – friendly places. 'How do, young man,' said an elderly and presumably myopic customer, 'how are you?' He waited for an answer because he really wanted to know. And, praise be, the pub had the great local speciality on the menu: Staffordshire oatcakes – a kind of wholemeal pancake which I had hot with melted cheese in the middle. It was delicious and cheap, which is what pub food is supposed to be. It is easy to sentimentalise about such places. Not all the traditions are good: I was taken to a pub where I was told there was a female customer about once in six months; I got the impression that that was considered excessive. Tradition can easily become dour conservatism.

There is a homogeneity about the pattern of the Potteries – factories and terraces, factories and terraces – but it can produce surprises. When Minton brought over his French artists, there were no brick terraces for them. They were given their own street, The Villas, a tiny enclave of Italianate houses prinked out in un-Stokelike pastels and surrounded by trees. It is as unlikely now as then, and just as pleasant.

There are fine parks to enjoy, invariably endowed by one of the great potters. My favourite is Hanley Park, if only because the Caldon Canal threads through the middle and there are few lovelier canals in the country. It too was promoted by the potters, Josiah Wedgwood prominent among them. There is a fine new theatre which at its best reflects the tastes and concerns of the community: they still talk about the play that was written at the time of the closure of the local steel works at Shelton Bar. This was drama with fire in its belly which made a deep impression, even on

A simple sign for a Potteries pub

Italianate villas built to house Minton's artists

those who might never have considered going to a theatre. The same local concern is shown in the great Man of Steel sculpture outside the Art Gallery, and the Spitfire inside, set there as a reminder that its designer Reginald Mitchell was a local man. But other cities have their pubs and theatres, museums and grand buildings. Stoke's appeal lies elsewhere, in an ordinariness which is itself extraordinary. It is a place very low on pretensions, but where local characteristics have never been swamped by anonymous development. No matter where you go, Stoke is recognisably Stoke.

I went to look at another town – Burslem – which has many associations with the great potters. In the early eighteenth century it was by far the most important centre. Writing the history of the industry in 1829, Simeon Shaw called it 'The Mother of the Potteries'. One can still grasp the old intimate relationship between the town and the industry which was the economic mainspring of its life. Bottle ovens peep over rooftops and are glimpsed down alleys.

Burslem was Arnold Bennett's Bursley and it is extraordinary how many of the features

85

he describes can be recognised today. Here The Leopard has changed his spots, for it appeared as The Tiger, 'one of the oldest inns in Bursley'. The Blood Tub, where the inhabitants could revel in gory melodramas, stood where the Queen's Theatre now stands. The replacement offers less sensational fare. The Town Hall has changed its use: once the pride of Burslem, a civic monument which had and has a pleasing and restrained dignity. It is now a recreation centre. Other transformations are even less likely: Clayhanger's print works have become the Kismet Restaurant, and the Conservative Club of which Darius Clayhanger was a member is now the Midland Bank. Perhaps that is not such a great change after all. But there is one building which brings the world of the potters and that of the novelist together. The Wedgwood Institute appears in Bennett's life both in fiction and reality. The Card attended its reincarnation as Bursley Endowed School and the author went there between 1877 and 1880. It is, given the Wedgwood preoccupation with the ancient world, no surprise to find it built in an Italianate style. A frieze shows what it was bound to show – the different stages in the manufacture of pots. It is a building which belongs completely to this place and it is good to know that it has been listed for preservation.

All these wanderings around the towns leave you wondering if there is anything even approximating to a city centre. There is: not in Stoke but in Hanley, where there are new shops, pedestrian precincts and a brand new shopping centre. They were still putting the finishing touches to this when I was there, and everyone was talking about the giant teapot which would be on display – the biggest in the world. That was a nod towards local tradition, but the centre is unabashedly of the new generation – light and airy, making use of that popular architectural device of the eighties, the atrium. But as I saw the decorators adding the last touches of paint, I was struck by *déjà vu*. Those pastel shades looked familiar. I enquired whether there was a shopping centre in Nottingham belonging to the same group. Indeed there was. It is sad that developers feel no need to make a distinction between centres in two such disparate cities.

By the end of my visit I was infected by the enthusiasm of the two guides who had helped me find my way around. They were not locals. One was Welsh and the other from Yorkshire, but I would as soon have told the Welshman that England would thrash the home team at Cardiff Arms Park and the Yorkshireman that Lancashire would win the Roses match as admit to either that there was anything to criticise in Stoke. Of course there are things to criticise, but it remains unique among the cities. It is parochial in the best sense, in that it has kept a hold on its identity. Something of that keen local pride came across when I left the new shopping centre in Hanley. It faces along a street to the sort of square which in Victorian times would have had a glum statue of Her Majesty. Not here – there is a new statue of a little man in baggy shorts with a football at his feet: Sir Stanley Matthews. By nature a modest man, he suggested that a more appropriate figure would be Mitchell the Spitfire man, who had saved England. Stoke had the answer to that. 'So did you, Stan,' said the local dignitary, 'lots of times.' I am not quite sure why that sums up Stoke for me, but it does.

BIRMINGHAM

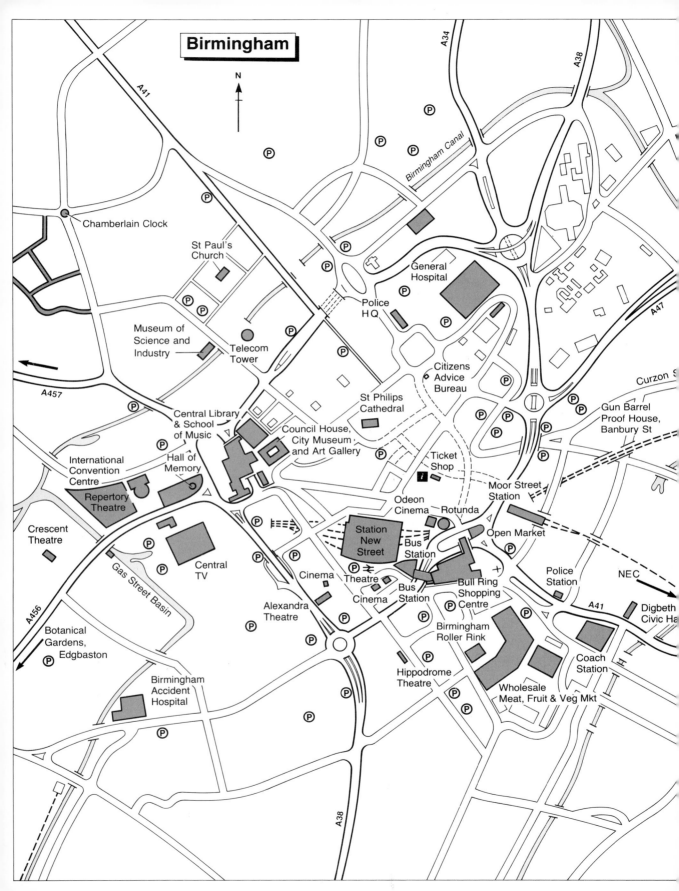

8

BIRMINGHAM

If there was ever a city which justified train travel, Birmingham is it. No matter which way you enter, there is something to catch the eye outside the carriage window. At the start of my Midlands tour I saw one aspect of the city – little workshops and factories arranged in no recognisable order and often crammed into the oddly shaped spaces at railway junctions. I knew one such site from the days when I used to travel up from Oxford: a burst of armorial colour and splendour as the train passed the Gun Barrel Proof House. I had promised myself that one day I would go to see it – this time I was going to do so.

Coming from the north is the best approach of all, though not everyone shares my enthusiasm. At the approach to Wolverhampton book or paper is put down and I cloud the glass with my breath, as eager as a young lad waiting for his first glimpse of the sea. I too look for water, the water of the canals, the BCN – Birmingham Canal Navigation, a complex network of waterways which enables the city to boast that it has more miles of canal than Venice. If anyone remarks that they are scarcely as attractive, the Brummies point out that they smell much the same. I wait for each anticipated treat: first there are the locks at Wolverhampton, up past the grandeur of the M & B Brewery; then the extraordinary crossing point where everything comes together – one canal crosses another, our train chugs

over the top and the motorway rides high over us on massive concrete pillars. There are deep cuttings which bring the country to the town and which in May were brilliant with gorse. You get a glimpse of Thomas Telford's magnificent iron span, Galton Street Bridge, which crosses the deepest of the cuttings; with luck you may even see a working boat on the BCN.

New attractions to look out for are metal horses cavorting by the trackside – galloping, leaping, contemplative. One of these sculpted beasts shares a field with real horses, who do not seem to mind the presence of their metal neighbour. And I was delighted by a scrapyard which had put up its own Welcome to Birmingham sign. One thing always puzzles me on this journey though: where does Birmingham begin? Wolverhampton shades into Dudley, Dudley merges into Smethwick, but where is the city of Birmingham? I have never understood the mystery of the boundaries.

Visually you cannot make any distinction between Birmingham and its neighbours. I know Black Country residents detest their area being referred to as Birmingham, but you really cannot blame us ignorant visitors. Everything seems joined together, stretched out along the lines of canals and railway tracks. The canals must have played a vital role in the development of the area: there are so many of them, and so much seems centred on their

The Farmer's Bridge flight of locks in the heart of the city

narrow, gleaming threads. The journey helps to form impressions and the idea that a major city lies ahead is strengthened by the drawing together of the railway web. On some routes you see miles of sidings and the lifts of the container yard; on others you get glimpses of the grandeur of the past. Curzon Street Station boasts massive Ionic pillars, an attempt by architect Philip Hardwick to complement his Euston arch at the other end of the line.

Euston lost its arch in a mindless act of official vandalism, and the Curzon Street arch has lost its station. The fine entrance leads only to the goods yard. It is sad, doubly so because I was about to be deposited at the most depressing station on the British Rail system: Birmingham New Street. This is no triumphal entry to the Second City, but a dive underground into dingy tunnels, and when you fight your way up to the light the station looks out on nothing in particular.

I arrived determined to find something to enjoy. The trouble is that here, more than anywhere in the country, the motor car rules. Like the trains at New Street, pedestrians are packed off into underground passages. I have never liked underpasses, largely because I am not competent at using them. I can see where I want to be, but when I get below my sense of direction seems to go astray. I was not going to get off to a bad start this time. I took a cab and was glad to be in the hands of an expert. We had an interesting conversation occasioned by a bus which carved us up. The opening up of bus routes to competition has apparently led to an influx of new drivers, not all of whom know the city. My driver told me one had stopped at his rank the other day to ask the way: it certainly brings a touch of adventure to everyday travel.

I was staying in the heart of the city at the Grand Hotel. This Grand, like Leicester's, lives up to its name – even more so, for it boasts a banqueting hall of breathtaking opulence. The other pleasing discovery was that I was now safely inside the ring road. I could move about in comfort and on the surface. The centre has the space and the buildings to convince you that you really are in the Second City, and a very intriguing mixture there is.

Birmingham, like Stoke, is a new creation, a creature of the Industrial Revolution, which shot up as rapidly as Alice when she drank the magic potion. One does not look here for signs of the distant past and ancient history. But opposite me, with space to allow its elegant simplicity to be appreciated, was the Cathedral of St Philip, designed by Thomas Archer in 1709. It is a lovely example of the English baroque: at first sight it seems a simple building, but the more you look the more complicated it becomes. It depends for its effect on a basic oblong plan elaborated by concave and convex planes which keep the eye moving up and down the tower and along the main body of the church. It has the flowing rhythms of the baroque, without the extravagances of many Continental churches of the period. The interior is cool and restrained, and for the second time in a week I made the acquaintance of Edward Burne-Jones and William Morris, who were responsible for the stained glass. I had not expected such a church in such a spot; the civic buildings not far away were less of a surprise.

Most cities are content to have one or two civic buildings together, but Birmingham has a clutch of them, grouped round a multi-level space, part city square and part amphitheatre. Everything is formal, yet friendly and optimistic – optimistic because many recent additions while not attempting to ape the styles of the past have taken them into account.

The most important building is the Town Hall, remarkable because it is so restrained even though it was built when most industrial cities were opting for flamboyance. Many others date from the high period of Victorian gothic, while Birmingham slides in at the end of the classical revival. Classical is what the Town Hall is, a Corinthian temple – no fuss, no elaboration, just itself. This restraint did not last: the City Museum and Art Gallery gives the impression that the architect threw

The classical formality of the Town Hall

stylistic devices at his drawing board and settled for whatever stuck – a touch of the classic here, a chunk of Italianate there; no surface undecorated and a huge clock tower stuck on the end. The clock tower is considered locally as imposing as the tower at Westminster and has been nicknamed Big Brum.

The square contrives to hold the disparate buildings together. A sweeping curve of steps turns part of it into a small amphitheatre, which goes well with the Town Hall; but in the middle is a sort of miniature Albert Memorial, much more in the tradition of the museum. Presiding over it from his plinth is James Watt, nonchalantly leaning on the separate condenser which revolutionised steam engine construction. He shares the square with Joseph Priestley, who would no doubt take an ironic view of the honour, because the local citizenry burned his home to the ground, together with all his scientific papers, and he was forced to flee for his life.

The square is completed by modern library buildings and some even more modern structures which are daring by English city standards. A pair of glass blocks face each other with entrances like glazed tents on their sides. This should be part of a continuous space which joins the Town Hall to the civic centre, but road improvements got in the way, so the curious little Hall of Memory and the jokily elaborate centre are left looking like the guests who weren't invited to the party. The whole area is now dominated by a newcomer, Alpha House – tall, curved and slender like a great aircraft wing stood on end. In the distance cranes nod in a stately dance, like some strange mating ritual of giant metal birds. Birmingham is a restless city, constantly changing, constantly on the move. This small area around the Town Hall is a crash course in the architectural styles of the last 150 years. Each age builds and rebuilds in its own image.

The fountain outside the City Museum and Art Gallery

Which modern building would one choose to epitomise post-war Birmingham? It would surely have to be the rotunda above the Bull Ring, but not for much longer. It is marked down as next in line for the bulldozer. And already attention is turning to the next major development for the city centre.

It is ironical that this new development centres on what was, years ago, my favourite place in Birmingham. Gas Street was then a little side road running off Broad Street. There was nothing remarkable about it, unless you noticed a red wooden door set high in a wall: unmistakably a fire door. The firemen could stick their hoses through to collect water from the canal hidden behind the wall. A separate door provided access to a secret, enclosed world – Gas Street Basin, where a small fleet of narrow boats floated under the shadow of the old warehouses. Then the warehouses went, knocked down early one morning before anyone knew what was happening, and the intimacy was destroyed.

For years, Gas Street stood next to a draughty car park. Now it is coming back to life.

A new pub has been built – the James Brindley – which uses motifs borrowed from the old working days, including a canopy on pillars which crosses the edge of the wharf, but this is no simple pastiche. Alongside it is a new, small-scale office development. The authorities have learned a lot in recent years: they now appreciate that the old boats brought colour and visual excitement to the basin and they have encouraged them to return. The fleet of narrow boats is back: a few trading, some running tourist trips, others adapted as floating homes. The scheme is still in its earliest phase. The whole area is going to be a huge, expensive conference centre – an inner-city enterprise to match the out-of-town National Exhibition Centre. The little secret canal I used to chug along will be a secret no more. The planners have also realised that locals may put up with dingy underpasses, but the international conference visitor will not. There is to be a reorganisation of the roads. People will be able to move on the surface, and cars will have to dip into the gloom. If only they had thought of that before!

It is hard work keeping up. A complaint often levelled against British cities and against the British in general is that they prefer sentimentalising the past to moving into the future. Birmingham has never had any qualms about abandoning the past if it stood in the way of where the city thought it should go. The rest of the country regarded this with suspicion and came up with the image of the Brash Brummy: flash car, flash clothes, flash jewellery – never mind the quality, look what it costs – one whose idea of High Culture was a sobbing rendition of 'My Way'. If that really is Birmingham, why has this city been able to attract and keep one of the brightest lights in the classical music firmament, conductor

Simon Rattle? The way to find out was to talk to the City of Birmingham Symphony Orchestra. Rattle has built it into a fine orchestra – not just good by provincial standards, but excellent by any standards. Presumably, given his abilities, he could have built a fine orchestra anywhere. Why stay with the CBSO when cheque books are being waved in centres such as Los Angeles?

One factor was the appeal of being in the provinces, where rehearsals can be organised without the constant drift in and out of players making money as session musicians in anything from soap commercials to pop record backings. But the principal appeal for Rattle seems to be the openness of Birmingham audiences to his ideas and enthusiasms. They do not demand a staple diet of the standard classics but are prepared, even eager, to accept newcomers. They are ready to listen without prejudice in a way that audiences in other cities often are not. The CBSO gives sixty concerts a year in Birmingham and could probably fill the hall for twice that number. It is an artistic success story as pleasing and satisfying for the conductor and players as for the audience. The CBSO is only part of the arts scene: there is the Midlands Arts Centre, set in Cannon Hill Park, where the emphasis is as much on participation as watching, the Ikon Gallery, one of the most ambitious outside London, the Birmingham Rep and more. But the CBSO best epitomises the new adventurous spirit in the arts.

It is easy to see Birmingham simply as a thrusting, dynamic city, but it has a past which goes some way towards explaining the present. It was built on the foundations of natural raw materials – coal and iron – but where other cities specialised this one diversified. They made the everyday things – nails and chains, guns and trinkets. They grasped the new. When James Watt developed his ideas for a new steam engine, the Birmingham entrepreneur Matthew Boulton drew him into a partnership which monopolised engine production for the last decades of the eighteenth century. When the canal age began in the 1760s, Birmingham established itself at the heart of the system and built a multitude of small factories and workshops along the strands of that watery web.

That old spirit has survived to a surprising extent. There is still an area of small workshops and back-street businesses which have kept their identity intact. The new Birmingham is there up front, but you have to hunt out the old, and it is no bad thing to have a local guide to help you. In my tour of the Jewellery Quarter I was led by Marie Haddleton, born and bred in the area and, it seems, on first-name terms with everyone who lives and works there.

At the heart of the Jewellery Quarter is the Chamberlain clock, a memorial to Joseph Chamberlain, the MP who had a long association with the area. Around it are streets containing a lot of jewellers' shops. So what? There are a lot of jewellers' shops. What is not immediately obvious is that there are also thousands of craftsmen at work in a honeycomb of workshops. Down an alleyway between two shops is a courtyard surrounded by buildings, each room of which hissed with the gas of burners and was suddenly lit by bursts of intense flame. Although there are places on the main streets where you can watch jewellery-making going on, it is mostly a hidden world which gives this district a unique character.

There are occasional flourishes, notably the Argent Centre, which has nothing to do with silver. Originally used for making gold pens and pencils, it was built in 1863 in the Florentine style, using an odd construction

technique. Individual floors were built of hollow bricks through which iron rods were threaded to provide strength and fireproofing. Today it houses a multitude of small units. The School of Jewellery and Silversmithing does this too, but it is not really the grand buildings which set the tone. Houses in Tenby Street – and Marie Haddleton was born at No 12 – were basic two-up, two-down terraces, but with a workshop tacked on to the top floor. In Albion Street the engraved glass windows still advertise such trades as pressing and stamping.

The Jewellery Quarter boasts one grand set piece – St Paul's Square, designed as a complete unit in the 1770s, with houses around the edge and the jewellers' church in the centre. Time was not kind to St Paul's: the growth of the quarter saw houses converted to workshops or demolished in favour of small factories. The residential area looked as if it might be gone for good, but enough survives to give a tantalising glimpse of how

A cast-iron urinal near the Jewellery Quarter

splendid it must have been. The church is a different matter – as unmistakably eighteenth century as the houses which surround it. The interior has all its original features, including the numbered pews once held by the leading industrialists of the day. Matthew Boulton had his place and so did James Watt, though Watt seems to have made little use of his. The east window is the work of Francis Eginton, who was Boulton's glass painter. It is a memorial to Birmingham's Industrial Revolution and belongs as firmly to that age as the workshops and factories which were turning out humble buckles and clasps, and, if it comes to that, the humble cast-iron urinal in nearby Vyze Street.

Among the multitudinous trades, the gun-smiths played an important part. It was time for my curiosity to be satisfied: I was to see the Gun Barrel Proof House. It was originally built in 1813 on the edge of town beside the Birmingham and Fazeley Canal, but was soon overtaken by development: the railways came and literally overshadowed the old buildings. Yet the place has never changed, neither have its functions nor its methods of working. Every gun offered for sale in this country, whether made here or not, must be proofed – officially tested and stamped as safe for use. Some European guns are accepted if proofed in their own country but others – from Japan, Russia and America, for example – must all be approved here. The trade supplies its own Guardians, whose role is defined by Parliament: they must be gunsmiths, men of property and live within ten miles of Birmingham.

When the trade was at its peak some 900,000 guns a year passed through the Proof House, but it is now down to 50–60,000, which is still a substantial number. Outwardly the place seems not to have changed at all. You enter beneath a big, colourful trophy, a sculpted group of armour and banners. Inside are panelled rooms and a series of outhouses grouped round a courtyard. It has an air of studied calm – one does not rush around when carrying firearms. I knew the place had a long tradition, but I expected a world of lasers and computers. Not a bit of it. They test a shotgun just as they always have: the manufacturer supplies a recommended cartridge load, so they simply overload the cartridge and fire the gun – with due precaution. If the gun comes to no harm, it has passed and is duly stamped; if it blows up, there is not much room for argument about the result. It is a comfort that in a city devoted to the gods of modernism and progress an institution exists which has scarcely changed in two centuries.

By way of complete contrast I went to Edgbaston. No squashed world of little workshops here, and the Botanical Gardens would seem to have little or nothing to do with gun barrels. Yet they stand close together in time, for the Birmingham Botanical and Horticultural Society was founded in 1829 and the site for the gardens was chosen two years later. It was part of the same movement to control and regularise, to apply scientific principles.

Bourneville: a rural idyll for factory workers

Plants would be collected on a systematic basis from around the globe and brought here to be displayed and studied. But it was always meant to be a place of beauty as well as a practical study centre, so laying out the gardens went to one of the leading landscape gardeners of the day, J. C. Loudon, recorder of the work of his even greater predecessor, Humphrey Repton. There were eventually to be hot houses for tropical exotica – the lily house, the palm house and the terraced glasshouses whose decorative ironwork vies with the plants for attention. But the main interest is the seventeen-acre gardens, partly formal, partly contrived to look natural. It was not so much the peace that I enjoyed, nor even the vivid colours, but the wonderful smells. Diesel and petrol fumes could be forgotten.

The gardens had become a touch dilapidated, but a major refurbishment culminated in a grand royal re-opening in April 1988. Experts revel in the variety of species here. Blissfully ignorant of all things horticultural, my lack of expertise was no handicap: that plant in the corner would look no more brilliant if I knew its Latin name, though it might increase my admiration for the gardeners if I had some notion of the effort needed to raise such exotica under the grey, cold skies of England.

The Botanical Gardens were an interlude, for I was still waiting to see the old Birmingham from which the new had grown. The system of motorways and ring roads, and the network of railways do no more than point up a vital factor in the understanding of the city's past. It sits in the centre of England and in the centre of the country's transport system. It had the advantage of important raw materials on the doorstep, but if you chart its explosive growth since the eighteenth century you can see how it has spread out along its transport connections.

It all began with the Birmingham I know best – the world of canals. Even without the historical justification, I was not going to leave without renewing acquaintance with the Birmingham Canal Navigation I had glimpsed so briefly from the train. I also wanted to delve back into the influence of the Industrial Revolution, so many traces of which have been gobbled up in the process of advance and replacement. Dudley is not Birmingham, but it is the place where the old values are enshrined. You can visit the Museum of Science and Industry down by the long flight of locks which hurries away from Farmer's Bridge Junction near Gas Street Basin. (There is a special magic in Birmingham names: where else could you find bucolic Farmer's Bridge next to plain Gas Street?) But I had a hankering after the more complete picture you can get from the big open air site, the Black Country Museum. So to Dudley I went, via one of my favourite canal spots.

It is not easy to explain to the uninitiated the attractions of these canals. They are black, greasy and contain a rich assortment of flotsam, from greying polystyrene to the occasional dead dog. But they create a world all their own, isolated and complete. The appeal is to a large extent the attraction of things designed for a practical purpose which manage to be attractive at the same time. This can be illustrated at a point on the canal near Rolf Street Station, Smethwick. The canal appears on two levels: the old wavering wandering line of the first Birmingham Canal which wriggled its way around every hump and hollow in the landscape, and its replacement, designed by Thomas Telford as a straight-line route in a deep cutting. The pleasures of the old are small-scale pleasures, a simple brick bridge rearing steeply over the water, its humped back ridged with bricks to provide a foothold for horses; the contrast between old dark red bricks and the crisp black and white of the lock gates. The old needed access to a point beyond the line of the new, so an aqueduct had to be built across the cutting. On the old, the materials were brick and stone and timber; here technology came into play with a wide iron span. This is no simple structure: the Engine Arm Aqueduct was embellished with an arcade of pointed arches giving it a curiously ecclesiastical look. Self-conscious artistry had reached the rough world of the first canal, foreshadowing the changes which mark Georgian Britain from its Victorian successor. It is not very often that the differences can be seen so clearly as in this quiet world behind the back streets of Smethwick.

I followed the canal down to Dudley and the Black Country Museum. Its aim is to show both the industrial and the everyday life of the region. There are big set pieces: a working tramway, a reproduction of the first Dudley steam engine used to pump out the mines in 1712, and examples of small workshops. The site is based on an old canal complex with towering lime kilns, and the pride of the place is the Dudley Tunnel – no mere hole in the ground but a mixture of narrow openings, down which boats slide like fingers slipping into gloves, and echoing caverns. A small village is being rebuilt, which re-creates the atmosphere of the turn of the century. The pub is a real pub selling real Black Country beer; they still bake bread in coal-fired ovens, and they will serve you food once standard throughout the area. I had to go

to a museum to buy home-made faggots and peas which were once widely available. It was worth going for that alone.

This is not a book about museums so I will not dwell on the attractions of Dudley, but one feature makes it special – the people who work there. For them, the past seems not to be a thing of artefacts and pictures nor even reconstructions, but one stage in a continuous process which incorporates the present and the future. It is possible to glimpse what the whole region was in the days before the motor car ruled. Its sense of individuality comes across in the personalities of the people who described it: the man setting up the rolling mill, for whom the past was an appreciation of the quality of the craft used in the machines; the man behind the bar who had seen a thousand rowdy Saturday nights, and the cooks and bakers revelling in the forgotten tastes of the past. It is easy to think of museums such as this as exercises in nostalgia. They are, in so far as they leave out the filth, the disease and the poverty, but that should not blind us to the qualities of earlier ages. Perhaps more than any other city, Birmingham needs to take with it in its headlong dash towards modernity a memory of what made it and gave it character. There was a time about twenty years ago when it looked as if everything might be swept away, but now a search is on for a balance which will find a place for the old canal, the jewellers' workshops and a testing house where they still pull a trigger with a piece of string.

Newcastle upon Tyne

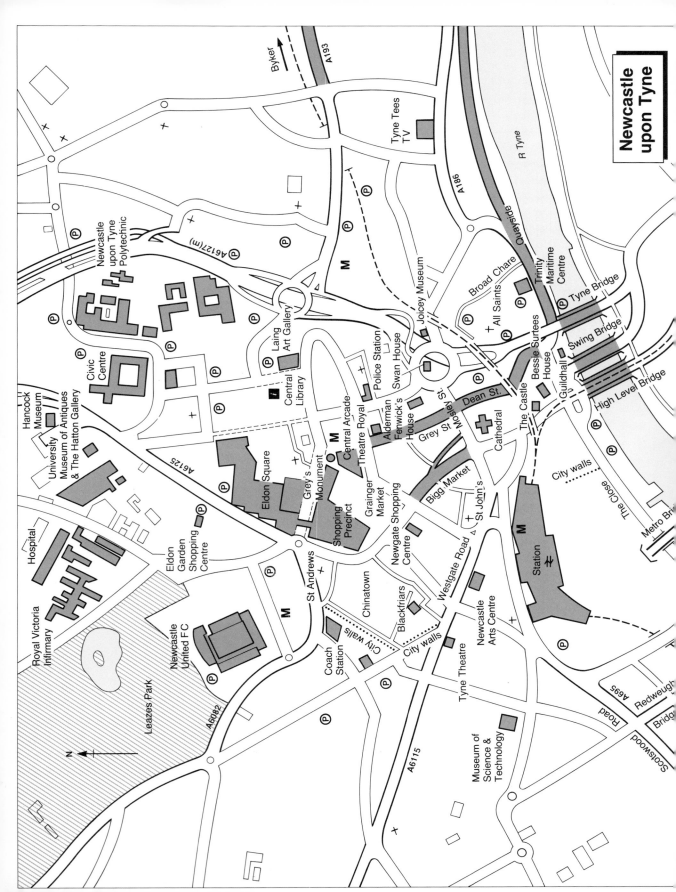

Newcastle upon Tyne

Byker
A193

Tyne Tees TV

R Tyne
Quayside

Newcastle upon Tyne Polytechnic
A6127(m)

Joicey Museum
Broad Chare
All Saints
Trinity Maritime Centre
Tyne Bridge

A186

Laing Art Gallery
Civic Centre

M

Police Station
Swan House
Bessie Surtees House
Swing Bridge
Guildhall

Central Library

Hancock Museum
University Museum of Antiques & The Hatton Gallery

Central Arcade
Theatre Royal
Alderman Fenwick's House
Grey St
Mosley St.
Dean St.
Cathedral
The Castle
High Level Bridge

A6125

Eldon Square

Grey's Monument
M
Grainger Market
Shopping Precinct
Bigg Market
St John's
City walls
The Close
Metro Bri

Hospital

Eldon Garden Shopping Centre

Newgate Shopping Centre
Westgate Road
Station
M

Royal Victoria Infirmary

Newcastle United FC

St Andrews
M

Chinatown
Blackfriars
City walls

Newcastle Arts Centre

A6082

Leazes Park

Coach Station
City walls

Tyne Theatre

N

A6115

Museum of Science & Technology

Scotswood Road
Redweugh Road
A695
Bridge

9

NEWCASTLE
UPON TYNE

Leaving the Midlands for the north is to change one world for another. This scarcely registers at first, although Derbyshire provides a brief glimpse of a landscape of hills and moors. The journey up through South Yorkshire brings a view of a desolate, ruined land, of worn-out houses leaning together in tired terraces. It is a scarred landscape of old spoil heaps – you can grass them, you can plant them, you can grow trees on them but they remain spoil heaps – rearing above land which is their reverse image, land which has sunk into its old mineworkings and left hollows full of motionless water. For one awful part of the journey it is a countryside with the goodness sucked from it, where wealth was created but ended up on someone else's table. It is only a short part of the journey, but it accounts for part of the attitudes in the north and towards the north: a defensiveness on one part, and on the other a patronising glance at a region whose day has gone.

As I anticipated the arrival at Newcastle, I could not get the image of the flat lands of South Yorkshire out of my mind. How easy to see the north in terms of stereotypes: cloth caps, Jarrow marchers, chip butties, Newcastle Brown and pigeon lofts. Even a more sophisticated line of thinking might dwell on the great figures of engineering, giants such as Armstrong and the two Stephensons. Yet even that is hankering back to a past overtaken by

events, with little more relevance to life in the 1990s than the cartoon world of Andy Capp. The image is still of an area in decline – grubby and worn out. I would say to those who have never taken the train to Newcastle: brace yourselves for a shock, for no city in the land boasts a more dramatic approach and few run so counter to popular stereotypes.

No matter how often I visit Newcastle I never tire of the moment of arrival. Nothing prepares you for it. The train threads its way through Gateshead and then suddenly there is the Tyne with its array of bridges and the city clambering up the steep hill from the river bank. You might expect a sense of anti-climax as you slow down for the station; not a bit of it, for the station too is magnificent. You sweep in on a gentle curve under a great roof of glass carried in three spans on delicate iron columns, as fine in its way as the palm house at Kew. It does have something of the look of a magnificent conservatory at the back of a stately home, for the buildings have their own grandeur, culminating in the dignified stone portico which leads you into the street.

The first thing to strike you in the street is a statue with the single name STEPHENSON. This is really not good enough. George Stephenson ('The Father of Railways') was certainly one of Tyneside's most famous sons, but what about his son Robert, whose

The Stephenson memorial

here in 1815 that George Stephenson demonstrated his miners' safety lamp, designed at the same time as the more famous version of Sir Humphry Davy. A Stephenson lamp is still displayed in the Lit. and Phil., but I see I am already falling into one of my northern traps, concentrating on the working world of pits and railway. Well, men like the two Stephensons did as much as any to shape our modern world, but Robert Stephenson's architectural colleague John Dobson had a major role in shaping Newcastle upon Tyne. As good a place as any to start an exploration of its different elements is the crossing point where Mosley Street divides Grey Street to the north from Dean Street to the south.

Looking back towards the station, down Mosley Street, the view is dominated by the cathedral. It started as a humble parish church in the twelfth century, though most of what can now be seen dates from the fourteenth and fifteenth centuries, including what is literally its crowning glory – the spire. The pointed steeple rests on a crown of arches which rise above the pinnacled tower. Visitors often remark how similar it is to St Giles in Edinburgh, at which point the locals point out that it predates the Scots version by over half a century. There is a further Scots connection: when Newcastle was under siege in 1644, the Scots threatened to blow up the church. The mayor filled the tower with Scots prisoners and said 'carry on'. The tower was preserved.

Drury Lane runs off the main street. Was there ever a Theatre Royal in this northern Drury Lane? There was indeed, though it has long gone, replaced in 1837 by the 'New' Theatre Royal. Down the other part of Mosley Street, to the east, the view is notably less interesting, culminating in one of those four-square developments in concrete found everywhere but belonging nowhere.

high-level bridge still carries the railway across the river? I forgive the designers their ambiguity because they have produced a statue of delightful incongruity. My favourite figure is the gentleman draped in Grecian robes who leans nonchalantly on a locomotive – *Planet* it looks like – at the base of the statue. But I had no need to explore further, no need even to leave the station, for I was staying at the old Station Hotel, which has a back door on the concourse itself. What a good introduction this is to the city, because the effect of the station depends on a happy marriage between the engineering skills of Robert Stephenson and the design of the architect John Dobson – and there is no way of telling where the work of one shades off into the other. The successful blend of the artistic and the purely practical was a key-note of much I was to see.

I went out and nodded my respects to Mr Stephenson, noticing that it was not only the station which made this an appropriate setting. He looks out over the Literary and Philosophical Society, a building whose exterior is only a hint of the fine library it houses. It was

To the north is Grey Street – one of the best city streets in all England, thanks to the skills of John Dobson. It runs away uphill in a smooth curve, designed to be seen as an entity, and the buildings conform to the proportions of the golden mean of classical architecture. Its focal point is the monument to Earl Grey, which those with good legs and sound lungs can climb and be rewarded with a superb view of the city. This is planned Newcastle, but my taste has always tended to an appreciation of the accidental effect, the unexpected conjunction, which is why my favourite among the four views is that to the south. There is nothing to compare with it anywhere else in Britain. The nearest equivalent I can think of is halfway round the world in San Francisco. It starts with an elaborate confection of a building in white and salmon pink, all plaster curlicues and

An ornate doorway near the Central Station

decorated columns, then zooms downhill to old warehouses and offices of dark brick, all but overwhelmed by the towering arch of the road bridge.

I was faced by four routes, four points of the compass to start me on my exploration. Perversely I chose what looked to be the dullest direction, but there is something to be said for starting low key and building up to a grand finale. In any case, I am an optimist when it comes to exploration, believing that almost everywhere has something of interest. Optimism is seldom as richly rewarded as it was on my walk down Mosley Street.

The dull office block at the end of the street was enlivened a little by a monument to Joseph Swan, inventor of the electric light bulb, which he developed with his American partner, Edison. This was once a grand corner of Newcastle and there is still a reminder of those glories. A little bit of Dobson's old Royal Arcade of 1831 has been reproduced in the heart of the new development. It is as handsome as ever but a trifle forlorn, a brave gesture among the concrete, like a soldier holding high the regimental colours which the enemy has already surrounded. But if one does not expect to find a gilded arcade in the middle of an office block, nor does one expect to look across the main road to see a gable end labelled 1880 Soup Kitchen. The 1880 charity was a continuation of a far older charitable tradition – the Holy Jesus Hospital founded by the Corporation in 1681 but standing on the site of a medieval religious house, the Austin Friary.

Having set out with nothing in view but an office block, I seemed to be scampering back through the city's past at an unseemly rate. But a point was being made: Newcastle is not a child of the Industrial Revolution at all. I may have started by thinking of the work of the Stephensons, but here I was back with medieval monks. It was time to take stock and as the old building now houses the Joicey Museum, devoted to the social history of Newcastle, it seemed as good a place as any to do it. In the event, a good half of the museum was taken up by restorations of rooms of different periods, which told you something about the development of English taste but little about the development of the town. It is a pleasant enough place but it did not advance my understanding very far. I decided that the city itself might give clearer messages.

Once I had managed to get under the new road system, I was faced with the remnants of the city walls rising above a cliff-like drop to the river. How splendid it must all have been, and how daunting to would-be attackers. Now the view is dominated by the neo-classical church of All Saints. On my way down the steep paths from the wall, I could see fragments of old buildings which gave the impression of a river bank once crowded with houses. This was a thriving area which had its own church as far back as the twelfth century. But the medieval church was declared unsafe, and the new one was erected in the 1780s to a design by David Stephenson (no relation to the engineering family). It is said that it stands on the site of a Roman pantheon, in which case it presents a suitably classical face to the world. It brought to mind some of the fine eighteenth-century churches of the City of London, except that where they are often hidden behind tall blocks, All Saints stands proud on its eyrie above the Tyne, having survived the decay which afflicted the area around it. With the disappearance of so many houses, it became redundant as a church and has been a teaching centre since 1985.

I almost passed it by, happy to enjoy its exterior but keen to get down to the quays on the river. I was glad I paused, for the interior

The elliptical interior of All Saints Church

is quite remarkable and nothing in the exterior prepares you for it. The auditorium is a perfect ellipse and still has its original mahogany box pews. There are cities where the straight line rules, where everything is set on regular grids, and others where the curve predominates. The railway tracks had bent in under the curved glass roof of the station; the new town plan of the 1830s had given the city the gentle curve of Grey Street and now here was this perfect eighteenth-century interior with a plan based on one of the most satisfying of all curved forms.

The way down to the quay was along Broad Chare. The chares are a distinctive feature of the Newcastle scene, the name being no more than a common medieval word meaning lane. There was once a whole series of them leading down to the quay, but the area was devastated in a fire in 1854. It began in a warehouse across the river in Gateshead, and crowds lined the Newcastle bank to watch the blaze. Then the wind began to carry sparks and burning fragments across the water and soon Newcastle was on fire. The area never recovered from the blow, but the biggest change lies with the river itself.

Newcastle grew up with its river trade: as early as medieval times, sturdy little sailing colliers were being loaded with coal for the fires of London. In 1861 there was a comprehensive scheme of river improvement, which involved widening, deepening and straightening the old Tyne. At the end of that process the river could take the biggest ships in the world and in 1907 the SS *Mauretania* was completed at the Swan Hunter yard and sent on its way down the improved river. I have a copy of the Official Handbook of the River Tyne for 1925. It is packed with adverts for shipbuilders and fitters, but the most romantic section deals with sailing out of Newcastle. Those were the days when you could pick your destination from Aalborg to Valparaiso. Not any more – the changing pattern of trade has left the river all but empty. The importance of Newcastle was reflected at Trinity House, established five centuries ago by a charter from Henry VIII and given responsibility for navigation lights and buoys over the whole coast from Berwick to Scarborough. It has a long and proud tradition and the old building reflects that pride, though there is little hint of it in the insignificant entrance on Broad Chare. This leads to a little flagged courtyard where stone steps go up to the porticoed entrance. Inside the wealth of the Tyne trade becomes a palpable presence. Charles I and Charles II both look down in stern portraiture from the walls, and the Low Countries are appropriately represented with a sumptuous Rubens. The banqueting hall has a fireplace around which mermaids and sea-serpents gambol, while a three-masted ship of the line sails the ceiling above the glittering chandelier. The tiny chapel is a gem, its ancient pews brought here, it is said, from Bede's at Jarrow. Everywhere there are reminders of the sea, for Trinity House was called into being

for the benefit of seafarers and its affairs were entrusted to seafarers, provided they were free men of the city and held a first mate's certificate. The old rules still apply.

Almost next door is the Maritime Centre, one of those small museums which make up in quality what they lack in quantity; not some grand municipal museum but one put together by individuals with patience and love. Even the building has a story to tell: it is a simple wharf building whose walls contain Flemish bricks brought as ballast by the colliers who needed the weight after they had unloaded their coal. Something of the maritime flavour has gone from the area and many of the courtyard buildings have been taken by barristers and judges, ready for the new court house being built across the road. The legal ladies and gentlemen have an unlikely neighbour. In between the Baltic pub and the Maritime Centre is The Live Theatre, which tells you almost all you need to know. The theatre is live, on the fringe and possessed of a strong social conscience.

At the end of Broad Chare are the Quayside, the river and Newcastle's most famous view: the Tyne bridges. For years they formed a classic trio, but have now been joined by newcomers including the Metro Bridge, which keeps itself apart but is just as important as its three predecessors. The Metro rail system is not just another transport route, but a sign of confidence in the future. Nevertheless it is the older bridges that demand attention.

First is the New Tyne Bridge, an arc of steel flying across the gorge, the deck slung below. If it looks familiar but you cannot place the connection, think of Australia; for Newcastle's bridge looks like a trial run for Sydney Harbour's span. Both derive their appeal from the simplicity of pure engineering with no frippery. Not everyone approves. There is a story, apocryphal perhaps, that when Sir

Thomas Beecham was conducting in Australia he was taken out to Sydney Harbour and shown the famous bridge. His only comment was, 'Can't you have it removed?'

Beyond that is Stephenson's High Level Bridge. What a brilliant concept it was for its time, and how daring to have a double-decker bridge with trains on top and a roadway underneath. In between the two lofty spans is the low-level bridge, which as no ship could possibly get under it swings on its central island to allow them to pass. There has been a bridge on this site since Roman times. That was replaced by a stone bridge, swept away in disastrous floods, and the Swing Bridge was opened in 1876. I went down to see the ma-

The Moot Hall

chinery, which is virtually the same as when it was built. The system is hydraulic, and it seems to be a minor miracle that water pressure alone can lift a weight of 1450 tons so that the whole bridge can be swung smoothly around. It is a lovely machine; the brass work is immaculate and all that has changed is the source of power for the hydraulic pumps: where once it was a steam engine, now it is an electric motor. How long will it be kept in working order, when the bridge has to be moved for at best one vessel a day? I hope that whatever happens the machinery remains *in situ*.

Even when you know the city's long history, it is easy to be beguiled by the modern bridges, so that it comes as a shock to find a seventeenth-century street scene under their nineteenth- and twentieth-century shadows. Here is the Guildhall of 1655–8; not much of the original design remains outside, but the interior is still very grand. The beautiful, timbered merchants' houses remain unspoiled. The Surtees House is famous for an elopement in 1772 when Aubone Surtees ran away with John Scott, a coal merchant's son from Love Lane. The parents later decided that the young man was presentable enough as a match for their daughter. Their confidence was justified: he went on to become Lord Eldon, Chancellor of England.

Less romantic, but possessing appeal, is the Cooperage, which has changed its role only slightly from making barrels to emptying them. It is a successful pub, which provided welcome refreshment for the next stage of the journey – the climb up Castle Stairs to the top of the gorge and the main city streets. But there was a chance to stop off by the Moot Hall, a Greek revival building of 1812, not so much to see the building but for the view down to the river. This is one of the most remarkable views in this remarkable

city, for the two Newcastles converge here. Beneath me was a jumble of steep pitched roofs and gables of the seventeenth century, above which the Tyne Bridge threw its great arc like a rainbow.

At the top of Castle Stairs I found the New Castle, a fitting place to give a name to a city. It is a great stone Norman keep which even the false battlements and roof of the Victorian restorers cannot diminish. Castle and river: the elements around which so many cities have developed seldom show their intimate relationship as clearly as here. I left the area by the thirteenth-century Black Gate, now quite overshadowed by the railway viaduct. The engineers may have done Newcastle proud in what they built, but they showed scant respect for the past in deciding where to build.

I was back in the centre, feeling I had found enough to satisfy any visitor, yet I had explored only one area to the south of my starting point. I had come out by the old market area – Groat Market, Cloth Market and Bigg Market, the latter not a corruption of 'big' but coming from an old word for barley. The old street markets have slipped into unimportance and others were swept away when a new covered market was built to hold butcher and vegetable stalls in 1835. The Grainger Market was John Dobson's work again, and when I went inside I wondered who influenced whom, for here again was a soaring glass roof to match that of the station. Was this Stephenson the engineer influencing Dobson the architect or was it the other way round in the first place? Either way it is a tremendous success, both as a building and as a market, and contains one genuine Marks and Spencer Penny Bazaar.

The covered market was built because the old market area was being pulled down as part of the development which did more than anything to give Newcastle its present character. It was an extraordinary scheme because virtually everything one sees in the central area was the work of two men. One was the entrepreneur and builder Richard Grainger. The phrase speculative builder conjures up images of get-rich-quick merchants throwing up rows of jerry-built shops and houses. Grainger was a speculative builder, but there was nothing cheap about what he did, and he had the good sense to leave the design work to Dobson. Centred on Grey Street, it is a scheme which can stand comparison with the area around London's Regent Street or Edinburgh New Town. It is not the quality of individual buildings which stands out, but the concept as a whole: the unity of line, the careful proportioning of details within each building and the setting of each building into the pattern. Some need to draw attention to themselves. The Theatre Royal is literally outstanding: the massive pillars of the portico stride across the pavement, deliberately breaking the line set by the other buildings.

The theatre has recently been refurbished and enlarged in a scheme which must be a model of its kind. Success here can be measured in the way that the majestic nature of a formal theatre has been retained and improved to allow perfect matching of old and new. The front-of-house facilities have been

The Theatre Royal at the top of Grey Street

improved by adding a separate grand stairway at one side, and nothing gives more of a sense of occasion than walking up a stairway like that. New bars and restaurants provide cheer for the customers and help to bring the theatre into the community. The auditorium remains in essence the work of Frank Matcham who re-designed it following a fire in 1899, and the modern paraphernalia for sound and lighting are tucked discreetly away. To visit the Theatre Royal is to enjoy theatregoing in a grand, formal style: something special. Having seen a production of *The Government Inspector* I can vouch that the theatre works, but it is not Newcastle's only grand one.

The Tyne Theatre and Opera House opened its doors in 1867, and was home to some spectacular productions. In 1889 *The Armada* needed thirty-two tons of scenery and props to produce the grand finale where Spanish galleons were sunk before the enraptured audience. That was surpassed by *The Prodigal Daughter*, which had real horses jumping real hurdles in the Grand National scene. But hard times came – it became a cinema and even played host to Sunday services, but by the 1970s it was unused and seemed unloved. Then a group of Tyneside amateurs came along with ambitious ideas: they wanted to stage musicals in the grand manner and the Tyne Theatre seemed ideal.

They hired it at first and then in 1980 they bought it – and acquired something unique. There are still a number of ornate Victorian theatres in Britain, but none can still boast a full complement of original stage machinery – the machinery which sunk the Armada. When I first saw it, I was like a character from the Blackstuff, shouting 'I can do that. Gi'e us a job,' not because I know anything about staging but because it was just like the tackle for raising and lowering sails on a ship. But no ship has a thunder-roll, a sloping metal tube with bumps, down which cannonballs were rolled

to produce the sound of thunder. In 1887 a cannonball jumped out of the run and killed a carpenter on the stage below; since then they have been kept in line by iron hoops. The machinery makes the theatre special, and is a magnet not only for enthusiastic amateurs but for professionals. How many small companies could persuade Placido Domingo to come to sing *Tosca*?

The nineteenth-century redevelopment has not been equalled by anything the twentieth century has done. The Eldon Square Shopping Centre is large but has little to offer which is not to be found in a dozen similar developments. It does have a charming statue of a man feeding the pigeons: these motionless birds were the nearest I got to the pigeon lofts of the popular image. The new civic centre is enhanced by sculpture, including the river god Tyne and a flight of swans representing the five Nordic nations. The carillon in the tower plays, amongst other tunes, Bladon Races, the Geordie anthem. Those who know the song will remember that the company set off from Balmbra's. The old pub is still there, though racegoers might not feel at home in its new manifestation as the Gaslight and Laser.

Newcastle has gone in for theme pubs in a big way, but they have a short life expectancy. For a season or two a pub is the 'in' place, then it fades and another takes over. Success means weekends when the place is packed by a young, free-spending clientèle. I would walk several miles over hot coals to avoid such places, but they are not meant for me. It is not just the pubs that are packed; life spills out right through the city streets – and makes me feel rather old.

The vivid life of the streets is only a part of the way Newcastle is revitalising itself. There is a little Georgian enclave at the back of Westgate Road which could have been overlooked and allowed to decay to the point where a developer could have knocked it all down. Instead it is being refurbished as a home for craft workshops and small shops, an exhibition space and a theatre. It is emphatically not about the sort of people who often inhabit such schemes – the potters who did a night-school course and decided to take up the mantle of Bernard Leach. The pottery produces work of real quality, such as the mosaic which has made one local ladies' loo the most colourful in Britain. Room has been found for a workshop handling film, video and sound.

Another area which has a new lease of life lies along the western line of the town walls which lead to Blackfriars, the old Dominican Priory of the thirteenth century. At the Dissolution it was leased to the town trade companies, which saved part of the buildings from destruction. Today, it houses craft shops, and a small museum. It is a peaceful enclave and the Smiths' Company still have their meeting-hall there, an extraordinary room with a central circular area where members sit, like the Knights of the Round Table, with no one having precedence. The surrounding streets are a Chinatown of excellent restaurants.

Newcastle never stops producing surprises. The Big Lamp Brewery is probably the world's smallest tower brewery. Its owners display wonderful ingenuity: the computer control system incorporates an old telly salvaged from a rubbish skip – which does not prevent the beer being superb. Then there is Jesmond Dene, a secluded river gorge across which Sir William Armstrong built a bridge at his own expense. The councillors were gratified and so was Sir William, for it opened the bank on the far side for profitable development. But the most remarkable feature is one of the most modern: Byker.

Like most people, I knew something about the Byker Wall, which had been hailed as a brilliant piece of design by some and condemned as Britain's answer to Berlin by others. I had always assumed that it was a straightforward council development, a variation on the tower block theme, where the tower had been laid on its side to make it less daunting. I went there and found I had only a fragment of the story. The wall is not just a friendly way of housing a lot of people in one unit: its sinuous, blank face is a sound barrier, protecting the people from the noise of traffic. Behind it is a village overlooking the Tyne. It is an area of colour and light, little streets and intimate squares. I have seen far worse executive developments where the houses cost a fortune. You can judge a housing area only by living in it, but the signs are propitious, starting with an almost total absence of vandalism or graffiti.

Newcastle has been blessed by its developers: the nineteenth century gave it a formal city centre of great quality and the twentieth century has provided a housing development of which any community could be proud. You cannot ask for much more than that.

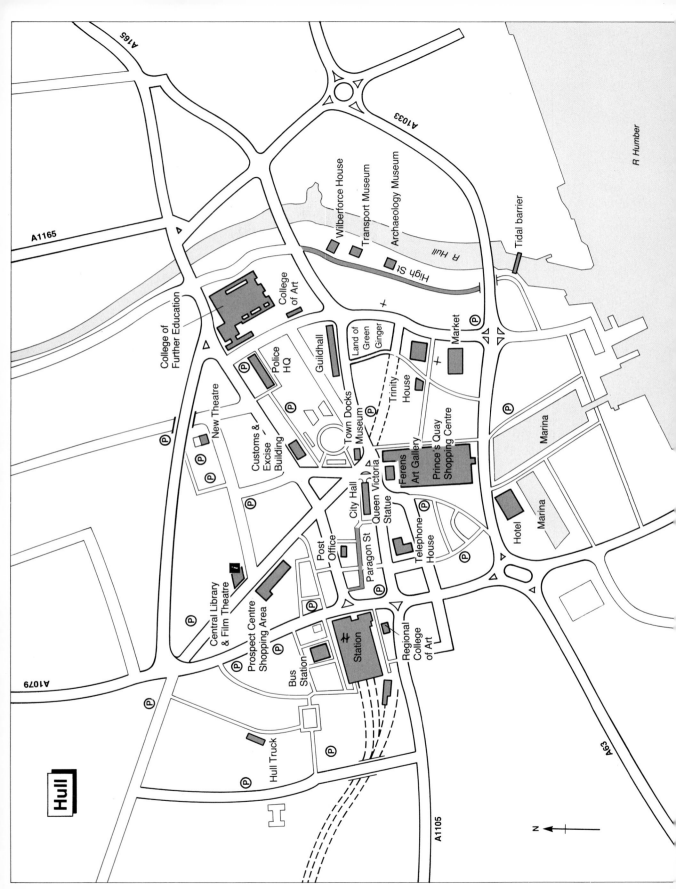

10
HULL

From Newcastle I headed south, then east through the rich agricultural lands of east Yorkshire. Nothing much disturbs the straight line of the horizon except the cooling towers of power stations and a glimpse of glory in the church at Selby. The train turned along the wide, muddy waters of the Humber and I saw the great bridge built to join this isolated corner to the rest of Britain. No one has disputed that it is an engineering marvel with a svelte, slender beauty, but there has been no shortage of critics condemning it as an economic folly. That seems harsh – and premature. A bridge may be a prerequisite to economic recovery, but it is not a miracle cure. Whatever Humberside has or has not become because of the bridge should be measured against what the region would have been without it. Whatever the accounting rights and wrongs, nothing can detract from the majesty of the longest suspension span in the world. I watched it until it was lost to sight behind a fun new housing estate.

Designs have been picked out in brick on the ends of the terraces – a ship, a steam locomotive and a Rugby player handing off an opponent. Since this was Hull, I took it for granted that he represented Rugby League. Then into the station, a few quick paces off the platform and into the Royal Hotel. There were pictures on the wall, not the customary stags at bay or polite pastel prints, but the flamboyant modern romanticism of Ivon Hitchens and the cool abstracts of Ben Nicholson. Very encouraging.

I usually prefer to meander around to get a general impression of a place and then catch up on the official view of the history. If I set out thinking that I know what to expect, I finish up seeing only what fits preconceived ideas; not that the first part of my walk produced any ideas about anything very much on this occasion. From the hotel I walked down Paragon Street, one of those broad, tidy post-war developments which adequately filled the gaps left by the bombs but did not create any sense of excitement. It led me to a square which looked more interesting and where I would probably have spent some time had the heavens not chosen that moment to open. The official view seemed suddenly inviting and I dived into the Ferens Art Gallery.

Downstairs were two touring exhibitions – one of Old Master drawings and the other of modern sculpture, but upstairs was centred on Hull, a celebration of the past. Local artists have painted the local scene with affection and knowledge: John Ward (1798–1849) pictured the docks and the busy traffic of ships on the Humber and knew what he was about. His rigging is accurate and you can tell which quarter the wind was blowing from at the time he made his sketch. Other scenes add

113

William III rides out over the city

up to a portrait of a bustling port where masts rose like saplings in a coppice beside a gaslit quay and where the river carried craft of all kinds, from paddle steamers to fully rigged ships. Two types of vessel can be distinguished: big sea-going ships and more modest craft, sometimes moving inland down a narrow river channel lined with windmills. This brought back happy memories, because it was just such vessels which first brought me to Hull.

Other ports I had visited all looked firmly out to sea, but Hull has always looked inland as well, to the Humber and the Trent, the Aire and Ouse. Special vessels were developed to work inland under sail as far as Sheffield. One

survivor of those days is the keel *Comrade*, as close as you are ever likely to see to a ship design of the Middle Ages. She is square-rigged: her single mast carries two square sails, one above the other. I sailed in her on the Humber with Fred Schofield, who spent his working life as a keelman on the waters around here. It seems extraordinary to look at old pictures and see vessels identical to one which still sails the waters a few hundred yards away. *Comrade* and her companion, the sloop *Amy Howson*, are survivors from those days. They are run and maintained by local enthusiasts and are as much a part of the city's history as the grandest building. I would have loved to have been out on the water again, marvelling at how well a ship's rig scarcely changed for centuries does its job. But I had to make do with paint on canvas. If the gallery did nothing else, it prompted me to head down to the docks. The rain stopped and I continued on my way, but I was glad it had come, because my visit had given me a standard against which to measure the dockland scene of today.

It is difficult today to look at the docks and see them for what they were, for there seems little connection between the pictures and the present scene. Prince's Dock was until recently a sheet of water without context, but now a new shopping centre on stilts is rearing up above it. Prince's Dock Street retains something of its old character. Hull, like Newcastle, has its Trinity House, responsible for navigation marks as far out as Spurn Point. In 1787 Trinity House also established a school to train boys for a career in the Merchant Navy. It is still in use and the uniformed students can be seen chatting in the courtyard between lessons on navigation.

It was obvious from the journey through the flat lands that this is not a stony region, so brick is, as expected, the principal building material, often enlivened by tiles and bright colours. What do you call a pub built of green glazed bricks? The Green Bricks, what else? I kept finding these interesting glazes, my favourite being beautiful smoky blue tiles adorning the Bedford and Ruskin Chambers in Scale Lane. Judging by the large numbers of solicitors I came across, Hull must have a litigious population.

Prince's Dock ends at the busy dual carriageway of Castle Street, beyond which are the old Humber Dock and Railway Dock, now the new marina. The tragedy is that change came too soon. All around this area you get glimpses of what might have been. Back in Prince's Dock Street a 150-year-old warehouse has been converted into the Waterfront Hotel, but has not lost that pleasing rhythm of wide loading bays rising up the centre of the building, flanked by smaller windows. Once the whole area was full of buildings with the same purposeful character, and the warehouses round Railway Dock were part of a comprehensive scheme designed by Jesse Hartley. His is a name we shall meet again because he was the engineer responsible for Liverpool's Albert Dock and anyone who has seen what happened there can only bemoan the fate of Hull's old buildings. If the clock could be turned back, I have little doubt that they would be retained, but what has gone cannot be recovered.

Hull marina is a splendid place to keep a boat if you are one of that comparatively rare breed of marina occupants who go out sailing. The river is well over a mile wide and offers sheltered waters all the way out to Spurn Point, but the surrounding land is so flat that one can generally rely on a good breeze. All kinds of developments are taking place. A new hotel has already been built and there is a restaurant at the end of the marina by the sea wall. Concessions have been made to the past: the old lock cottage has been restored and the Spurn lightship of 1927 has been moored and opened up to visitors. Some of the old hydraulic dock machinery has been set on a plinth as a sort of quasi-modern sculpture. But nothing can disguise the fact that the marina has at best a slender relationship with the past.

At least the old Minerva Hotel came in for refurbishment; it occupies a corner site and is an ideal spot to sit and watch the traffic of the river. I knew *Comrade* was somewhere out there, but caught no glimpse of her tall mast and wide spreading sails. Other comforts, however, were on hand. The pub has its own beer, and Hull is one of the last bastions of the genuine northern pint. I was brought up to appreciate beer with a head on it, which left a frothy, lacy pattern down the sides of the glass as you drank. It does not work properly in dimpled glasses with handles, which is why we always use straights. In the Minerva they do things in the old style. A half pint is pulled, and allowed to settle; more beer is added and there is another pause before the final top-up leaves a glass full of liquid with the foam rising above the rim. Add to that traditional food – in this case a local speciality called cobblers – minced beef topped by a sort of cheese-flavoured scone – and you have somewhere to cherish.

From outside the Minerva you can look upstream towards Albert Dock, home of Hull's deep-sea fishing fleet. The area was once crowded with passengers waiting for the Humber Ferry. The new bridge put an end to that trade and the last of the old vessels was pensioned off. It all seems so long ago that it is impossible to believe that up to 1978 you could still make the trip across to New Holland in the paddle-steamer *Lincoln Castle*. All that is left now is the booking office of 1880 with its monogram for the Manchester, Sheffield and Lincolnshire Railway Company – a few years later they could have saved on the lettering because the company was re-named the Great Central. Now the area has been turned into a pleasant walkway and new houses have appeared behind the waterfront buildings. But by far its most striking feature is what looks like a set of giant goalposts across the River Hull. This is the tidal surge barrier which can be lowered across the river to protect the town from flooding by the high spring tides.

To reach the river I walked past the Pilot Office of 1820, still in use, and past the entrance to the market area – a happy reminder that this is a port with international connections. The directions to the fruit market appear in four languages. But nothing could deflect me from my main objective, Hull River. Long

before the enclosed docks were built, the river provided safe moorings for craft plying the Humber; it still does. One has become so accustomed to dead rivers or rivers which, at best, carry the fluttering sails of yachts and dinghies that it is a joy to find wharves lined with working boats. There are so many, moored side by side, that only a narrow channel is left for passage. It was a sight which lifted my spirits in a way that no marina could.

Accidental sculpture: a barge on the River Hull

I have often tried to analyse what it is about working boats and their environment that is so appealing. Size has something to do with it and the shapes formed by long use. Bollards are grooved by a thousand mooring lines and the lines are dragged by their own weight into long, slow drooping curves. Nothing is there to create an impression, everything is there to do a job. Yet for all its signs of a busy life – and when you stand here you can believe that there are still 30,000 commercial movements on the Humber in a year – the river front is changing. Old warehouses are finding new and successful uses as shops and offices. Peering through archways reveals a different world from that of the waterfront: a quiet courtyard here, a narrow alley there and even a sculpture garden. It all contrives to sit comfortably together, the new blending with the old working world. There seems nothing incongruous in a shady garden looking out across the river to a lighter being loaded with gravel, or a sculpture on the quay repeating the patterns of the immense lift bridge which closes off the river view upstream. A nearby pub sign has reminders of an older generation of movable bridges: the Kingston shows a scene which could as easily be Amsterdam, with a wooden bridge topped by a tall balance beam. The connection between the two countries goes back a long way, and there is still a Dutch consulate close to the wharf. Here is the true heart of the ancient port, and glimpses down alleyways suggest that behind it must be the old town.

The old town is there and is Hull's prize. The dock area may have slipped away by default, but here there has been tremendous effort put into conservation and renewal – and the two are not the same. It is possible to conserve by putting buildings on public show, but renewal requires imagination to find new uses, to adapt the old without losing its character. Most of the old town has been declared a conservation area, but with the declared objective of encouraging active use. So far it seems to be a resounding success, an area full of visual pleasures, where it is a joy to walk and enjoy the scenery.

The numerous alleys or staithes lead away from the river and join it to the High Street. Two worlds come together: the commercial and the private. The tall warehouses rise above the cobbled alleys, and behind them are the houses and offices of the merchants who made their money from trade. There

is no mistaking the sense of opulence. No 6 High Street was home to the Blaydes family, shipbuilders and merchants. Though they lived in splendour, they never lost sight of the source of their wealth: their counting house was practically next door and they could oversee the movement of goods in and out of their warehouse without leaving home. It is this close relationship between trade and traders, work and domesticity, which gives High Street its special character. Two buildings in the street take up the twin themes.

The Corn Exchange is a newcomer, built in 1856 in a rather ponderous Roman style, on the site of the Old Customs House. Today it houses a museum of archaeology and transport, Hull and East Riding Museum, which has a reminder that river traffic is no new phenomenon. In July 1984 a team of archaeologists working at Holme upon Spalding Moor discovered the remains of a log boat. The popular idea of a log boat is of something like a dug-out canoe, but this was a cargo vessel made from a hollowed-out oak tree over forty feet long, five foot beam and weighing around six tonnes. She was built in the Iron Age around 450BC. A visit to the museum gives the city's maritime history some perspective.

It would be interesting to know what one occupant of High Street thought of having his house close to the Black Boy pub. It was here that reformer and abolitionist William Wilberforce was born in 1759. The house is partly seventeenth century but it was modernised by the Wilberforces in the 1750s, and is now a museum. The building is extremely fine, still maintaining much of its original character, but is chiefly visited for the exhibits telling the story of the fight against the slave trade. Whatever he might have thought about the pub up the road, where slavers were said to meet, Wilberforce would be delighted that the peaceful gardens next to his house are named

William Wilberforce's statue in the garden of his house

after Nelson Mandela.

One side of Bishop Lane is an almost perfect Georgian terrace which has seen hard times but is coming up in the world again – though most of the houses seem to have been taken over by yet more of Hull's army of solicitors. I made my way to the Market Place at the heart of the old town. You get glimpses of every aspect of the city's history here. It is a public square, open and airy with a magnificent parish church which speaks as clearly of the wealth of the city as the rich houses of High Street. There is an old grammar school – among its pupils were men as diversely famous as Wilberforce and the metaphysical poet Andrew Marvell. Maritime life is represented in the handsome façade of Trinity House; archways give glimpses of the medieval complex, and the Kingston pub, with its old bridge on the sign, stands at one corner.

Holy Trinity Church has one of those slightly meaningless claims to fame: it is the largest parish church, by area, in Britain. More interesting is that this splendid edifice, consecrated in 1425, is, like the rest of Hull, built of brick with stone reserved for the dressings. The first impression inside is of light and immense space. But a beautifully carved marble font has been preserved, and some wonderful carvings on the bench ends. Churches have their obvious ikons, but the early builders seemed to feel a need to give them a common, earthy touch as well. So here are beasts, real and imagined, and human faces, grotesque and grimacing, as if to say, 'it's all right for you saints smiling up in the windows but down here life is one hard slog.'

The Elizabethan grammar school is now a museum. Trinity House has a splendid sculpted pediment showing the royal coat of arms with Neptune and Britannia. But the most intriguing building is No 10^1/$_2$ King Street. It really is half-size, its façade almost filled by a Venetian window above an arch through which an old street curves away. It was an invitation to explore. Prince Street turned out to have more fine eighteenth-century buildings, and it is extraordinary how much of this period has survived: the old Neptune Inn, now prosaically 11–14 Whitefriar Gate, and Boots the chemist in majestic isolation, whereas Parliament Street comes as a planned unit, complete terraces which would not look out of place in Bath. The old town is old but the Georgians rebuilt vast tracts of it. When we talk of conservation (and this is a conservation area), we usually think of preserving beautiful buildings like the Georgian terraces. What would have happened if a similar policy had been applied two centuries ago? There would have been no Georgian terraces – would we have preferred the medieval streets? Were the Georgian developers condemned as vandals? Why is it that we have no objection to what they did and yet fight modern proposals

Trinity House

for similar wholesale changes? Perhaps we simply do not have confidence in builders of our age: a sad thought.

The old town does have its share of shops and commercial buildings and some add touches of interest to the scene: three Viking ships sail stonily out from the front of Marks and Spencer's. But the formal centre has shifted away. As Hull prospered it could no longer be contained within the town walls, so a new area of civic buildings was developed beyond what is now the excavated site of the Beverley Gate. Here in 1642 Sir John Hotham refused Charles I permission to enter the city, one of

those acts of defiance which multiplied to the point of war between king and Parliament. It was the last time the walls and gates played any significant role in the life of the city.

The first of the new buildings is one of the more recent additions, the Edwardian Guildhall, built when architects had turned away from the excesses of the nineteenth century in favour of a less cluttered style, but still looked back to history for their inspiration. It has a sense of official pomp, which on a bright Sunday morning provided the backdrop for official ceremonial. Local dignitaries marched in procession, with no one to admire them but bored policemen on traffic duty. Behind the

The Guildhall

Guildhall the formal Queen's Gardens lead on to Queen Victoria Square, which is where I had intended to start poking around before the deluge hit me.

Queen Victoria rules the centre of the square, which contains an interesting mixture of buildings. The Concert Hall is imposing, with marble everywhere. It is somewhat gloomily Victorian, and one cannot imagine anything frivolous being performed as one walks in under the gaze of several stern Victorian worthies. Across the square is the Town Docks Museum, equally solemn on the outside but housing a lovely collection of models, paintings and artefacts which tell the story of the city and the sea. Amid this seriousness of purpose there is a note of frivolity – the Punch Hotel, loud and brash in colourful terracotta. Another item caught my eye: the telephone booth, which was the wrong colour – white not red. I had forgotten that Hull had refused to join the rest of Britain and ran their own exchange instead of leaving it to the GPO. Now they too have been privatised, and the old exchange machinery has been replaced but will not be scrapped. It is probably going to Hull's twin town – chosen because of the Wilberforce connections – Freetown, Sierra Leone.

Newcastle had whetted my appetite for things theatrical and I was assured that Hull's citizens enjoyed the thespian art. The designer of the City Hall certainly thought so, for the façade has a statue of Drama holding the two masks of Comedy and Tragedy. The old Assembly Rooms were converted into a theatre, and work was completed in 1939, just in time for the bombing of Hull. It fell on hard times but was taken over and refurbished by the council in 1985, and a good job they made of it. It is an unpretentious building with a colonnaded façade and an interior where everyone in the audience gets a good view. That may seem an obvious requirement, but

I can think of many theatres high in prestige where several of the audience are lucky if they see more than half a performance. The setting is on one side of Kingston Square, flanked by Albion Street, yet another Georgian terrace which has survived intact. Others have been less fortunate: Hull Co-operative Institute of 1833 survives only as a façade, and the old Anchor Brewery has kept its buildings but not its function. The most flamboyant building is the Catholic church of St Charles Borromeo, with its portal carried on Corinthian columns. The theatre fits well with its rather formal surroundings, but Hull's main claim to theatrical fame lies elsewhere.

Hull Truck was founded in 1971 by Mike Bradwell because, he said, no one would let him work as he wanted. He recruited actors in London, but when he announced where they were going half of them vanished. The company survived the first few years on hard work, commitment and little money. They performed in pubs and clubs and seemed little different from other small fringe companies. They were also inward-looking, and it was when they widened their scope – when they turned to characters outside the immediate environment known to the cast – that they discovered an ever-growing audience. Hull Truck are now known throughout Britain and have a well-deserved reputation as one of the country's liveliest companies. You know what to expect when you go to see *Up 'n' Under* or *Bouncers*: I had no idea what to expect when I went to see *A Midsummer Night's Dream*. It was Shakespeare's play but unmistakably Hull Truck's production, with the characters treated as though they were newly written by one of the company's writers. The lovers inhabited a real world and faced a menacing forest where they looked likely to break a leg among the twisted roots. But their style was most impressive with the supernatural characters: Oberon was a bare-chested Mafia boss, loaded with menace, and Puck was no mischievous imp, but a magical bovver boy, a poetic football hooligan. From the bar conversation it was clear that some of the audience had never before watched Shakespeare for pleasure and were loving it.

Local officials have all the statistics to show that Hull is thriving again. There is a growing industry processing the seeds from the rich agricultural hinterland. The deep-sea fishing fleet is growing. The city is well placed for trade, looking out across the North Sea to the container port of Rotterdam and inward to South Yorkshire and the Midlands. The council took the initiative in building small factory and workshop units, of which most are let. The grim tide of economic depression seems to be receding. Sadly, as with so many provincial cities, people elsewhere have an image of a dour, unsavoury place. When Hull Truck lost half of its company at the mere mention of the city's name, those who left were sharing a common misapprehension: 'From Hull, Hell and Halifax, Good Lord deliver us' is still a sentiment which lingers in the popular imagination. Hull has long since given the lie to the old rhyme, and if you are not convinced, where else would you find a street name as enticing as The Land of Green Ginger?

LEEDS

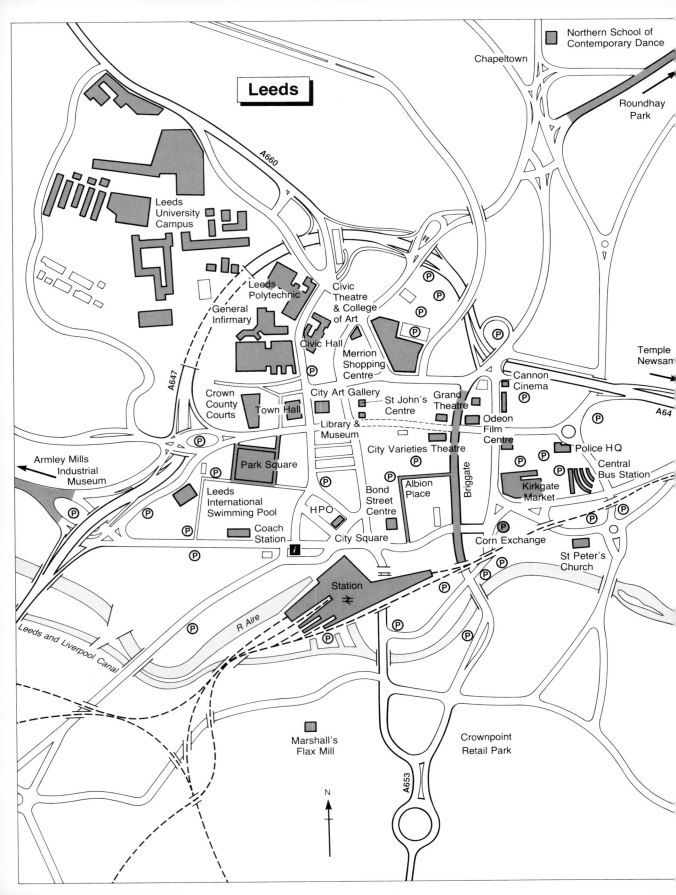

11
LEEDS

Of all the cities I visited Leeds was the one I knew best. All through boyhood it was *the* city, the place I went for those things not available in a small provincial town. In the town hall I heard the Yorkshire Symphony Orchestra play classics and Humphrey Lyttleton play jazz; the Grand Theatre offered a stage which could take the big touring companies – everything from opera and ballet to the spectacular Christmas panto. Best of all was Headingley, where the cricketing heroes of Yorkshire were on display. Leeds meant big city excitement. As an undergraduate I went to live in the city and gained a different perspective. So I was returning to a city I thought I knew, but when you arrive with the aim of looking hard, you see much that you had not previously noticed or had dismissed as of no interest. And, of course, the cityscape had changed dramatically since my time, when trams still trundled up the streets. I was not rediscovering Leeds; I was discovering it.

The rail journey took me back over the flat lands. I stared at the level horizon until the tower blocks announced the imminent arrival of the city. It was not an exciting introduction, but things began to change as the train looped around on a high-level route, splitting the city apart with its embankments and viaducts. On one side were set-pieces: the parish church, the dome of the Corn Exchange and often quite ornate commercial buildings, including a jeweller's shop with a giant clock on which a gilded Father Time perched. In the distance was the tall white tower of the university. On the other side of the tracks was an incoherent jumble of buildings, sooty redbrick works and warehouses, stumpy chimneys rising out of cluttered yards. The railway is the boundary between two worlds, but there is an older boundary as well, the River Aire, which in the eighteenth century became part of the Aire and Calder Navigation.

The first sight outside the station was of an expected Leeds, a Victorian city square in what most people think of as a typically Victorian city. But look again: the statue in the middle may be Victorian and certainly the coy, topless maidens holding up their lamp globes could come from no other period. Only the Victorians could express prudery while filling their public squares with statues of naked women. The centrepiece, however, was not Queen Victoria – who would not have agreed to appear in such company – nor even some local worthy, but the Black Prince. Leeds was sending out a message: our city may look Victorian but it has a long, proud history. Yet it was the Industrial Revolution which ushered in the great period of growth, so other figures around the square point up a different message.

Among them is James Watt, the steam pio-

Tempus fugit: ornate clocks on the Time Ball Building

neer. He had an obvious role in Birmingham's history, but why should a Scot who set up business in the Midlands have a place of honour here? Well, Leeds had a special role in the development of steam power. Newcastle has its Stephenson statue, but long before the 'Father of Railways' designed his first locomotive he came here to see the world's first commercial steam railway. The Middleton Colliery Railway is not as well known as the Stockton and Darlington but it began work thirteen years earlier, in 1812. Its lack of fame stems from its method of construction: the engines worked on the rack-and-pinion principle like those of a mountain railway. Some writers have suggested that the engineers did not believe smooth wheels could grip smooth rails. This is nonsense – they were built that way because other locomotives had smashed the brittle iron track. It worked successfully, and it is still remembered. A preserved railway steams old locomotives on the line of the pioneering route just south of the M1 – but on rather more conventional track.

The two aspects of the city signalled in the square keep recurring, sometimes in conflict. Nowhere is this seen more dramatically than in the parish church. There is ample evidence of an ancient foundation: the churchyard contains a first-century Saxon cross with Norse inscriptions, and a parish church certainly existed here in the tenth century. But all traces of the medieval past were submerged in the reconstruction of 1841. This was not so much gothic as gothick, creating a darkly theatrical mood. Sermons were delivered from the top of the elaborate sixteen-foot-high pulpit. Outside the church, however, the two worlds – ancient and Victorian – collided. The churchyard stood in the path of the proposed new railway and in the contest between God and Mammon, material progress came out a clear winner. But what was to happen to all those bodies and their memorial stones? You can see the compromise solution: the headstones were relaid like paving slabs up the side of the new embankment.

Much of the city centre remains very much as I remembered it. At the station the most impressive sight to greet you is a vast hoarding advertising Joshua Tetley and his beers. If there is one thing I look for it is a traditional Tetley pub with traditional beer and traditional fare to match. I found all three in the Adelphi with its engraved glass windows, multiplicity of bars and a good pint to wash down a bowlful of pie and mushy peas, served as it should be, spattered with mint sauce. Those looking for that other famous local delicacy, roast beef and Yorkshire pudding, can find it in Leeds' most famous pub, Whitelock's, tucked down a little alleyway off Briggate. For a time I was overwhelmed with personal memories and nostalgia for the traditional elements in the city scene, but I decided to leave other familiar pleasures for later. I collected one of those odd but fascinating bits of information – like knowing that Birmingham has more miles of canal than Venice. I discovered that Leeds has a greater area of green open space than Vienna. That seemed worth investigating.

My way towards the edge of the city lay through Chapeltown. Much of Leeds' prosperity has been built on the clothing trade, which pulled in a large number of immigrant workers, mostly Jewish. This was their part of town. In recent years, other immigrants have come from other parts of the world and the old Jewish quarter has changed. Many of the synagogues became redundant, so what do you do with a redundant synagogue? One answer was to transform it into an exciting centre of artistic work: the Northern School of Contemporary Dance. The school is as multiracial as the surrounding area and seems to zing with energy. Everyone works like demons but with boundless enthusiasm. An old Jew came back on a visit to see what had happened to his old synagogue, and was delighted with what he saw. The synagogue exists to give thanks for the beauties of life, he said, and the beauties of life are still there. This is a school which exists not only to promote excellence but to show it to the local community. It is winning on both counts.

The first green objective was Roundhay Park, a huge open area with all the space you could wish for – and the trimmings. There is an amphitheatre capable of staging the biggest concerts: Michael Jackson was on the way and concerts do not come bigger than his. The profits from such extravaganzas do more than keep the park running; they pay for things like the new restaurant over the boating lake. The lake is no old village pond but a sizeable sheet of water, seventy foot deep in the middle. The music profits also keep other attractions open and free. The latest is Tropical World, which began modestly with the building of the Coronation House in 1911 when George V came to the throne, and pleasant hothouses they are even if they were a year late. New and exotic tropical displays have now been added to the original buildings. They start with the Butterfly House. Here the organisers at first miscalculated and several hundred colourful insects disappeared from view among the luxuriant plant life. Hundreds more were released but there are still not all that many, which is fine because there is a sense of discovery every time one is spotted. But the real draw is the Tropical House, with an atmosphere like an Amazonian rainforest. The plants have taken

Marshall's Flax Mill, built like an Egyptian temple

to the artificial sauna under grey northern skies and have shot upward and outward, filling the whole area with colour and scent. Add to this aquaria and insect displays and you have an attraction which gives immense pleasure to thousands of visitors. And it is largely thanks to Michael Jackson, other stars and their enthusiastic fans.

Temple Newsam fell outside my objective of staying within inner city limits, but it was such a beautiful day that I gave in to temptation. It was interesting to see such a place no more than a couple of miles from the centre and within the limits of the built-up area. The grand house was once home to Lord Darnley, who married Mary Queen of Scots. The park is by Capability Brown but it was neither stately home nor park that brought me here. The Home Farm has a serious function as a breeding centre for rare varieties of farm animals, and it provides a wonderful opportunity for city kids to see the beasts. Children who believe pork chops and steaks come readymade in stretch-wrap can see snuffling pink pigs in a sty they share with immaculate white doves, and can gasp at the lowering glances of heavy-shouldered bulls. The farm has magnificent views over the city – including some grassy piles with the unmistakable shape of spoil heaps. It was time to tear myself away from the farm and to head for the other, sterner Leeds.

I had intended to go straight to the Industrial Museum, but I was waylaid by three oddities – buildings which proved that the world of industry need not wear a solemn face. Park Square is a quiet and charming Georgian square, once one of the more fashionable residential areas, but now entirely taken up by offices with polished brass plates next to the door. Commerce had already appeared by 1878, when a wool warehouse was built on its south side. Now warehouses often have solid virtues, but they can seldom be described as exotic. This is an exception. Quite why a Yorkshire wool warehouse should imitate a Moorish palace is a mystery, but that is what it is, complete with minarets. It has recently been refurbished as offices but the exterior has been left just as it was – though some patching was necessary and a keen eye might note that some of the terracotta details are now fibreglass replicas.

Another building of interest in the square is the Yorkshire Water Authority's headquarters of 1938. It is plain enough, but has a splendid ceramic plaque on the façade showing river barges and dredgers. The third surprise in the city was that extreme rarity: a Grade I listed textile mill. Marshall's Flax Mill was built in the early nineteenth century to treat flax for linen manufacture. Flax was made in ancient Egypt, so John Marshall turned away from fashionable gothic and built his mill in the style of an Egyptian temple, with massive palm columns copied from buildings at Tanis. In its working days it was an even stranger sight. The processing of flax required even temperatures, so it was decided to insulate the flat roof by laying soil on top. Soil, left to itself, would blow away, so grass was sown and to keep that under control a flock of sheep was given a home on the factory roof. Alas, they are no longer there.

The most pleasant and interesting approach to the Industrial Museum is along the towpath of the canal as it winds its way up the Aire valley. The walk has a dramatic beginning. I left City Square by the Dark Arches, which are indeed gloomy, but here I was not just under the railway but under the station itself. What makes these arches unique is the thunderous roar of the River Aire sweeping down through this same dark space, speeded to a torrent by being pent and confined. The arches lead out to a small dock area and a pleasing little porticoed building which was once the canal company office. The way may be urban, but it seems a world apart. Just beyond the railway bridge I came to Armley Mills; there could be no better place to discover the basis of Leeds' prosperity.

Warping frame at the Industrial Museum

There has been a textile mill on this site since Tudor times, though the original was not a mill as we think of it today. Spinning and weaving were done by hand in the workers' homes and only the finishing needed special buildings and special equipment. The cloth had to be 'fulled', shrunk and felted by pounding under giant hammers worked by a waterwheel. In 1805 the mills were rebuilt by one of the most powerful men in the Yorkshire woollen industry, Benjamin Gott. Use changed over the years: the new manufacturing techniques of the Industrial Revolution were introduced as the old handicrafts were moved from home to factory. The power of steam replaced the power of water. Then, in 1969, after four centuries in the textile trade, the mills closed and found a new role as a museum.

This is what I would describe as a serious museum. It knows exactly what its function is: to tell the city's industrial history in all its aspects. The textile industry has pride of place – the buildings ensure that – and among the machines are some of the most beautiful I know: spinning mules. The delight I get from them is not unlike that from the Emett clock in Nottingham – pleasure in seeing intricate parts moving in stately arabesques. Leeds made machines as well as using them – everything from the locomotives of Hunslet to cranes for the Zambesi Bridge – and has a long history of supplying them to foreign parts. A magnificent ploughing engine was found in the Sudan, where it had survived because the climate was dry and there is no market for scrap metal. But it is woollen cloth and the clothing trade which provide the main theme. They began making clothes in factories as early as 1856 and the big names of the trade – such as Burtons and Hepworths – set up in business. The important companies had a party piece for visiting VIPs. The dignitary would be measured up, taken on a tour of the works and presented with a made-to-measure suit by the end of his visit. All these stories and more are told here and they explain the wealth of the region.

The energetic can walk to another site farther along the canal, where the long history of Leeds is given physical expression. Kirkstall Abbey is extraordinarily well preserved and would now be as famous as Tintern or Fountains but for its setting, which long since turned the ancient stones a sooty black. Industry made use of the Aire here as well as at Armley Mills: a mighty forge used water power to turn its great hammers pounding out iron under the control of a foreman who was my great-great-grandfather. I must have inherited my love of old machines from him, and no doubt other tastes were fed into genes from the nearby Kirkstall brewery.

*

The prosperity was built on the River Aire, both as a means of transport and a source of power, and that prosperity finds its expression in the city centre. What is not so immediately apparent is how much of the present city has followed the patterns laid down in the past. Briggate, the principal shopping street, has been important since medieval times. It was here that the clothiers set up their stalls for trading, and the narrow burgage plots – thin strips stretching back from the main road – can still be recognised in the complex network of alleyways and arcades. The arcades, which are such a feature of the city, are true reflections of the past and quite glorious – narrow medieval entries transformed into little palaces of glass and gilded iron.

Leeds has a reputation as a shopping centre and was a pioneer of pedestrian precincts. When the plans were mooted, traders indulged in much wringing of hands and protestations of imminent doom. They have long since been accepted and widely copied and the new shops which have opened are a mark of commercial confidence. There are some fine examples of conversions of old buildings, notably the former Church Institute in Albion Place, where the tall arched windows at ground-floor level have been projected out on to the pavement to provide shapely display cabinets. There are brand new shopping areas, but the old also survive.

It is interesting to compare Newcastle's Grainger Market with Kirkgate Market. The former was designed by an architect but has the simplicity of good engineering in its plain, glazed roof. The credit list for Kirkgate puts city engineer Thomas Hewson's name above those of the architects Leeming and Leeming. Again a large area is covered by a roof of glass and iron, but the effect is more ornate. Red and gold lions stand guard over the colonnades which carry the elaborate curves of glazed domes. Newcastle still has its penny bazaar, but Leeds has its commemorative clock to record that it was here that Marks and Spencer first set up shop.

The area near the market is full of interest and of reminders of a long history of prosperity. The Corn Exchange is an elliptical rotunda of 1862. Its dome covers an open trading floor and offices are set around the perimeter, but these days there is only the occasional conference. I once saw a notice announcing that a meeting on psychic phenomena had been cancelled due to unforeseen circumstances. I cherish that memory. This is a building which deserved to find a new use, and now it has. It is being converted to provide shops and restaurants.

Just behind the exchange are the Assembly Rooms, a touch of Georgian formal dignity now too restrained to make any impact when set against their Victorian neighbour. The rooms have found a new use as an antiques market, though the proliferation of small cubicles has meant that the interior has lost much of its original character.

The eighteenth-century rooms never stood a chance of competing for attention when a great outburst of civic pride engulfed Leeds in the nineteenth century. In 1852 a competition was held for the design of a new Town Hall and the winner was Cuthbert Broderick. The building heaves itself up above the traffic of the Headrow on a grand podium of stone. The main hall is surrounded by Corinthian columns and the whole is topped with a baroque domed tower. There is no mistaking the main function of this building: it is intended to create the impression of great wealth resting on a reassuring foundation. When I lived in this area I never doubted that it was built of black stone. Then it was cleaned, and a

One of the city's famous shopping arcades

hundred years of soot and grime were washed away. That filth was as much a part of the story of Leeds as any carved detail, for the soot had been dumped there by the ever-smoking chimneys of the factories. The new *persona* never seemed quite right somehow, but Broderick would have been pleased that his building was once again the shining monument he had planned.

That applies not merely to the outside but to the Concert Hall, which must rank as one of the most ornate in Britain. The painted vault of the ceiling springs from marble columns which echo those outside, but the most striking feature is the concert organ, topped by a sunburst, while angels dance on the decorated organ pipe. It was designed in the days when a good evening of music meant massed choirs singing 'The Messiah'. The nearby Civic Hall, built in 1933, may gleam brightly in its Portland stone, but in this shop window of architectural confectionery it is a meringue beside a wedding cake.

The Art Gallery next to the Town Hall looks plain in this company, but it benefits greatly from its connection with one of Yorkshire's famous artistic sons. Henry Moore's bronze reclining figure lounges outside, peering across the swelling curves of her body at thoughtful chess players moving oversized pawns on the square below. The Moore is a fitting introduction to a gallery which has always had a character of its own, featuring artists such as Frank Brangwyn, whose great slabs of colour sit uneasily beside the fey works of the pre-Raphaelites. There is a spattering of Impressionists, but the overwhelming presence is that of Moore.

The Headrow is formal, grand Leeds with a saving touch of irreverence: it is also home to the famous music hall, the City of Varieties. Leeds still has its Grand Theatre but, thanks

Reclining figure by Henry Moore outside the Art Gallery

to television, it is the music hall that everyone knows. This is a creation of the past, where the audiences go to as much trouble as the cast to turn back the clock. It is all jolly good fun and a chance to dress up. In the old days there was a good deal more hearty vulgarity: for many years the Varieties was home not to ladies in crinolines but to ladies in nothing at all, who stood, under pain of heaven knows what penalties, as immobile as the statues in the city square. A show might be called 'Naughty Nights in Paris', but the law decreed that not a nostril should twitch to disturb the 'artistic tableaux'.

I did not really feel inclined to end my tour with civic grandeur or even with wicked Parisiennes. I had seen the wild rush of the river through the dark arches and the river that turned the wheels of industry, but there was another river I had seen only as a view from a carriage window – the old trading route of the city. It was on the crossing point of the Roman road from Chester to York that the hamlet of Loidis in Elmete was founded before the Norman Conquest, and Leeds Bridge stands on the site of a Roman ford. The riverside still has strong associations with the trading days in its tall warehouses, which until recently seemed doomed to a gentle decay. Instead the council decided to revive the waterfront, to bring it back to a position of importance in the life of the city. London's dockland has shown that such areas can have immense appeal, but Leeds rejected the yuppie solution, and old warehouses have been converted into workshops and offices. New houses for sale stand next to other conversions of apartments to let at reasonable rents. It seems too good to be true. But it is true, and one can see how successful the early schemes are proving. It seemed a suitably optimistic note on which to end, but on my way back to the station one last detail caught my eye. It seemed to be a Florentine campanile, complete with ornate windows. But the windows were false, and no bell would ever ring, for it was nothing but a mill chimney in disguise. I added it to my list of curiosities, a fitting companion for a Moorish warehouse and a rooftop pasture.

BRADFORD

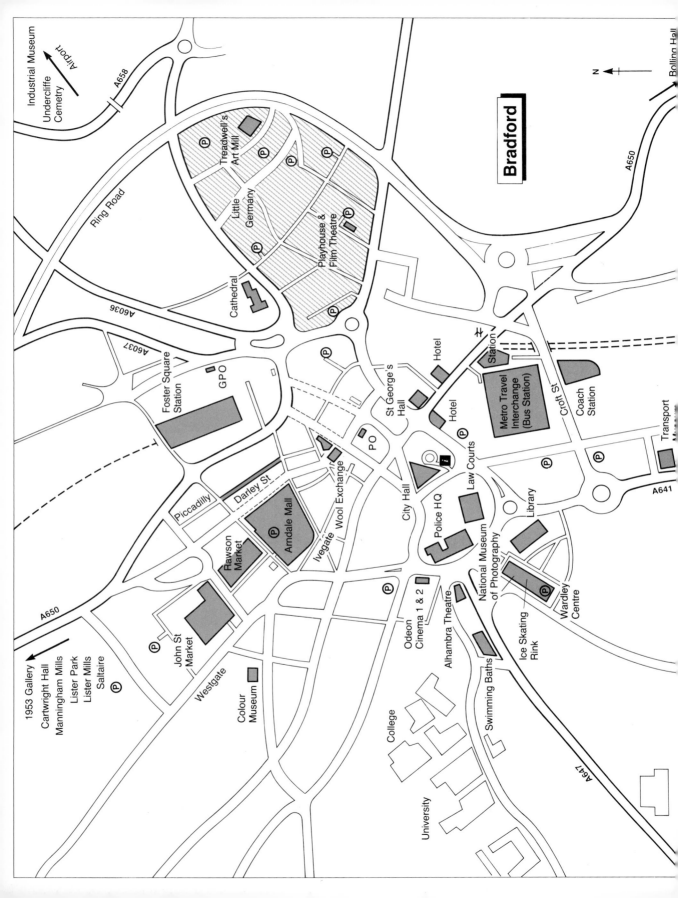

Bradford

N

Industrial Museum
Undercliffe Cemetery
Airport

A658

Ring Road

A6036

A6037

Treadwell's Art Mill

Little Germany

Cathedral

Playhouse & Film Theatre

Foster Square Station

GPO

St George's Hall

Hotel

Station

Hotel

Metro Travel Interchange (Bus Station)

Croft St

Coach Station

Transport

A641

PO

City Hall

Police HQ

i

Law Courts

Library

A650

1953 Gallery
Cartwright Hall
Manningham Mills
Lister Park
Lister Mills
Saltaire

Piccadilly

Darley St

Rawson Market

Arndale Mall

Ivegate

Wool Exchange

Colour Museum

John St Market

Westgate

Odeon Cinema 1 & 2

National Museum of Photography

Alhambra Theatre

Wardley Centre

Ice Skating Rink

Swimming Baths

College

University

A647

A650

Bolling Hall

12
BRADFORD

Bradford probably comes closest to everyone's idea of what a northern city is, so much so that when the city launched a campaign to attract tourists southern journalists fell about in collective hysteria. There were jokey news items on radio and television and you knew the journalists were not local because they put a funny sort of diphthong vowel in the middle of the word 'Bradford', whereas everyone knows it's 'Bratfud'. The publicists did not mind; they had achieved their first objective: the city was being talked about and journalists did come to see for themselves. Nobody laughs very much any more and Bradford has made its point. Yet it does remain one of the most distinctively northern cities, and I find nothing wrong in that.

On the short journey across from Leeds there could be no mistaking which part of the country I was travelling through. It took a while to clear the suburbs, then there was a flash of countryside near Pudsey: fields of tussocky, coarse grass marked out by drystone walls, and a hard margin to the land where the millstone grit pokes through the thin soil of the hilltops. Then Bradford appeared, set in a hollow which sprouted mill chimneys, like struts holding up a dark, overbearing sky. The view was lost as the train plunged into a stony cutting: a dour approach on a dour day which seemed specially chosen to confirm the worst prejudices about the wool city.

Bradford has a long history, but it is a history in two parts, and the second has overwhelmed the first. For many centuries it was a quiet spot where not a great deal went on. There was a busy woollen industry in the cottages of the surrounding hills, but with no river for power and transport it lacked the advantages of Leeds and Halifax. Even at the end of the eighteenth century, when the Industrial Revolution was well under way, it was still a small rural town.

Then came the steam engine, liberating the textile mills from their dependence on river sites. By 1810 there were 5 steam-powered mills, an ironworks turning out steam engines and a population of around 16,000. By 1840 there were 112 worsted mills, 8 other mills and a population of nearly 70,000, many of whom were immigrants from Ireland. That set the pattern. Mill work was never highly paid, though it could seem good if you came from an area where wages were much lower or non-existent. The Asian immigrants of the twentieth century are the latest actors in a long-running story. So, long though its history may be, what one sees today is an industrial city which in the nineteenth century overwhelmed its past. The idea that it might have anything to offer apart from muck, flat hats and an incomprehensible accent seemed ludicrous to those who had never seen the place.

Bradford has retained its nineteenth-century

character. Emerging from the railway station or, as it is now known in a rare burst of official pomposity, the Transport Interchange (which simply means that there is a bus station here as well), I found myself looking down into the bowl of the city. There is absolutely no doubt as to the dominant feature – the Town Hall, now grandly called the City Hall. The argument often used against the Victorians is that their great civic buildings were never given a style of their own, but were always pastiche, based on some earlier period. In Leeds the origins were classical; Bradford looks back to the great gothic town halls of northern Europe, such as Bruges or Gdansk.

Attitudes have changed: they had even begun to change when I was an undergraduate in the Fifties. A friend was an assiduous reader of John Betjeman; moved by his description of the splendours of Victorian architecture, he insisted that we set off then and there on a pilgrimage to Bradford Town Hall. That it was already getting dark was no deterrent. We arrived to find the building shining pallidly in the light of a full moon. More recently, I visited the Taj Mahal at full moon, but I was no more entranced by that wonder of the world than Chris by his first sight of the nineteenth-century town hall built in the style of the thirteenth century. He was so taken with it, so insistent that we should not overlook a single detail, that we missed the last train and had to return to Leeds with the milk churns in the dawn. I could never have recaptured that excitement, because I had known Bradford for years but the town hall was simply the town hall, always there. I had needed to see it through the eyes of a new and zealous convert to the doctrine according to Betjeman. Looking at it now, what seemed remarkable was just how good a re-creation of the gothic it is, and how self-confident and dominant it remains in the city.

The centre is quite small, but the geography of the area ensures interest. Whichever way you look, the streets climb steeply, offering constantly changing perspectives, while the big buildings huddle together in the bottom of the saucer. The Wool Exchange was completed in 1867, with little of the outward flamboyance of the town hall just six years later. It has something of the air of a pantheon, though the gods on display are a very secular lot. At the entrance are Bishop Blaize, patron saint of woolcombers, and Edward III who encouraged the wool trade. Ranged around the wall are a fine assortment of gentlemen, who at first seem a very strange mixture: Raleigh and Columbus, Arkwright and Watt, Palmerston and Gladstone and many more. Then a pattern emerges: the explorers opened up the world for British trade; the local worthies such as Sir Titus Salt used the machines designed by men such as Joseph Jacquard of the Jacquard loom. They were all the gods of wool.

The true grandeur of the exchange is inside: a vaulted porch leads through to the main hall, built like some medieval guildhall with marble pillars and hammer beam roof, but with some Victorian additions of wrought-iron staircase and balcony. The presiding genius is Cobden, who stands beside the motto: FREE TRADE. PEACE GOOD-WILL AMONG NATIONS. The marble columns are all numbered, a reminder of the days when the exchange was so crowded that assignments had to be carefully arranged – one merchant would meet another at pillar number 4. The room is still used for business, but there is no need to make arrangements in advance. At best half a dozen wool men will turn up, more for a chat than in the hope of doing real business. In the age of electronic communications there is no need for numbered marble pillars.

The area around the exchange has the

kind of rich commercial buildings one would expect, notably the big banks, once all local, now nationals such as Midland and NatWest. The Prudential Assurance buildings were the first to arrive with their national style already set. The architect Alfred Waterhouse, whom we shall meet again in Manchester, used brick and terracotta, materials quite new to Bradford in the 1890s but already part of the Pru image. But my eye was drawn away from these to the shopping streets leading up the hillside.

Piccadilly starts promisingly with the Old Exchange Rooms of 1828, which began as assembly rooms offering everything from billiards to dancing; they were briefly the wool exchange and even more briefly the post office. On the other side is the Shoulder of Mutton pub of similar date. The hillside has a curiously odd mixture of buildings at the top end. The Church Institute matched the Old Exchange in providing public facilities, except that where the one had decadent billiards, this had a healthy gymnasium. There is an air of moral improvement here, with the dauntingly entitled Bradford Subscription Library and Literary Society. Even the statue off Northgate was erected in honour of one of the great social reformers, the 'Factory King'

The Yorkshire Penny Bank

Richard Oastler. He fought for the Ten-Hour Bill, to limit the hours worked by mill children, and is depicted pointing benevolently at the sad figures of a young girl and boy. But there was still room for commerce among the benevolents: the old Yorkshire Penny Bank was built here and there is a glorious shop front, a real Victorian extravaganza, in Manor Row.

In between Westgate and Darley Street is the market area – John Street Market, rebuilt in the 1970s after a fire, Rawson Market, also rebuilt, and the modern Arndale Mall, a sort of small-scale tryout for Manchester's Arndale Centre. I suppose if anyone had to pick on a building to reinforce the Bradford stereotype they could find it here: a little shop which faces out on to the road and inwards to the market – Hey's Tripe Shop, specialists in quality tripe and black pudding. Tripe is one of those dishes thought comical or repellent by those who have never tried it. I was once informed that only uncouth northerners would dream of eating the stuff, and when I pointed out that it was one of the great traditional dishes of Florence and could be found in any good restaurant in Normandy my news was greeted with ill-concealed scepticism. I hope Hey's shop will be around for a long time to come. I was disappointed that I could find no local menu which featured tripe, and had to wait until I got to a Chinese restaurant in Manchester where there were three variations. It was good, but I can think of easier things to eat with chopsticks.

My route back downhill brought me out by Forster Square, an area scheduled for redevelopment and badly in need of it. There are extensive plans for change in the city centre. Forster Square is to see a major new commercial development with a £60-million shopping centre. There are also plans for more

The Alhambra Theatre

pedestrian precincts and extension of the ring road system, the closure of some streets to cars to free them for public transport and the provision of new off-street car parks.

A lot of thought has gone into the social implications of the changes. The planners have looked at the problem of making the city centre safer for women, by improving lights in car parks and designing pedestrian areas which will not turn into deserted and menacing alleys at night. But what impressed me most was the effort to involve the community. Information leaflets were being handed out to everyone in the streets and they included a prepaid form so that people could show approval or disapproval of the new schemes – and there was plenty of space for individual comments. A mobile exhibition centre showed in more detail what was planned. As befits the new Bradford, the information was available in different Asian languages as well as in English.

Meanwhile all I had to look at was glum Forster Square Station and the Midland Hotel, whose chief claim to fame was that Henry Irving expired there after collapsing on stage at the Theatre Royal in 1905. The far side offered a more attractive prospect, with a flight of steps leading up to the cathedral. This is perhaps the one corner of the city where you can believe there was a Bradford in existence before the nineteenth century. Part of the building dates back to the parish church of the fifteenth century. There are a great many nineteenth-century additions and changes and, more unusually, a good deal of the work of extension was done in this century. The different periods are more obvious outside than in the interior, which has a calm, well-ordered appearance. There are few elaborate gothic gestures, so one finds a basic simplicity of form such as one might expect in a far older building. The

cathedral marks the start of a special area – Little Germany. There were many German merchants here before the rampant jingoism of the First World War made it unhealthy to have anything but an English name on your brass plate.

This was the commercial heartland of Victorian Bradford, the merchants' quarter of streets lined with monumental offices and warehouses. Like many such areas, it became run down. It might have made sense when the canal came up to the edge of Church Bank and the railway was just across the road, but no one wants a warehouse in a city centre in the motorway age. So there was an area of historic importance and self-evident character, which showed great unity because it was all built around the 1860s. What was to be done? Little Germany was made into both a Conservation Area and a Commercial Improvement Area, which meant that firms were encouraged to take over the old buildings, and while there was a limit on what could be changed externally, grants were available to adapt the old while keeping its character intact. The first results are encouraging.

The conservation theme came up again in the context of what is Bradford's best-known landmark after the Town Hall – the conspicuous dome and turrets of the Alhambra Theatre. It was completed at the start of the First World War and represents the end of an age of big, ornate municipal theatres. Like many of its kind, it had a fine auditorium, a not-so-grand front-of-house and what can best be described as an inadequate backstage area. For a time its future was in doubt, but there were many who argued that everything should be done to preserve the distinctive outline and the splendid decorated auditorium with its domed ceiling and frescoes. Once agreement was reached on that, it was necessary to rebuild within the original framework, replacing and adding on as necessary. The result is striking and more than a little surprising. The new has echoes of the art deco style of the thirties, but has brought a new lightness to the stuffy atmosphere of the old foyer. New facilities included the incorporation of the old Majestic Theatre as a full-size rehearsal room, which ensured that the Alhambra can take virtually any production and provide accommodation to meet the standards of the most demanding performers. In many ways, the story is similar to that of Newcastle's Theatre Royal: what was worth saving has been saved; what was not has been replaced in style.

Close to the Alhambra is a building which has helped to dispel Bradford's cloth cap and whippet image – the National Museum of Photography. Its arrival was closely connected with the fate of the Alhambra. When it looked as though the theatre might simply be allowed to close, attention was concentrated on building a new civic theatre. But the Alhambra was saved; a new theatre was not needed after all, so it was scarcely finished before it was mothballed. At about that time it was generally agreed that Britain needed a museum covering photography, film and television. The government indicated that support would be available if it were sited outside London and run by an existing national museum. The Science Museum was the obvious parent body. They already had a basic collection and experience of running a major provincial museum in the shape of the National Railway Museum at York. In 1977 the director Dame Margaret Weston was in Bradford for a conference, saw the unused civic theatre and the enterprise was born. The Science Museum wanted it, Bradford wanted it, and together they have given the city one of the most exciting museums in the country.

This is not an exhibits-in-glass-cases estab-

Undercliffe Cemetery: a Victorian necropolis

lishment. Visitors find out what is what by doing as much as watching. If you want to know what it is like to read the nine o'clock television news, they give you the chance. You sit in the studio, the credits roll, the regular announcer says, 'over to our Bradford studio', and off you go, reading a story about a rail disaster from the teleprompt. After that comes the embarrassing moment when you see the playback of your efforts. This is one example of the many ways in which the visitor is involved in using and exploring the exhibits.

There are more conventional displays, including changing photographic exhibitions – on my visit they were showing the work of the great portraitist, Karsh. Images one had seen reproduced countless times appeared with a fresh crispness and sparkle. The show proved that photographs need proper exhibitions as much as other works of art. For many, the great attraction is Imax, where 70mm film is projected on to a giant screen more than fifty feet high. It has remarkable clarity and immediacy, but has not quite lost a suggestion of gimmickry.

This is a genuine national museum setting the highest standards.

Outside there were memories of an older town. Queen Victoria, that inescapable presence, looked out over the city; her companion this time was not Albert but that great chronicler of Yorkshire life, J. B. Priestley. I wonder what he would have thought of the new Bradford. He remembered it when there was still a strong German influence, when it was 'at once one of the most provincial and yet one of the most cosmopolitan of English provincial cities'. He enjoyed the old mixture

and I am sure he would have approved the new.

The Asian community has brought a whole new aspect to local life, though one wonders how long they will still be called that. A second generation has been born and brought up here; they have the same broad vowels as their neighbours, but there are still differences. Food is the most immediately obvious example, for Bradford is famous among lovers of Indian cooking, not just for its quality but for its cheapness and authenticity. I went for a meal at the Kashmir, what I can only describe as a caff in a basement up from the Alhambra. The décor was practically non-

Lister Park from the Cartwright Hall Art Gallery

existent, the tables were formica-topped and there was no cutlery, just *nan* bread to scoop up the food. I had last eaten like that in an open-air restaurant in Ahmedabad – and the flavours in Bradford were just the same. The cost of my two-course dinner was less than £2. One surprising up-market restaurant, Bombay Brasserie, has re-created a Moghul palace in what was once a United Reformed Church. It is exotic, but I will remember the Kashmir with pleasure for a very long time.

Food is important, not just for its flavours, but because for many of the community it has a religious significance. Muslims need to know that what they are buying conforms to the Islamic code of purity. Panorama Stores began through an overheard conversation, when a non-English-speaking old gentleman was patiently waiting while his grandson translated the list of ingredients on a packet of biscuits from English into Urdu. It was clear that there was a need for a store where everything sold was guaranteed to conform to Islamic law.

A co-operative was formed to sell Islamic food and run on Islamic principles – which meant, among other things, no loans, not even a small overdraft at the bank. The first thing that struck me was the wonderful smell, the rich scent of spices. After that, it was the sheer bulk of everything: ghee in 15kg buckets, rice in 10kg sacks. People come here to shop from all over Britain, for it is unique. No one is surprised when a family arrives from London and fills a big estate car with food. But there is nothing exclusive about the Panorama, no discrimination over who should be employed, and more and more European faces are to be seen among the customers. The store offers superb value for money.

The new Bradford is multiracial, but dependence on the woollen industry has not been entirely broken. In their time, the mills brought wealth for some and poverty for many. One of the dignified gentlemen who look down from the walls of the Wool Exchange is Sir Titus Salt, mayor from 1848–9. Horrified by the slums, he decided to build a new mill at the edge of the city and surround it with a model town for the workers. His new town, established on the banks of the Aire, is Saltaire, and it still looks much as it did when the mill opened in 1853.

The style is Italianate and is carried through everything, industrial buildings and houses alike. Sir Titus was the universal supplier: almshouses, hospital, library, church and a handsome park over which his statue presides, flanked on one side by an angora goat and by an alpaca on the other. Sir Titus's mill spun mohair not wool. The one thing Saltaire does not have is a pub – not that its founder was a teetotaller, but he did not believe that what was right for him was necessarily right for the lower orders. One thing has changed in recent times: the mill has stopped work. Only one building now remains in use, re-named Gallery 1853. It is a part of the original mill but is now devoted to showing the work of another famous son, David Hockney, and is surprisingly successful. The building is a typical fireproof mill, where the upper floor is carried on brick arches springing from iron pillars. The regular, rhythmical pattern of deep red bricks finds an echo in the formalised ripples of Hockney's famous swimming pools.

Saltaire is one image of the old industrial life. Bradford also has an industrial museum, based as in Leeds on a former mill building. It is up on Moorside Road to the north of the city, in a genuine moorside setting, and it brings home one of the features of Bradford life. Down in the bowl, the mean Victorian terraces sat under a canopy of smoke from the mill chimneys. But the moors – Ilkley Moor itself, where as all Yorkshiremen know it is

The mill at Saltaire

fatal to go hatless – are a mere half dozen miles from the city centre. The old spinning mill which now houses the museum has much in common with Armley Mills, for both are concerned with telling the story of local industry, and that has to mean a concentration on worsted. Here are the machines which turned a fleece from a sheep's back into fine cloth and the great engines that powered them, the steam monsters on whose back Bradford rode to prosperity. Outside, local kids had painted their view of the city and what they saw was still a Victorian town of terraced houses striding down a hill until the way is blocked by the vast bulk of a spinning mill, and trains on viaducts riding high above a forest of smoking chimneys. The city is changing, but it will be a long while before it shakes off the old image.

145

There is another Bradford. The city boasts a baroque art gallery, Cartwright Hall, built in 1905 in Lister Park. Some of the old rooms are being restored as appropriate settings for the nineteenth-century collection. In a way this is still an aspect of the mill town, but it shows the reverse of the Victorian coin – public money spent for the public good. Bolling Hall is a more surprising survivor, a manor house which started with a medieval tower, was built up in the seventeenth century and was given a Georgian wing in the eighteenth. It is a west Yorkshire manor which the spreading city swallowed up.

I walked back to the centre on a route which took me past a spot where all the traditional elements came together. Undercliffe Cemetery stands on the side of a hill and here more than anywhere else one feels the full weight of the Victorian past. Pinnacles and gothic towers, pedestalled urns and weeping angels, stand in ranks, and there is even an exotic tomb in a style borrowed from Egypt's Valley of the Kings. The monuments are avowals in stone and marble of the solid worth, virtue and wealth of those who lie beneath them. From these monuments to the prosperous dead I looked out over the tightly packed terraces to what is the grandest of all Bradford's buildings, grander than the town hall itself. It dominates the whole region as an unmistakable landmark – Manningham Mills.

The huge bulk of the building and the tall chimney soar above the surrounding streets. Mills and terraces may be the northern cliché, but clichés have a basis in truth. It is still the same place that grew up around the manufacture of worsted, and there is nothing to be ashamed of in that. Bradford can be proud of the fact that it produced woollen cloth of a quality matched nowhere else in the world.

MANCHESTER

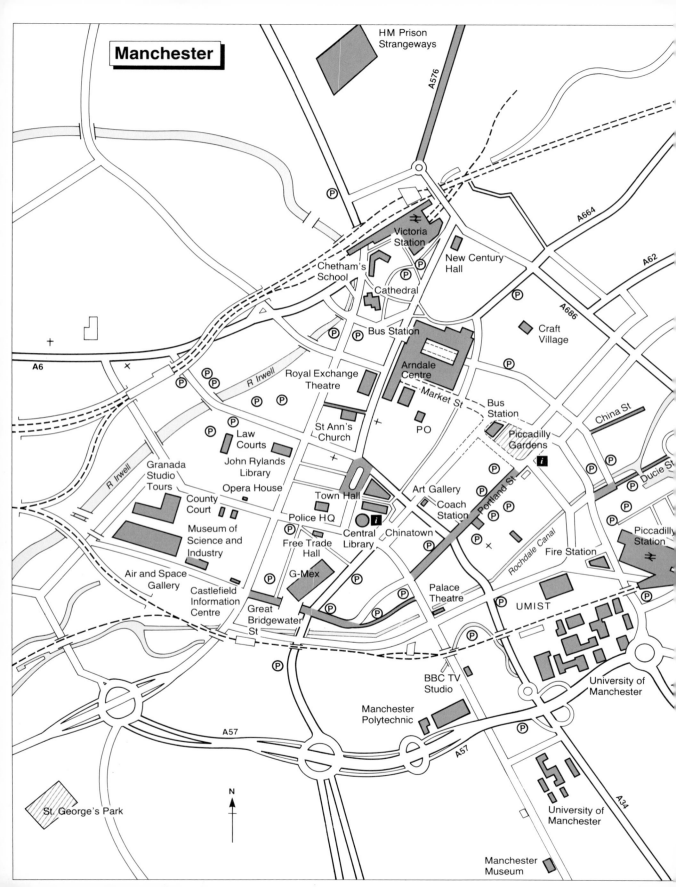

13
MANCHESTER

The journey from the wool towns of York-shire to the cotton capital of Lancashire – Manchester – was retracing a route I had followed on foot the previous summer. The railway threads the same line through the Pennines as the earlier Rochdale Canal whose towpath I had walked all the way from Sowerby Bridge. The engineers had little choice where to go; geography dictated their choice because the hills rise steeply around the narrow river valleys. This is a landscape of high, stone-rimmed hills and tightly bunched mill villages. In the distance I saw the hill farms in their stony webs of walls and the little groups of weavers' cottages; close at hand, the mills had grabbed the space near the all important transport routes.

At Littleborough, the mood changed as the line left the hills for the flat plain. The stone of the hills gave way to livid red brick as the chimneys of the cotton mills vied for attention with church spires and the tall tower of Rochdale Town Hall. The spread-ing suburbs of Manchester took over until I arrived in what seemed at first glance the rather ordinary building of Victoria Station. The first impression was partially banished by the concourse, where everything is labelled not in BR plastic but in art nouveau ceramics. Without that touch, the station would have little to commend it.

Manchester is not a city where patterns are easy to discern. I have discovered on more than one occasion that it is easy to get lost here. The streets have something of the feel of New York: the buildings may not be so high, but they are just as effective in closing off the view. What is striking is to find how much there is to admire. The builders of offices and warehouses may not have gone in for flourishes as exotic as the Moorish building in Leeds, but everywhere there is a love of embellishment and the grand effect. Nowhere was grander in scale and concept than S. & J. Watts' cotton warehouse of 1851. The style is renaissance, or should one say styles? – each of the four floors represents a different phase of the architecture of the period. It is now the Britannia Hotel and I had no doubt that this was where I would stay. The interior is as flamboyant as the exterior: a wealth of blue and gold with a staircase fit for a royal entrance winding from the lobby. The new luxury trappings do not look ridiculous or out of context in the converted warehouse. But then when Lancastrians were cotton spinners to the world the accepted thing to do with wealth was to flaunt it.

The city once served the world and ex-pressed its connections in streets and build-ings. Down by the canal are China Street and Bengal Street, and the ornate warehouses pick

The Britannia Hotel was originally a cotton warehouse

up the themes – Byzantine here, Moghul there. Details tell stories of trade. Chepstow House has a ship with a Neptune figurehead above the entrance, while a merchantman weather vane sails the winds of the city. Warehouses turn streets into gloomy canyons as they cut out the sun. You could once see the power of the city and its industries all around the

150

world: I have watched cotton being ginned in India on machines shipped out from here; I have seen it woven into cotton in America on Lancashire looms; and I have even seen wool pressed and baled on the other side of the world, in the Falkland Islands, using Lancastrian know-how.

Manchester could afford to send out machines, because it seemed that the millions of whirring spindles in the local mills would go on turning for ever, sending millions of miles of thread around the globe. It did not last. The cotton-growing countries became cotton-manufacturing countries, and the city which had raised the philosophy of free trade to a religion found itself undercut by traders as far away as Japan.

Lancashire exported its ideas, its styles and its philosophy as well as its machines to the East; now the East is returning the compliment. Just around the corner from the Britannia Hotel, marked by a triumphal arch in a traditional Chinese design, is Chinatown. Across the road, a mundane car park has a junk, picked out in brickwork, sailing across a gable end. Street names are duplicated in Chinese. There is colour and life in the streets and the aroma of cooking from dozens of restaurants, each offering regional specialities. All of it is squashed into a small area bounded by Portland Street on the one side, where tall modern blocks overshadow the Britannia's exuberance, and on the other by the formal area of official buildings around the Town Hall.

The first building I visited was the Art Gallery, which has a huge collection of Victorian paintings. After a while I began to feel like the child in the sweet factory, and was overcome by the cloying colours and sentimental themes. But there are other things to enjoy. Leeds has its tribute to Moore; Manchester pays homage to L. S. Lowry. The old rent collector's

rooms have been reconstructed within the Art Gallery with all their atmosphere and clutter intact. There were more echoes of the Orient, not so much China as Japan, in some exquisite prints which combine great formality with tangible sense of reality. Waves form classical scrolls yet one feels them heave against an unfortunate, foundering ship. Lancastrians took out their machines to Tokyo, but did well in what they brought back. There is much to enjoy here from English ceramics to a gorgeous, swirling seascape by Turner, but what made my day was the discovery of an Impressionist painting which not only pre-dates the works by the French masters but is an Englishman's view of a Welsh beach. David Coxe's painting of Rhyl Sands in the 1850s could easily pass for a Boudin, and if I were a local resident I would long ago have signed up for the gallery's picture lending scheme.

Travelling around the different cities, one gets the feeling that there must have been a nineteenth-century competition to see who could produce the grandest, most flamboyant town hall. Sir Nikolaus Pevsner has pointed out that the municipalities poured money into establishing an outward show of prosperity which might more profitably have been spent on relieving the squalor in which so many of their citizens lived. But the Victorians were no different from any other powerful group, and if those precepts had been followed in earlier times the world would have no Pyramids, no Parthenon and no Taj Mahal. So the money was put into the showpieces, and Manchester's Town Hall must come high on any list.

The style is gothic, similar to that of Bradford, and only half a dozen years separate the two buildings. It is not Yorkshire prejudice which makes me come down in favour of the Bradford building, but given the aim of re-creating styles of the past the Bradford

The high-tech theatre inside the old Cotton Exchange

turret tower is more happily integrated into the design than Manchester's spire. Having said that, architect Alfred Waterhouse showed great ingenuity in unifying a building which occupies an awkward triangular site – and the outside is only part of the story. At the centre of the building is the great hall, lit by surrounding courtyards, with the main offices grouped around the outside. In many ways it is more visually exciting than the exterior, with vaulted corridors, great spiral staircases and elaborate decoration.

Above all, it benefits from its setting, facing out over a piazza of generous proportions, though that has become apparent again only in recent years with the redirection of traffic to keep Albert Square an open space. It also has good company: the extension built in the 1930s managed to bridge the exuberant gothic of the original Town Hall and the classical simplicity of the adjoining Library, by using overall shapes which echoed the former while keeping detail starkly simple.

South from the Town Hall is a building which says more about the city's past than any other single structure – the Free Trade Hall. It commemorates the rising power of the industrial world over the old order of landed aristocracy. The hall stands on the site of the infamous Peterloo Massacre when a peaceful demonstration against the Corn Laws was attacked by the yeomanry and eleven demonstrators were killed. The struggle against the laws was led by local men – Cobden and Bright – and led to their repeal in 1846. The movement was always about more than removing an agricultural subsidy; it was about the freedom of industrialists to manufacture and trade as they wished, untouched by interference from the legislature. This was a vital part of Manchester's thrusting, aggressive drive towards wealth and influence. The Free Trade Hall has few of the attention-grabbing devices of the Town Hall, but it is a building of solid worth and richly carved. As much as any warehouse or great mill, the Free Trade Hall is a monument to the success of the Industrial Revolution, which changed the social order of Britain as decisively as the Civil War changed the political. It is not insignificant that it should now be the home of one of the city's artistic successes, the Hallé orchestra. Perhaps the only other building to match it in significance is the Royal Exchange.

The present building is Manchester's third exchange, which in itself tells a story of growing demand for space as business developed. The second exchange was greatly extended and virtually transformed in the 1870s, to become a building whose pomp and finery could match any in the city. Here was conducted the cotton business of the world, and at its peak the exchange had 11,000 members, representing everything from shipping insurance to machinery manufacture and spinning. Twice a week the great hall was packed out and members, like those of Bradford's exchange, arranged meetings using numbered and lettered columns. They were like a set of map references: one set of columns had letters, the other numbers. If you had arranged a meeting at B7, you had to find a spot where the two imaginary lines intersected.

In the twentieth century, depression led to decline and the exchange closed its doors to traders. Its new use is more bizarre than anything the old cotton men could have imagined. The great pillared hall is still there, but in its centre is what looks like a giant spaceship, the auditorium of the Exchange Theatre, a structure of steel suspended amid all the Victorian splendour.

So much of the city is filled with buildings of great elaboration that it is a relief to find something both simple and impressive. That we can see such a structure is a piece of good fortune, or perhaps one should say bad fortune. Central Station, the Midland Railway terminus, has a train shed covered by one great span of iron and glass, 220 feet wide, which arched over tracks and platforms and showed itself to the world, unmasked by any other architectural details. St Pancras, at the other end of the line, has a similar dramatic structure, but that is scarcely noticed behind the fantasy of the Station Hotel. Central Station could similarly have been tucked out of sight, but the cash ran out before the hotel was built. When there was money in the coffers again, the hotel was given a different site across the road, and if it cannot match St Pancras it does its best. The architects have left no surface undecorated and were never content to use one type of decoration where three could be fitted into the space. The two styles of the age, the purely practical and the highly decorated, are seldom seen in such clear juxtaposition.

The old station is not quite what it was. It was closed in 1969 and we have now not so much a restoration as its re-creation as an exhibition and events centre – G-Mex. It is triumphantly successful and worth exploring further, particularly the car parks underneath – a complex of arches, tunnels, platforms and turntables where the mundane business of moving goods went on out of sight of the passengers above.

If I were to choose an area to show what Manchester was as well as what it is and might be, this would be it. The passenger station and the hotel's commercial importance are matched by the towering Great Northern Railway goods warehouses to complete the transport story. They were all overtaken by events, and Manchester has moved on, but has had the commonsense to realise that the past can be re-used rather than jettisoned. New buildings are being added, not just office

The Central Library

blocks but houses. Hundreds of homes were swept away to make room for the railway. Now neat rows of neo-Georgian houses stand a little self-consciously under the shadow of the G-Mex arch.

Great Bridgewater Street runs down the side of G-Mex and leads to an area of unique importance in transport history. The Bridgewater Canal was the first in Britain to take a line quite independent of any natural waterway and its success led to the great period of canal building which lasted from 1760 to 1830. Then the first public railway on which everything – passengers and goods alike – was moved in trains hauled by steam locomotives, was opened between Liverpool and Manchester. Down the road, within a few hundred yards of each other, are the old canal basin and the world's first passenger station, and it is only in the past few years that anyone has taken much notice of them.

The Museum of Science and Industry is centred on the original terminus of the Liverpool and Manchester Railway. It has all the things one might expect in such a museum on such a site: stationary steam engines are steamed inside the building, while locomotives on the tracks outside give passengers rides up and down the line. It also has things one might not expect: a whole section on the generation of electrical power and an almost too realistic exhibition of sewers. This is, in fact, very imaginative and visitors walk down a reconstructed sewer complete with nasty trailing fronds and a definite whiff in the air. But the principal exhibit remains the site, its old warehouses and the restoration of the world's first station booking office. Just across the road, in the old market hall, is the Air and Space Gallery, a typical nineteenth-century market, iron pillared and glass roofed, and now packed with aircraft. I cannot imagine how they manoeuvred them all into place, but there is not an inch of space in the main hall for anything, no matter how small.

The area where the museum stands is Castlefield and it has now become an Urban Heritage Park, a concept which has some rather odd features. Certainly the word 'heritage' is not out of place, because this has been an important centre since the Romans established a fort here. The north gateway has now been reconstructed. I am sure it is a very accurate reconstruction, but it looks like a bit of the set for *Quo Vadis* which someone forgot to remove. The surviving genuine fragments are scant but more evocative. Other buildings have been pressed into service to reinforce local messages: a gable end carries a huge mural showing the Stephensons and the *Rocket*, while other houses have now become a visitors' centre and an art gallery. Once again it is the area and the story that it tells which are more important than the explanatory exhibits.

At Castlefield Junction the Rochdale Canal meets the Bridgewater in a flurry of docks and warehouses, and the Bridgewater in turn is joined by the Ship Canal, once a vital link in Manchester's trade, now unused. Over the canals, the railways stride on iron viaducts. The high-level railways have called for a whole range of bridges in different styles: tubes of riveted iron plates hold up one viaduct; a conventional iron span runs between castellated towers farther down the canal. Some of the lines are in use, others abandoned, and some are destined for revival as a light railway system. The abandoned lines have become urban wildernesses, where orchids can be found, but refurbishment is going on at a great pace. I hope the essential ordinariness of the area can be retained. It is historically important because those who created a transport complex thought in terms of practical problems and practical solutions. If that atmosphere goes, the cleverest exhibits and the most brilliantly designed museum will never be a compensation.

The walk back to the city centre brought me out of the world where money was made and back to the one where it was spent, to the shops and offices of Deansgate, where every conceivable style of building can be found. I went through a narrow passageway beside the *Manchester Evening News* offices to a little square with a bold modern sculpture and was confronted by a stepped glass tower, culminating in a glazed round-headed turret. It belongs as much to the 1980s as the building opposite belongs to a century ago. The Rylands Library is pure gothic, inside and out. It is meant to have the same air of ancient learning as, say, the Bodleian in Oxford; having done research in both institutions, I have to say that it succeeds. Deansgate is the home of the big department stores, in which the

Railway bridges across the canal at Castlefield

library seems something of an anachronism, but the streets behind offer more of a sense of intimacy.

Here I found one of Manchester's rare examples of a pre-nineteenth century building, St Ann's Church, though the Victorians did their best to drag it into their age. Alfred Waterhouse, the Town Hall architect, did nothing much to the exterior but altered the interior radically, removing the old box pews and adding new stained glass, quite out of keeping with a light Georgian church. Nearby is a pedestrian street, a fashionable shopping area where the lunchtime crowd were strolling or sitting in the sun, while a tenor saxophonist provided the entertainment.

The effect of Manchester can be overwhelming. Street after street boasts buildings on a monumental scale, so that you tend to lose all sense of where you are or in what relationship you stand to where you have just been. The Town Hall forms one recognisable nucleus but there must, one feels, be another, older centre. The obvious choice would seem to be the cathedral. But this, although medieval in origin, is once again a reconstruction by the Victorians in their version of gothic. At least they were true to the feel and spirit of the original and I finally had a context for the city, a point of growth from which so much else must have sprung.

I had arrived on the high ground above the

River Irwell, once a vital part of the life of the city but now all but forgotten, receiving even less attention than the canal system. The canals are at least regularly used by boats and provide a unique way of seeing the city: travellers on the Rochdale Canal find themselves diving underneath office blocks from which they emerge to an enclosed world, an unnatural gorge of warehouse cliffs. By comparison, the Irwell seems wide, open and pleasant. It also marks a clear division in the city, for across its waters is not Manchester but Salford. The names of surrounding streets have their stories: Hanging Ditch was once a deep ditch protecting the side of the cathedral, and Market Street does mark the old market area. But the days when the cathedral tower dominated the landscape have long gone. The old market has gone too and Market Street fronts its modern equivalent, the Arndale Centre.

The Arndale Centre is development on a gargantuan scale, covering a twenty-five-acre site. Unlovely it may be, but it boasts of being the largest covered shopping area in Europe and attracts nearly a million customers a year. There is nothing wrong with what it does in the daytime, but at night and weekends it kills a huge area of the city. Everything is locked up and closed down, with the corollary that everything in its shadow tends to die when it dies. One is left with a huge building of no use and no discernible architectural merit.

One problem which faces all city centres is that of keeping them alive, not just in the hours when offices are open but afterwards as well. The saddest thing about the Arndale Centre is that it has the opposite effect, as if one quarter of Manchester puts up a 'closed' sign every evening. The developers would point to 800,000 shoppers who disagree. Almost every city I visited had its shopping centre or was planning one, and no one spends tens of millions of pounds without being certain that they are meeting a demand. I still find them depressing and would prefer to wander down the pedestrian precinct of King Street to leaving daylight for the artificial lighting and canned music of the centre.

So I set off to enjoy a nostalgic glimpse of an earlier and different market. Not far from Arndale is what was the Wholesale Fish Market. Now only the façade remains, but it is very fine, with carvings showing fishy scenes: men hauling in their nets and girls gutting the fish at the quayside. As part of a general move to improve the area, one building has become a craft market. I am always dubious about the craft market idea, because so many people in the movement seem to have neither much artistry nor much mastery of their craft. Here everyone seemed competent and a few were much more than that, which was very encouraging. I still saw nothing that I liked as

The façade is all that remains of the Fish Market

much as the carvings on the front of the old fish market.

Manchester is like Birmingham in that it is too big to absorb in a few days. I began to feel that I was on a whistle-stop tour as I peeped in on the Jewish Museum, based on a gorgeous Spanish and Portuguese synagogue, and took an even more cursory look around the Transport Museum practically next door. It is a city where, in a way, one comes closer to its true character by not going very far but looking at one area in detail. The previous year I had walked down to Castlefield on the canal towpath and the effect created then by the imposing commercial buildings full of telling details still seems to say much of what needs to be said. Again, like Birmingham, it is a city which is always changing, where new

development is accepted as a constant part of life. Yet there is an awareness that this is a unique city, that in outward appearance it is still Cottonopolis, a centre which once controlled a whole world of textiles. So buildings are preserved and adapted; thought is given to the past as well as to the future. It is a policy which I can only applaud, but it is ironical that in this great commercial city, which was built on gritty realism, the great new tourist attraction is a pure fantasy. Coronation Street is accepting visitors at the Granada Studios, just over the wall from the industrial museum. The world created by the engineers of the nineteenth century sits next to a pretend world of the twentieth century. It will be all right so long as they remember that the real pub opposite the museum is every bit as valuable as the Rover's Return.

LIVERPOOL

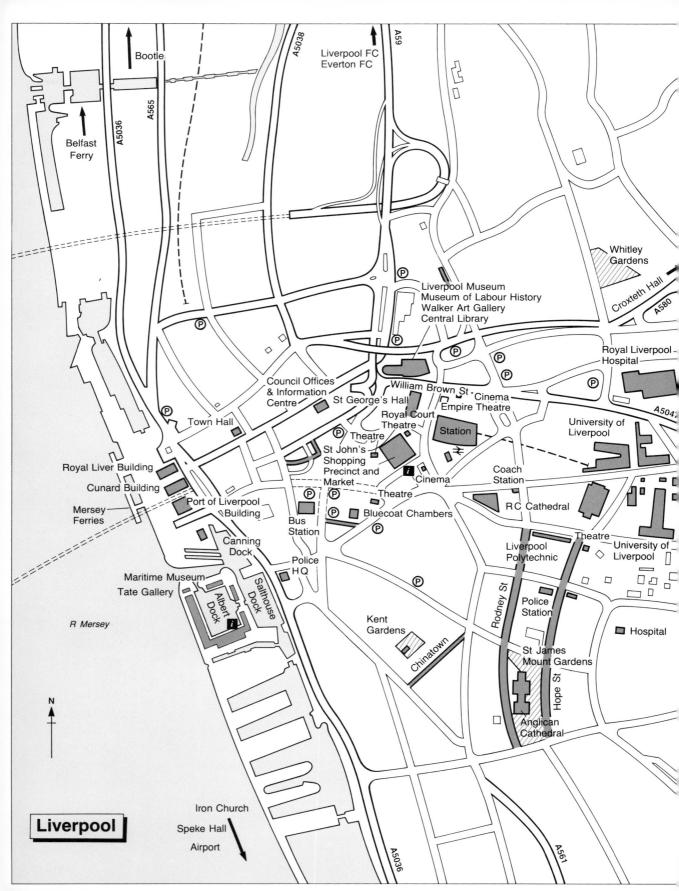

Liverpool

14
LIVERPOOL

The last stage of my English journey was on the historic railway line from Manchester to Liverpool. I came through Rainhill where Stephenson's *Rocket* beat all the competition and set a pattern for locomotive construction which was to be elaborated and improved but not fundamentally changed until the end of the steam age. Arrival is down the immense rock cutting of Olive Mount where the sheer walls are as daunting now as they were when the navvies blasted and hacked their way down a century and a half ago. As a piece of engineering it is impressive; as an introduction to the city it is less satisfying. But once I left the train and stepped out into Lime Street I was confronted by a group of formal buildings which form one of the best, unified classical groupings in the country. Yet it is typical that the immediate surroundings are a contrast – bearing no relationship to the coherent group of St John's Gardens. So there are worse places to start looking at the city than right on the station doorstep.

The immediate area around Lime Street looks out on to a modern hotel and a department store, though not every department store has an over life-size statue of a nude man on the front, standing in the bows of a boat and apparently trying to direct the traffic. But I was drawn to a precise group of buildings, dominated by St George's Hall which is just about the finest neo-classical building in England. A competition was held in 1839 for a building to house two concert halls, one to seat 3000 the other 500, and the rules specified that they were to be in the 'Grecian or Roman' style. The winner, Harvey Lonsdale Elmes, was only twenty-five years old and he also won a second competition for new assize courts. The two functions were eventually brought together in the one building, a magnificent Corinthian temple. It was to be his one great achievement, for he died in 1847 and the work was completed by Charles Robert Cockerell.

The building is as remarkable for the way it works as for the way it looks. The entrance up the broad steps to the podium with its equestrian statues creates an expectation not disappointed. The main concert hall is visually stunning, with a massive organ, the biggest of its kind then, and the decorative details include a frieze suggested by the Elgin Marbles, granite Doric columns, ten chandeliers each holding more than a hundred lightbulbs and – a happy reminder of the Stoke visit – tiles by Minton. What you do not see is just as impressive. The building was designed to be as comfortable as it was impressive. A central heating system was built in, using air blown over hot water pipes and directed by flaps in the air ducts. More remarkably for the time, there was also air conditioning. Air was drawn in at street level, cooled by fountains and circulated around the building by steam-powered fans. Hollow tiles in the floor and outlets in the ceiling panels aided ventilation. The hall looked superb but there is still a question to be answered – what is to be done with it now?

No such problems affect the buildings which face the hall across William Brown Street, all of which took their design cues from the neo-classical masterpiece. A row of four buildings are, from the top of the hill to the bottom, the Museum of Labour History, the Walker Art Gallery, the Central Library and Liverpool Museum. Three of the four are very much what you find in any city, so I concentrated on the first.

There is something very pleasing about a museum which tells of bitter fights by groups such as trades unions and suffragettes against the laws of the time and which is housed in the old County Sessions House. The section on the education of the poor is reached through a fine doorway labelled Barristers' Room and Library, and the court room is bright with union banners. It shows another Liverpool from that on display in St George's Hall. Here you can learn that when the hall was built there were 170,000 slum dwellers in the town, many living in cellars twelve feet square and six feet high, where the lucky ones had stone flags and the rest bare earth. It tells the story of the immigrants, not just the Irish but the Chinese who established a community here in the 1860s, and the West Africans who

The Walker Art Gallery

followed shortly after. It also explained a name I had never understood before – 'scouse' was a cheap stew which was standard fare in the workhouse.

The principal story tells the history of the port: 27,000 dockers were employed as casual workers before the First World War. Now containerisation and mechanisation rule. An old docker recorded his impressions for the museum: 'I went on to Seaforth. The cargo they shift there is colossal, but there's no one around. It's frightening.' It was here that I picked up the background to what was to become one of the principal themes of the Liverpool story.

What is notably absent in this area is a town hall. That is down in the city centre and comes as something of a surprise, no Victorian extravaganza but a dignified and quite small building of 1754, built at a time when Liverpool had scarcely entered its first great period of expansion.

The main streets run in an easily recognisable pattern: broad ways leading straight down to the Mersey, with a series of smaller streets running across to complete the grid. In among them, down Mathew Street, is a small shopping complex – Cavern Walks – which now occupies the site where the Beatles launched their career. All there is to see is a statue of the quartet, but the Beatles are still the basis of a thriving tourist trade, taking visitors to such spots as the Salvation Army Children's Home, Strawberry Fields and Penny Lane. The street signs have been replaced by the names painted on a wall: replacing stolen signs became a little too expensive. Liverpool's Magical History Tours seem particularly popular with the Japanese. But this was only a temporary stop; the real lure was the Mersey and the docks. If Liverpool has no grand town hall it more than compensates with the snow-white

palaces which line the waterfront: the Port of Liverpool building, Cunard and the Royal Liver Building, with its golden liver birds perched on the towers. Beyond is the Pier Head and the busy shuffle to and fro of the ferry boats.

This is one of those areas which suffered what appeared to be irreversible decline, first as the sailing ships gave way to steamers, then as the passenger ships grew ever bigger until, quite suddenly, they stopped altogether. This was where Liverpool started to grow in the eighteenth century, when the natural pool, an area of shoals and shallows, was enclosed behind a sea wall. The old town was set well back in a small square centred on the Town Hall, until gradually the foreshore was reclaimed and the docks created. The earliest are by the Pier Head – Canning Dock, Salthouse Dock and the grandest of them all, Albert Dock.

I was here in 1981 to film the newly created Maritime Museum, and Albert Dock was a set of semi-derelict buildings surrounding a sea of mud. All kinds of plans were being put forward, including a proposal to drain Albert Dock and create a car park. What many of us hoped and prayed was that the buildings could be restored and the dock dredged and refilled to bring back the finest example of nineteenth-century dock engineering in Britain. It has happened, and no one can accuse Liverpool of hyperbole when they describe Albert Dock as the jewel in the crown of Merseyside.

The Maritime Museum has grown and developed since that early visit. The attraction is still the site itself, the docks where historic ships can be floated, the dry docks, the wharves and quays with their machinery and the buildings such as the Pilotage Offices. Inside the city's maritime story is told in every aspect. There is a special display area, featuring live performances by actors, who tell the story of the hordes of emigrants who left for America. There is the story of the ships built on the Mersey which plied their trade here. But the greatest difference has been the extension of the museum to occupy one part of the warehouses which surround the Albert Dock. No maritime museum could have a better setting and the story of this section of the museum is only a part of the whole story of the dock.

Sculptures by the Mersey

It began when Jesse Hartley was appointed Civil Engineer and Superintendent of the Concerns of the Dock Estate in 1824, an imposing title for an important post, which Hartley held until his death in 1860. He gave Liverpool 140 acres of wet dock and ten miles of new quay, but the Albert Dock was his masterpiece. Before Hartley's time, theft from the open town quay was a major problem. So he introduced a new concept of fortress-like docks, hidden behind high walls, and built secure warehouses all around the quays. The warehouses are carried out over the wharf on iron colonnades, with hydraulic

cranes and hoists fitted neatly away into the arches. It was in every way a bang-up-to-date development, using hydraulic power for the machinery and iron absolutely everywhere – the portico at the dock office is iron, and even the roof is an undulating sea of iron plates.

What gives the scheme its character is the regular pattern of the colonnades and the contrasting materials: the huge stone blocks of the quay wall and the smoothly worn iron bollards are set off by reflections in the great sheet of water they surround. I came here on a morning when the whole area was alive with activity. The museum was doing a roaring trade, the shops which occupy three sides of the dock were busy with customers, and there was considerable interest in the latest addition to the docks' attractions, the Tate Gallery.

The northern Tate opened the first phase of its development with three major exhibitions. The first was a room devoted to the series of paintings by Mark Rothko, originally commissioned for the Seagram building in New York. They seemed almost childlike, devoid of real substance, huge blobs of dark colour – yet they have a magical presence which needs time to work. The rather dim, plain rooms of the old warehouse might seem to be wrong for these brooding paintings, but when you sit and look in the cool, peaceful room the pictures come alive as delicate brush strokes and nuances of colour emerge. This would make the ideal permanent home for the Rothkos.

The Surrealism exhibition was a total contrast, covering every aspect of the movement from the animalistic intensity of Picasso's 'Three Dancers' to the dry, sly wit of Magritte. Both were free and Liverpudlians were crowding to see the new gallery. They were not impressed and said so loudly in terms which allowed no argument. But they did come, they talked about what they saw, and perhaps some at least will come again. They were lucky

The India Building

in that they did not pay, as I did, to see the third show, 'Starlit Waters' – British sculpture of the last twenty years, most of which was as sterile and meaningless as its title. No new gallery, especially no new modern gallery, can be an instant success; time will provide its verdict on the northern Tate.

Gallery, shops and museum are part of the Albert Dock development but housing is also included in the scheme and I could easily be tempted. The dock behind, Salthouse Dock, has another role to play in providing space for sailing, and how pleasing it is to see lunchtime sailors enjoying the water in dinghies and on sailboards within sight of their offices.

This new core of development, however, represents only a fraction of the dock area. I went on to the north: it is a daunting sight – acre upon acre of dock, rows of old warehouses, all full of character and interest which spreads outside the area. Pubs have their own stories to tell: the Pig and Whistle used to specialise in supplying food for the emigrants; the Dominion has a bold colonial type standing on the roof, his dog at his side; while the A1 at Lloyds and the Cunard scarcely need explanation. I was intrigued a little farther on in my travels by a pair of pubs which faced each other across Scotland Road; the Hamlet on one side and the Hamlet Hotel on the other. Unfortunately, I had no time to investigate.

You get the impression that trade on the Mersey has gone. It has gone from the old town centre docks, but the closer you move to the mouth of the river the more signs of life there are. The old days of the Cunard line will never return, but a less romantic trade continues. Mountains of scrap for export waited on one quay; Dublin and Belfast car ferries still run; but the most important development was the opening of the Freeport in 1984, which is already carrying £160 million worth of trade a year. Liverpool has not yet lost its reliance on the Mersey.

The area to the north shades off into the terraced houses of Bootle, where two lads were having a fine time in a pavement paddling pool. This led me on to the other area which has done almost as much as the Beatles to spread the city's name around the world. A bunch of local lads used to kick a ball around in Stanley Park. In time they split up and developed into two neighbouring football teams. One lot became Liverpool, the other Everton – they are still neighbours and still rivals.

Having explored one side of Liverpool, it seemed reasonable to see what there was to look at in the opposite direction. Once again, dock reclamation is being given priority, and part of the area was given a mayfly moment of glory when it became the site of the Garden Festival. What is left is a park and a riverside which have been opened up for the locals to enjoy. This is one of those areas which does not fit with the popular image of Liverpool. Every television documentary, every newspaper article, seems to depict a run-down, rowdy, troublesome place where no one has a job because no one wants a job. Well, here was an area of pleasant leafy suburbs with the advantage of a river at the end of the road. It also turned out to be an area of surprises.

I turned away from the river up a quiet road in which the houses seemed to have an unusual quantity of decorative cast-iron work. That was nothing compared with what I was shown in the parish church of St Michael village. It looks ordinary enough, a simple brick building, but the brick is only a skin, purely cosmetic. This is a cast-iron church. Church and village were built by the Mersey Iron Foundry, who had their works by the river on what locals used to call the Iron Shore. Cast-iron churches were a speciality

The Liver Building seen from the Maritime Museum

of theirs. They were pre-fabricated buildings which could be crated up and sent off to missionaries in distant corners of the Empire, who had only to bolt the bits together to have their very own gothic church in the jungle. It was more than worth the short journey from the centre to find such a remarkable building.

The way back led through Toxteth, where the riots did more than anything else to defile Liverpool's name. At the same time, they brought home the miseries which accumulate and fester when a whole area is faced by massive unemployment, decay and prejudice. Nothing on the outside sends out signals to suggest that this is an area which will again suffer the horrors of violence, but that is not something you can read in bricks and stone. What can be seen is that there is a decent basis here for renewal, for Toxteth is not a distant suburb but sits next to some of the most attractive properties in the city.

I had now reached the area dominated by the two cathedrals. The only part which I did know was Chinatown, based on Nelson Street. It has none of the outward show of Manchester, and is much closer in feel to some of the Indian and Pakistani areas of Bradford. One finds restaurants first opened to serve the local population rather than tourists, where on a summer's evening you eat to the accompaniment of excited conversation and the click-clack of Mah-jong tiles. This time, for my last exploration, I walked up Mount Pleasant to Rodney Street. What I did not expect to find, knowing that Toxteth was just round the corner, was Liverpool's Harley Street. Rodney Street has supremely elegant houses, the fanlighted doorways of which could be sold for a fortune without a house attached.

At the end of it stands the Anglican Cathedral, in a dramatic setting on a high sandstone bluff. Sandstone is the principal building material of the church, which is a massive but simplified version of the classic English tradition. It took a long time to build, with the result that different styles were adopted for different periods, which is not surprising since almost every great church in the land shows a similar pattern. The older part is gloomier and more highly decorated than the new, with a reredos by Scott and a less than imposing Te Deum window. Other windows are more impressive. A St Cecilia window celebrates English composers from Tallis to Elgar, but my favourite is a mixture of ancient and modern Biblical characters in a local setting. You can see river traffic on the Mersey and the Liver building, together with Francis of Assisi, Mary Magdalene and the Israelites. Overall the effect of the building is of great spaciousness, with a tall central arch pulling together the disparate items. It still seems surprising to realise that it is modern. It seems unlikely that anything will again be constructed in such a style and to such a scale.

From the cathedral I walked down Hope Street, where you could easily pass the Philharmonic Hall without paying it much attention. In fact, it is a wonderful example of Thirties' architecture, complete with most of its original details right down to the light fittings. Its chief glory is the engraved glass with figures in that peculiar stylised mode which shows borrowings from Cubism and more than anything else typifies the period. What Sir Thomas Beecham, whose bust looks out on this exercise in modernism, thought of it is not recorded.

If the hall is discreet about its attractions, the same could not be said of the Philharmonic Hotel, where audiences can have a drink. It was built between 1898 and 1900 and is as good an example of its period as the hall is of the Thirties. It proclaims its style in the entrance, where the arch has a highly decorative iron screen, full of writhing shapes, heads and motifs which include the liver bird. The architect was Walter Thomas, but the decoration was entrusted to the students of the University School of Applied Art. They were clearly not instructed to exercise restraint. Every surface is treated: mosaics and tiles are alongside wood panelling, pillars are carved and glass is stained or etched. It works somehow, because the pub is made up of small divisions and separate rooms. This love affair with decoration leaves no part of the building untouched; even the Gents is given the full treatment. They sell a decent pint too, so this is a pub no one should miss. Across the road is the Everyman Theatre which, apart from putting on plays, provides one of the city's best eating places – the food is cheap and good and the atmosphere is friendly.

The Metropolitan Cathedral is the Catholic counterpart of the Anglican Cathedral at the other end of the road. Where the architects of the latter opted for tradition, the designers of the Metropolitan decided on a modern style. The building is circular with a conical roof rising to a tower topped with pinnacles, a clear representation of a crown. It has earned the irreverent nickname, 'Paddy's wigwam', but there is no doubt that it impresses those who go inside. The effect is like being under water with coloured lights; the overall tone is bluish, flecked with colour from the stained glass of the windows. The main structure is as simple inside as out, but around the perimeter are a number of individual chapels, each with its own style. It could scarcely be a greater contrast to the Anglican Cathedral. It is possible to admire or dislike both the Liverpool cathedrals, but the remarkable fact is that the city should have built two in such a short time.

The major public buildings of Liverpool helped to create its image: the two cathedrals are symbols of the way in which the population has grown through immigration; those on the river front are monuments to a prosperous past. But there is much more to the city than that. It was almost by accident that I decided to visit the Bluecoat building in School Lane

The former Bluecoat School is now a flourishing arts centre

– the city's oldest and one of its most beautiful. It was built in 1717 as a school 'dedicated to the promotion of Christian charity and the training of poor boys in the principles of the Anglican church'. The design is strictly formal: you approach via a courtyard, the two side wings setting off the main block, which has tall, round-headed windows, a pediment and a little cupola on top. This public face is a great contrast to the private garden at the back, tree-shaded and peaceful, as informally delightful as the front is formally handsome. The school was moved to larger premises in 1906 and the old buildings were taken over by artists. But for many years they survived under the constant threat of demolition. Now they are a well-established arts centre.

I went there after seeing the sculpture exhibition at the Tate, and the contrast was extreme: not the obvious one between a nineteenth-century warehouse and an eighteenth-century charity school, but between two sculpture exhibitions. The Tate offered up-to-the-minute art establishment thinking; Bluecoat had sculpture by Sokari Douglas Camp, a Nigerian-born artist whose work combines a preoccupation with the life and ceremonials of the people of the Niger delta with modern sculptural techniques. Her work had all the vivid life so sadly absent at the Tate. I make the comparison to point out that modern art did not arrive overnight as the gift of a benevolent body in London. Provincial cities are not pale imitations of the capital: they have a life of their own. If this is true of Liverpool, I was soon to discover that it is even more true of the cities of Scotland and Wales.

Above: *The Baroque interior of St Charles Borromeo, Hull.*

Right: *The River Hull.*

Above: *Hockney on display in Sir Titus Salt's old mill at Saltaire.*

Opposite: *The Victorian opulence of Leeds Town Hall.*

Top: *The ornamental gateway that leads to Manchester's Chinatown.*

Above: *L.S. Lowry's room recreated in a temporary display at the Manchester City Art Gallery.*

The splendid interior of the Philharmonic Hotel, Liverpool.

Top: *Mackintosh design in the Willow Tea Rooms, Glasgow.*

Above: *The Burrell Collection, Glasgow.*

Cool classicism in Dundee's City Square.

Dundee cake and castle at Broughty Ferry.

*The Grand Theatre epitomises
Swansea's wholehearted acceptance of
modern stylishness.*

This bizarre combination of clock tower and lighthouse is in Cardiff's Roath Park.

GLASGOW

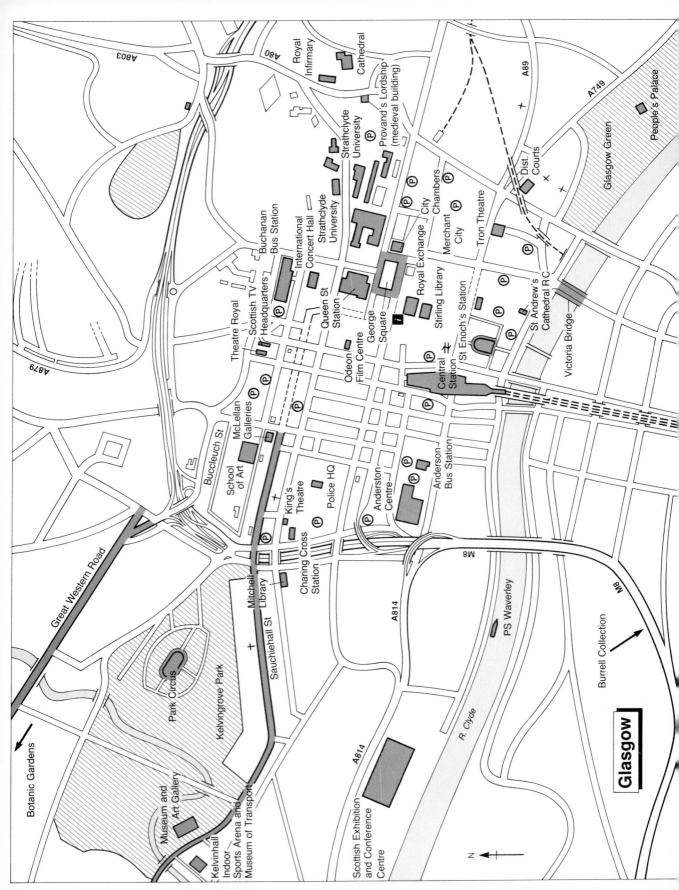

Glasgow

15
GLASGOW

The journey to Scotland always induces a sense of occasion. But by the time I took the trip, the first part – up through the Midlands – seemed as familiar as a commuter route. The remainder had a character all its own. There was the flat land of Lancashire, spiked with mill chimneys; after Lancaster there were the distant mountains of the Lake District and the bleak grandeur of Shap Fell. As we rumbled past Carlisle and over the border, we seemed to be entering an ever emptier land, empty apart from the stream of heavy traffic on the adjoining road, occasionally dammed to a sluggish flow. Few parts of England have such tracts of almost unpopulated country; what houses there were displayed a style very much of the region – low built of stone, with only dormer windows to light the upper storey.

Ignorant visitors sometimes think of Scotland as England with a funny accent, bagpipes and tartan. It is nothing of the sort, but a different country entirely. Its ways are particularly noticeable in the small, everyday things. The familiar becomes faintly unfamiliar: the fish and chip shop becomes a fish and chicken shop; the takeaway, the carry-out. Glasgow turned up the sign at an Indian restaurant 'European carry-out', which suggested an unusually lethal curry. But the real difference for me is in the drinking establishments. In Scotland they are not pubs: they are bars or lounges and the difference is more than

semantics. Outwardly, they are dreary, often with blanked-out windows; inside, the stranger has to grapple with the mysteries of 70/- and 80/- beers and the ubiquitous 'pint of heavy'. It may seem a small point, but a nation's drinking habits and the places where they drink say a lot about attitudes. The differences between Scottish bar and English pub are so striking that one is at once aware that they are very different countries. Other differences are not hard to find.

Crossing the Clyde may not have the grandeur of the Tyne crossing, but it announces the arrival of Glasgow city centre as clearly, and the station has a fine richness. It stretches over the top of Argyle Street and ends in a wide concourse. The surrounding buildings – restaurants, booking hall and the rest – are panelled in dark glowing wood, irresistible reminders of the saloons and staterooms of the great liners which started life on the slipways here.

A taxi took me out of the centre along the Great Western Road, lined with neo-classical sandstone buildings, very formal and correct. Northern classical styling seldom has the *élan* one finds in, say, Bath. There is an austere stiffness, a sense intensified by the rain slicing up the dusk. Once the taxi driver and I had finished the essential discussion of the weather, he began to extol the virtues of the city. He enthused over the changes of recent years, the refurbishment and revitalisation of the city. It was a theme I was to hear echoed by many others.

There has always been local pride, but often tinged with the need to establish a claim to be different from if not better than Edinburgh. My favourite Glaswegian comment is that in Edinburgh they think sex is what you put coal in. Edinburgh is refined; Glasgow was content to be down to earth. Now the attitude has changed – they still relish their special character, but now point to a city which can stand comparison not only with Edinburgh but with any other city in Britain. When I first visited the city many years ago, the notion of Glasgow as the cultural capital of Europe was risible. Not any more, and in 1990 it is officially European City of Culture for a year. The title reflects a new, vigorous artistic life as well as the vital changes in its fabric.

My hotel was on the western side of the city in a quiet, elegant crescent and, in spite of the downpour which had scarcely eased overnight, I decided to take a devious route to the centre. I retraced in the grey damp light of morning the route I had taken in the grey damp light of dusk, along Great Western Road down to the Botanic Gardens. I love this corner of the city, for it contains one of my favourite buildings – the Kibble Palace, where art, engineering and the natural world meet.

The palace is no more than a large greenhouse for tropical plants, but inside it is like a giant transparent sculpture. A complex pattern of iron arches culminates in a vast glazed dome. The technique is reminiscent of the sweeping roof curves of a Victorian railway station, but here tree ferns climb up to brush the glass panes of the dome. Peeping out coyly through the leaves are several nude ladies, statues which seem more prim than sexy. The

The Kibble Palace in the Botanic Gardens

only other occupant on that dank morning was a tame blackbird which had discovered the advantages of living in a waterproof garden. The palace is such a fixture here that I was surprised to discover that it was moved to Glasgow in 1873 from its original home at Coulport on Loch Long. It remains, however, as essentially Victorian as the Crystal Palace which it in many ways resembles.

I walked back to the Great Western Road and down to the River Kelvin, which had curled around from the gardens and was heading in a rumbling torrent down to the Clyde. I decided to take a detour to the south and, as the rain dripped off the end of my nose, Kelvinbridge Station seemed very inviting. I was going to the Transport Museum, so it seemed appropriate to take an underground ride. It is a modern, efficient underground system, though I know of no other railway where you can not only hear the roar of a river as you wait for your train but can see water flowing in a fast channel between the rails. A short ride took me to Kelvinhall, where I emerged to find the most striking feature of the city – tenements. The name conjures up the worst of the old Glasgow, when the name Gorbals was synonymous with degrading slums. But tenements are no more than flats which, unlike most post-war developments, were not relegated to some distant suburb but integrated into the city centre. There are tenements which exist as overgrown stone houses and others which rise above the shops of the city streets. The restoration of these is breathing life and vitality into the centre of the city. For the moment, however, I was more concerned to see the new Transport Museum.

The museum's new home is part of the Kelvinhall complex and very good it is too. The old home had the edge in atmosphere because it was originally a corporation tram depot, which, having lost one function, is to gain another. It was pressed into service to house the astonishing Peter Brook production of *The Mahabharata*, which was so successful that it was decided to convert the building into the Tramway Theatre. The move has been to everyone's benefit: the city has a new and exciting theatre, and the Transport Museum has space to spread and develop.

Museums can easily suffer from a lack of identity, but there is no such problem here. This is not just a museum of transport, but a museum of Glasgow transport with a few concessions to the rest of Scotland. You can find everything from the oldest surviving pedal cycle in the world to steam locomotives, and it was a revelation to an ignorant Englishman to discover how much had been built here. My knowledge of early Scottish motor cars is slight, but here they were, the genuine horseless carriages: buggies with petrol engines instead of nags. Goldsworthy Gurney's steam drag was supposed to pull a sixteen-seat trailer between Glasgow and Edinburgh at the speed of ten miles per hour, which was pretty swift for 1831. In the event, the journey took three days and they needed a horse to help.

A street scene of the 1930s gave the first hint

Ship models in the Transport Museum's Clyde Room

of the antiquity of Glasgow's subway system. It opened in 1896, with cars hauled by cables powered by mighty steam engines. Electricity took over in 1935 and in 1977 work was begun on the present system. But pride of place has to go to the Clyde Room, home to a magnificent collection of ship models: everything from the homely Clyde puffer and the river paddle-steamers to some of the finest ships the world has ever seen – the resplendent liners built for Cunard. It is a museum tinged with sadness. The day of the ocean liner has ended and the shipyards are no more than pallid reflections of their past, a forest of motionless cranes.

It was with some reluctance that I left and emerged into the downpour, still heavy enough to encourage a dive from one museum into another. Across the road in Kelvingrove Park is the Art Gallery and Museum. My first scribbled note reads 'the Victorian museum in full solemnity', and then I discovered that it was nothing of the sort, having been opened in 1902 – though perhaps the design crept into the end of the queen's reign. It is château style on the outside, but the interior is a pseudo-renaissance hall, redolent not of history but of an elaborate Hollywoodish view of history. What came to mind was Citizen Kane and his great mansion Xanadu.

It is extraordinary as a building but not well suited to being a museum, where the prime purpose is to display exhibits not conceal them in stygian gloom. Modern lighting at least ensures that the pictures can be seen, and it is a curious experience when one comes to the fine collection of works by the Impressionists and their successors. The stunning colours stand out all the brighter from the surrounding gloom. But the biggest contrast must surely come in the room devoted to what is now known as the Glasgow-style. This name was given to the Scottish version of art nouveau practised by the group of architects and designers led by Charles Rennie Mackintosh. The contrast is startling because the work is contemporary with the museum building. Here everything is light, bright colour and sinuous lines contained within stricter geometrical patterns. It is a world away from the surrounding pseudo-gothicism. How ironical that Mackintosh has so belatedly come to fame and prominence. He was there to be commissioned, having already proved his worth. Now modern versions of his designs need to be advertised by no more than the initials C.R.M. I was moved to go off in search of more 'C.R.M'. After all, not every city has its own art style.

The rain had cleared and I made another discovery about Glasgow: it is a city of splendid parks. Kelvingrove, as the name suggests, is centred around the River Kelvin, but the name tells you nothing about the splendid quality of this urban green space. Paths twist up and down hills and between groves of trees. The views change constantly, from the splashing Kelvin to the tower of the University proud above the trees. At its eastern end is Park Circus, a superb example of mid-nineteenth-century town planning which does for Glasgow what John Wood's Circus and Royal Crescent do for Bath. It is stylish in terms of individual houses but also imposes a coherent elegance on the entire area. If it has a certain solemnity about its detailing, that is perhaps not inappropriate for a northern city and it is in any case counterbalanced by the richness of the stone, varying from a pearly grey to a deep salmon pink. Most of the houses now serve as offices for architects and surveyors, who recognised a good thing when they saw it – which is more than can be said for local property developers. The unity is broken by Park House, a crashingly dull office block at the end of the Circus, but at least the church

Kelvingrove

tower has been retained and forms a focal point for the area.

At the end of Kelvingrove Park is the motorway, which effectively defines the limits of the city centre. But here it is only emphasising the division which was clear before the arrival of the motor car, for the circles and crescents now give way to a strict, regular grid of streets. One might expect that commercial buildings would have taken over such a region, but the tenements still march on. To the north of Sauchiehall Street, visitors can see the tenement block as it was at the turn of the century. Buccleuch Street boasts typical sandstone tenements, where one flat has been preserved by the National Trust for Scotland. A fortunate accident led to its preservation. The building dates from 1892 and the flat was occupied by one family for over fifty years. It was bought by the actress Anne Davidson, who recognised and appreciated its unique atmosphere, which she carefully preserved.

When she moved out, she sold it to the Trust. It is quite small, but a masterpiece of managed space. Box beds, which can be closed away behind doors or curtains in daytime, make rooms dual purpose, so that even the kitchen doubles up as a bedroom. Other surprising features include a large coal bunker in the kitchen. Coal was delivered directly to each flat, which meant everything had to be covered in sheets on delivery day. This is a middle-size tenement. They could have as many as ten rooms, and at the opposite end a single room with no facilities might have served for a whole family.

Buccleuch Street was a deviation from my main objective, because it was more than time to come to terms with the city centre. Sauchiehall Street is to southerners the archetypal Glasgow city street, and most of us find it difficult to pronounce without incurring the mirth of the locals. I chose it as the approach to the centre because it provides an opportunity to see the very best of Mackintosh.

Just to the north is the School of Art. The design was decided after a competition which was won by twenty-eight-year-old Mackintosh in 1896. Plans had to wait on finance and it was not completed until 1909. It is not just Mackintosh's masterpiece but one of the finest twentieth-century buildings in Britain. It has the sweetly flowing lines that mark all art nouveau, but where in some works of the period everything is subordinated to the aesthetic effect, here it is held in place in a rectangular frame. The result is a building which is lovely without being mannered. Just as importantly, the building works as a functional school. Back in Sauchiehall Street, Mackintosh used a more frivolous style for a more frivolous purpose. The Willow Tea Rooms (Sauchiehall means 'lane of willows') are a delight. I can remember little about the tea for I was too busy enjoying the atmosphere. Those who want to see more of the master's works can turn back towards the University and the Hunterian Art Gallery, where rooms from his house have been re-created.

The label 'Glasgow-style' has become a commonplace in city shops, covering everything from furniture fabrics to jewellery, but it has never dominated the city's buildings. The true dominant style there is that Victorian neo-classicism seen at its best in Park Circus and in some of the important buildings in the centre. First impressions are of squashing together, even bridging over streets, creating a sense of intimacy which balances the grandeur and opulence of a great Victorian city. The centrepiece, in terms of importance, is pushed away to one end of the street grid, so that you see a good deal of the city before you arrive at its civic buildings.

George Square is a familiar set piece, a city square with statues, bounded on one side by City Chambers. The date is 1888, the style Italian Renaissance and the interior of the chambers is even grander than the exterior – in the main hall you get a sight of splendid marble staircases. One clue to a city's view of itself and its aspirations is provided by its public statuary. Whom does it choose to honour? If we ignore the ubiquitous Victoria

The Stirling Library at night

and Albert, the collection is quite interesting. Like Birmingham, it honours James Watt the engineer; homage is paid to numerous politicians, for favours received or anticipated, but pride of place goes to writers. A Scottish version of Nelson's column holds up Sir Walter Scott. Beneath him, sculpturally, are Burns and Thomas Campbell. I had to look Campbell up, and discovered he was author of such epics as *Gertrude of Wyoming* and *Lord Ullin's Daughter*. He also penned a line which I quote without comment: 'Now Barabbas was a publisher'. It is hard not to warm to a city which honours poets above generals.

George Square has a satisfying unity, but behind it the other civic buildings jostle for space. Arches built across John Street link the courts to the main administrative block, and the arches form a miniature triumphal way. Such areas in most cities have their grand gestures, but seldom much in the way of fun. Glasgow has its fair share of odd public buildings, none more astonishing than the Stirling Library. It did not start life in that role. The original building was a sumptuous Georgian house, Cunningham Mansion, built for one of the city's tobacco barons. The Great Hall, with its ornate panelled ceiling, pillars with gilded capitals and elliptical atrium, was added in 1829. In 1949 it took on its present role as the city's main public lending library and surely the grandest to be found in Britain. Its partner, the Mitchell Library of 1874, is less dashing, but is a magnificent reference library holding over a million volumes.

One of the pleasures of wandering aimlessly is that you pick up snippets from one place and relate them to another. It was by accident that I came across a survivor of the nineteenth-century subway system. St Enoch's Station is now a travel centre but it is a delightfully quirky little building. The style is Jacobean

with miniaturised Scottish baronial in the corner turrets.

Equally surprising in a different way was Prince's Square. Some bright-eyed developer spotted this forgotten square of decayed and unappealing buildings lurking behind the main shopping street. Its inside was cleared out and remodelled as a 1980s shopping centre. My usual grumble about such centres – that they have no relation to the surrounding city – does not apply here. The motifs are all Glasgow. The classical city is represented by columns and porticoes; the glazed roof has overtones of Victorian markets and the Kibble Palace, while the decoration is Glasgow style. The overall plan is still the modish atrium with shops grouped round the edge, but even here a welcome local touch is a specialist whisky shop and stalls to balance the larger shops.

My meanderings took me down to the river. The Clyde is so much a part of the image that it is a surprise to find how little impact it now has on city life. One tradition lingers on: going doon th'water by paddle steamer, though only the *Waverley* now remains of the once great fleet of paddlers. The elements are there to make the river front as important as it once was: a handsome Customs House in Clyde Street and Victoria Bridge, with its five sandstone arches given a granite cladding, is particularly fine. But there are problems about such areas. Where do you start? Will you be able to attract people to developments off the beaten track? Time will tell.

My journey from west to east ended at Glasgow Green. To a visitor's eyes this is a dull, flat piece of municipal grass: to many citizens it is redolent with history, the scene of great rallies and the home of radical movements. It has been a park since 1662. Arguments for and against change resound, in a domestic quarrel from which the sensible outsider tiptoes quietly away. The green does

The new 'Glasgow-Style' shopping centre based on Prince's Square

boast two more of my favourite buildings, which I like for very different reasons. The first is the People's Palace and Winter Gardens. The Winter Gardens is a great glass conservatory which though not as grand as Kibble Palace is grand enough and serves a wonderful mug of tea – just the thing after a long walk on a damp day. The People's Palace is a museum of the ordinary life of Glasgow, similar in many ways to the Museum of Labour History in Liverpool – less overtly political but sharing the same preoccupation with everyday life, including the life of the factory. To some people that sounds dull; the very name 'factory' suggests gloom and drabness. They have never seen Templeton's carpet factory at Glasgow Green. It looks like something out of the Arabian Nights, a polychrome brick extravaganza, a Victorian recreation of a Venetian palace. Its old use has ended, but I remember coming here with a photographer and being bombarded with wit by the girls in the factory. The building is as exuberant as ever, but the new inhabitants are a lot more staid.

My first journey had a pleasant symmetry, west to east, glasshouse to glasshouse. I set out to fill in some of the gaps. Some things I regret missing out on, like the great weekend street market The Barras. I have never found myself in the area at the right time, and everyone always tells me what I have missed: the noise, the colour, the character. I would also dearly love to have seen the Citizens' Theatre's widely acclaimed production of *Richard III*, but it was sold out. I did take in two other theatres with widely differing characters. The Tron Theatre is housed in an old church and is a fine example of adaptation, but there was no production to see during my visit. The bar is a friendly place to stop for a pint and a snack. That evening was altogether more formal: the

Theatre Royal and *The Magic Flute*. I know people in London who say they could not live anywhere else because nowhere else has the same amenities, the same rich cultural life. The only difference I can see is that in Glasgow I can afford to go to the opera. I would not complain if my operatic diet were limited to Scottish Opera – or come to that the Welsh Opera or Opera North – what they may lack in international stars is compensated by thrilling and imaginative productions.

Other wanderings took me through the old Merchants City where refurbishment is going on apace. This is one of the most intriguing areas of the town. It boasts some handsome eighteenth-century churches with typically Scottish tall narrow steeples above rich red stone tenements. Not so long ago this was an area of neglect, and there are few parts of the city where the transformation is so clearly visible. It is still going on: a warehouse is being converted into flats, while the adjoining building site serves as temporary car park and open-air sculpture gallery. I kept on up the High Street and Castle Street to the cathedral. It is a paradoxical building, for though its proportions are on the grand scale, with a nave roof 100 feet high, it seems to have infinite solidity, great massiveness and weight. This is partly because the nave is divided by the choir screen and partly because of a strong horizontal division. The main church stands on a lower church, not a crypt, where the great weight above is spread over a multitude of sturdy pillars and arches, from the simplest stone vaulting shafts of the twelfth century to the fifteenth-century elaboration of the Blacader Aisle.

The cathedral's qualities seem very much those of the city itself: solid worth rather than inconsequential show. The same could be said of Provand's Lordship, the only other surviving medieval building, a fifteenth-century house of stern aspect. But it is far from true of another feature of this quarter – the Necropolis. Wealthy merchants were buried here and they advertised their importance in death as in life. The tombs look out over the city which is itself a monument to the wealth created in the great days of trade and industry.

I began with a notion of looking at what made Glasgow into a cultural capital, and if any one thing brought it into new prominence it was the Burrell Collection. Sir William Burrell was a great shipbuilder, but he was also a great collector. His house, Hutton Castle, was an artifice constructed from the remnants of the past. He gave his collection to the city in 1944, but it took until the 1980s to find a home for it. The new museum is one of Glasgow's glories and one of its surprises. It is in a park, a tranquil rural setting in the south of the city. The building is not exciting from the outside but the inside is magical. The glazed walls seem no more than a flimsy barrier between woodland and field and the great works of art. One sees the earthy colours of Chinese pottery against a background of earth and trees. Away from the glass, intimate spaces have been created to display the great art of the world, and at the heart of this very modern building is a recreation of the original rooms of Hutton Castle. It is a *tour de force*.

No wonder the rest of Britain woke up to realise that the city which had resounded with tales of gloom and depression for so long was changing. The museum will not replace the jobs lost in the shipyards and engineering works, but it has lifted Glasgow's spirits and helped to build the new confidence to be seen on every hand.

DUNDEE

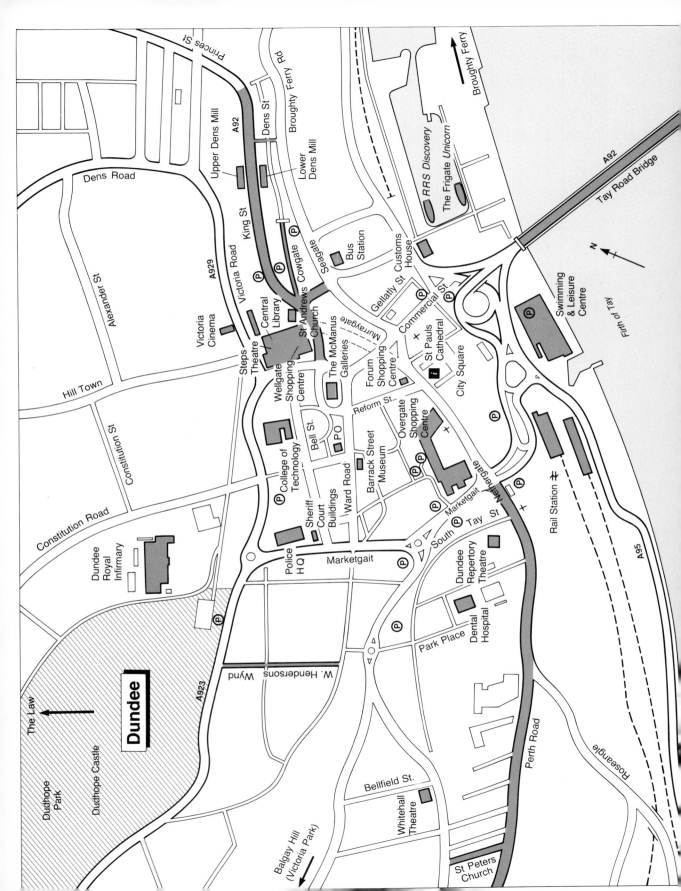

Dundee

Princes St

Dens St

Broughty Ferry Rd

A92

Upper Dens Mill

Lower Dens Mill

RRS Discovery

The Frigate Unicorn

Broughty Ferry

A92

Tay Road Bridge

Dens Road

King St

A929

Victoria Road

Alexander St

Seagate

Bus Station

Customs House

Firth of Tay

N

Hill Town

Victoria Cinema

Central Library

St Andrews Cowgate

Gellatly St

Commercial St

Swimming & Leisure Centre

Constitution St

Steps Theatre

Wellgate Shopping Centre

The McManus Galleries

Murraygate

Forum Shopping Centre

St Pauls Cathedral

City Square

Constitution Road

Bell St.

PO

Reform St.

Overgate Shopping Centre

Dundee Royal Infirmary

College of Technology

Sheriff Court Buildings

Ward Road

Barrack Street Museum

Nethergate

Marketgait

Rail Station

A95

The Law

A923

Police HQ

Marketgait

South Tay St

Dundee Repertory Theatre

Dudhope Castle

Dudhope Park

W. Hendersons Wynd

Park Place

Dental Hospital

Perth Road

Roseangle

Balgay Hill (Victoria Park)

Bellfield St.

Whitehall Theatre

St Peters Church

16
DUNDEE

Leaving Glasgow by train, one is impressed by how close it lies to some magnificent hill scenery. The hills are an accompaniment for the rest of the journey – on past Stirling, its ruin like a rotting tooth high on its own hilltop, to Perth and the Tay. The river widens into the Firth of Tay, across which a railway bridge snakes. Almost everyone knows that the first Tay railway bridge fell down, thanks to the incomparable chronicler of the event, Dundee poet and tragedian William McGonagall:

> Beautiful Railway Bridge of the Silv'ry Tay!
> Alas, I am very sorry to say
> That ninety lives have been taken away
> On the last Sabbath day of 1879.
> Which will be remember'd for a very long time.

Countless tragedies have been commemorated in worthy verses which are promptly forgotten; the Tay bridge disaster is remembered as something comical. It was, in fact, horrific, caused by a mixture of poor design and incompetent workmanship. The stumps of the original piers can be seen at low water. What strikes the passenger about the replacement bridge is its length – two miles – and the elegance of its sweep away from the main line in a gentle curve across the racing river. The river was streamed with foam where it and the tidal water met and even on a fine, clear day the force of the water was evident. The new bridge looks reassuringly solid, whereas photographs show the original balanced on flimsy trestles. It is not hard to imagine the wild night in 1879 when it collapsed, plunging the train into the water. The locomotive was retrieved and, until it left service in 1917, was known as 'The Diver'. Dundee's other Tay bridge, carrying road traffic, is as impressive as the rail bridge, but before the train reaches it, the station arrives.

Having admired the distant prospect of the Tay road bridge, opened in 1966, I now faced the consequences of its building. It not only serves Dundee but forms part of a larger road system, so it had to connect with that system. The bridge was brought to the centre of the city, which probably seemed a good idea – but where do you put your connecting roads? They were placed between the city and its river, so the first thing I saw when I left the station was a dual carriageway and a complex interchange. Dundee has been divided from its waterfront, which is especially sad because the Tay is a beautiful and majestic river. A vital link of city life has been truncated, but Dundee is working on plans to repair the damage.

First impressions were less than favourable but that is not a cause for despondency. Not every city displays its attractions to a casual glance, so I set out to explore. I began with visits to two old friends: the first much as I had left her; the second having returned only recently after a long stay in London. Down in the docks, again separated from the city centre by the busy road, are the frigate *Unicorn* and Scott's ship the *Discovery*. It was *Unicorn* which first brought me to Dundee when I filmed the TV series The Past Afloat. She has the distinction of being the oldest British warship afloat, the 'afloat' part distinguishing her from others such as *Victory*. This is an odd-looking ship: instead of the customary masts and spars above the hull, there is a roof. The explanation is that she was built in 1824 when Britain was at peace and looked like staying that way. So she was started but not finished. Below decks she is full of interest, which increases the lower you go, until at the bows you see the beautiful sweeping lines of wood and iron which define

The Tay railway bridge

and shape the hull.

Unicorn is an attractive feature in the Dundee scene; *Discovery* is central to the new thinking about the city, and pulls together two threads from the past. The port was engaged in trade with Europe, especially the Baltic, for centuries. Then, in 1754, the Dundee Whale Fishing Company was formed and developed into a thriving business. At much the same time, the city began building ships, both for the Baltic trade and for the new, dangerous work of whaling in Arctic waters. When Scott was looking for a vessel to take to the South Pole, he turned to a city where there was expertise in navigating the polar seas and a tradition of building vessels which could withstand the rigours of that icy world. Scott got his ship, which could work under sail – the sailcloth coming from Dundee's own mills – or under steam. Now restored, she has come home. *Discovery* represents a movement towards bringing a story to life. The Dundee Heritage Trust has been formed to tell that story, and her return to her native city is only the first stage of a more ambitious project. Before looking at that, I set out to find what that heritage is and what it means in terms of the modern city.

The city centre at first seemed ordinary if not downright dull, but here first impressions are deceptive. Dundee does not separate into neat compartments. A shopping street may be indistinguishable from a dozen similar: the same shops with the same names and the same goods, which spread a blanket of uniformity over Britain, but in Dundee one is never quite certain what to expect around the corner. City Square has been refurbished, but is itself something of a newcomer, dating back only to the 1930s. Before that the old parish church stood here and the original Town House, designed by Adam and completed in

The bowsprit and figurehead of HMS Unicorn

1734 – please note this was William Adam and not one of his famous sons. None the less, it is difficult to believe that such a building would now be destroyed, however pressing the needs for municipal office space. But walk a short distance from the square in any direction and you will find a wholly different character to the buildings. One corner offers a superb example of this diversity.

At the corner of Cowgate and King Street stands the surprisingly elegant St Andrew's Church, surprising because other major buildings suggest gravity in both senses of the word. They sit squarely and heavily on the land, and they have an air of dour northern solemnity. St Andrew's is unmistakably eighteenth century, from its ornate iron gates – their posts topped with decorative urns – to the tip of its tall delicate steeple. It was built in 1772 at the expense of the Nine Trades Guild, and the trade emblems are shown in the windows. It is unusual in providing a rare glimpse of Georgian architecture in a city otherwise dominated by nineteenth- and twentieth-century styles. What is even odder is to find a second church on the same corner site which was built only seven years later.

Nowhere near as grand as St Andrew's, this was a Glasite church used by the followers of Reverend John Glass who parted company with the Church of Scotland in 1728. The Glasites are no more, and it is now used as a church hall.

From this delectable Georgian church I looked down Cowgate to an intriguing view. One might not be too surprised at seeing an old city gate, except that here 'gate' means street and a gate is called a port – all very confusing. But I only noticed this gate, the East Port, because I had been impressed by the street. The northern side is dominated by vast mills. Facing directly on the road is one complex, the façade enlivened by round-headed relieving arches, while behind it rises up an even taller building topped by a cupola. I am used to cities where manufacturing and commercial and shopping areas are clearly defined. Not here: one steps straight out of one world into another.

I had arrived at one of the three Js on which the city's prosperity was built – jute. The other two were jam, the famous Dundee marmalade, and journalism. Jam-making ended recently, but journalism thrives and jute survives, on a sorely reduced scale. What remains are the few small working factories and the majesty of the nineteenth-century mills. In the eighteenth century there was a flourishing industry turning flax into linen cloth; then in the 1820s they began to use jute from India to make coarse cloth and sacking. It was not a romantic trade, but it was immensely profitable and for a time Dundee was the fastest growing city in Britain, earning the nickname 'jutopolis'. The decline of the industry has left the buildings and a familiar problem: what do you do with a huge Victorian mill when its working days are over? Dundee has found some excellent answers.

The mill with the cupola is Lower Dens and behind it one could have found, not too surprisingly, Upper Dens Mill and a cluster of smaller buildings. Upper Dens was demolished, leaving a large empty space surrounded by apparently useless buildings. A consortium stepped in to convert the area for housing, but not on the familiar yuppie pattern. The partners were Dundee City Council, the Scottish Development Agency and three housing associations, looking to satisfy special needs. A listed mill building has been converted into flats and the vast empty space filled by parkland and housing. Special groups have been catered for: there are flats for singles, sheltered accommodation for the elderly and flats for the mentally handicapped, where support is always available. Two of the houses have been specially designed for wheelchairs.

Elsewhere there is a mixture of conventional and unconventional use. It is not difficult to find small-scale commercial use in a divided-up mill – but who wants a big tall building with no lifts? Answer: artists if the rent is low enough. Meadow Mill of 1874 in West Henderson's Wynd has been let out to artists who each have their own studios but benefit from a friendly, supportive atmosphere. There are thirty-nine spaces over two floors for potters, painters, sculptors and other types of artist. The project was set up by WASPS, the handy acronym for Workshop and Artists Studio Provision Scotland, and there are plans to take on a third floor as well. Its success is in the mixture of a good building offering spaces at reasonable rent and in the diversity of the artists and their arts.

I was tempted to say that Dens Street Market is at the opposite end of the scale of use, but that would not be true. In common with most of the market users, artists generally lack money. Dundee has more than its share of unemployment and low wages, and the market meets many needs. It is neither an

The new housing development based on the Lower and Upper Dens jute mills

ornate Victorian hall nor a street market, but a collection of stalls housed in old weaving sheds, and has everything from food to furniture, second-hand clothes to bric-à-brac. Occasionally a southern dealer arrives to look for a bargain which can be turned to profit. The Dens Street stallholders know all about that: the hint of an English accent sends prices soaring.

Other jute mills still stand empty, and it is hoped that the Dundee Heritage Trust will use a mill for its textile project – not as a museum or a fossilisation of the past, but as a centre where past and present can meet. There will be restored machinery and displays which tell the jute story; these will exist alongside other activities related to textiles. There will be workshops and meeting-rooms, educational facilities and a library. This is a scheme typical of the best of Dundee, in that it displays an awareness of the past, a recognition of what is wrong in the present and a determination to learn from experience in moving to the future. There is one grand reminder of the greatness of its old industry. The Camperdown works have long been disused and some demolished, but the main building boasts a lovely ornate cast-iron cupola. What grabs the attention is the mill chimney, which was built in red and white brick in the style of a campanile and soars to a height of 280 feet, an outstanding monument in every sense of the word.

Exploring the remains of the jute industry would involve hopping from one side of the city to the other, for mills pop up anywhere and everywhere. I decided to take a slice of Dundee, much as I had of Glasgow, by walking from the hotel out to the west on the Perth road. A strong wind was whipping the waters of the Tay. The wide river ensures that however crowded the city centre may become there will always be a feeling of openness, a sense of being a city where the countryside has a physical presence. The houses down the Perth road seemed rather poky stone bungalows, but this was a delusion. The land slopes away steeply towards the river and on the downhill side the 'bungalows' are revealed as handsome tall houses showing their faces to the river. One house in particular, close by the railway bridge, has a splendid turret offering superb views.

Perth Road runs through the Blackness area, described in the official guide as having been 'drab and workaday'. Personally, I found it an area of considerable character, but I have no objection to its being improved if that takes the form of good, inventive public art. All kinds of media have been employed, many using ceramics to create lively murals, but the most impressive work is at the end of the terrace of houses in Peter Street. The gable end is covered by a mural showing different aspects of Dundee life. The top, in subdued grey, shows whalers, but the main painting depicts jute, shipbuilding and that other J – journalism. Newspapers roll off the presses for the citizens down at street level who are reading their *Courier*. This daily paper must be one of the last to continue the tradition of having a front page devoted to small ads. It did, however, show its modernity during my visit by having colour photographs of Dundee's latest and spectacular visitor: a huge oil platform towed up the river for repairs.

The steep streets enticed me down for a closer look at the Tay railway bridge. The metal piers are sturdy, but as they march off across the river they diminish in perspective until they seem insignificant, hardly disturbing the broad expanse of water. I also discovered that to reach the bridge involves a 'life in your hands' dash across a busy main road. There is little inducement to walk along the river bank: all you see is an area of dereliction, of

Inside one of the city's jute mills

abandoned goods yards. It is a cruel waste of a magnificent riverside site.

The Dundee Project was launched in 1987 as a co-operative venture between Dundee and Tayside Councils and the Scottish Development Agency. This area sits squarely in its sights, but a delicate balancing act has to be performed: on the one hand is the Dundee Project, knowing what is needed to improve the city environment; on the other are the developers who know what has to be done to make a profit. Project and developers agree that the area needs to be brought back in touch with the city, and not just by isolated walkways. But when it comes to the site there have to be trade-offs. The Heritage Trust

want a new museum with a permanent berth for *Discovery*. The developers would like the whole site for commercial use, but accept that a good development with museum and other facilities is better than no development at all. One can only wish them well, for nothing would do more to bring renewed vigour than reuniting the city with its waterfront.

I turned away from the wasteland and made my way back towards the centre. The main road, Nethergate, has one of the few reminders of an older Dundee – Morgan Tower. This is a nineteenth-century tenement block with shops on the ground floor which would not be out of place in Glasgow – and that is intended as a compliment. It is, however, distinguished from similar buildings by a central curved tower graced with Venetian windows. It was probably part of the old town defences. Elsewhere, the interesting buildings seem to belong to the Victorian era and the jute age.

Eighteenth-century and earlier buildings were simply overtaken by events, much as the old town hall made way for its larger replacement, but some Georgian buildings survived. The Exchange Coffee House was built down by the quay in 1828 as a combination social and business centre, where merchants could chat over their coffee or conduct the serious affairs of prices and sales. The new, grander Royal Exchange brought an end to that and the building went from jolly music hall to the home of Winter's Printing Works. But it survived, adding a touch of grace to a corner dominated otherwise by a dull office block.

Dullness is not a charge that could be levelled against other public buildings. Scottish architects seem to have had a penchant for an imposing neo-classical style, and local stone was well suited to it. Dundee has its share: the Court House with its Doric portico is memorable, but grandest of all is the Customs House down by the docks. For true Victorian grandeur one has to turn to the work of Sir George Gilbert Scott, who was always true to his dictum that the principal occupation of the architect should be 'to decorate construction'. Decorate he did, in no uncertain terms. He was one of the leaders of the gothic movement and looked with contempt on any style later than 1400. The Cathedral Church of St Paul shows Scott at his strictest and most severely gothic, which makes the reredos, aglow with colour and richly gilded, all the more striking.

However, the cathedral is modesty personified compared with the McManus Galleries, originally the Albert Institute to Promote Arts and Sciences. It would be worth preserving for the entrance alone. The main staircase divides to sweep round in two semi-circles carried on gothic arches to reunite at the grand porch. Scott said of the building, 'I have followed the best period of pointed architecture,' and so he has, because the pointed arch sets the pattern for the whole building. It works surprisingly well as a museum; unlike the Kelvingrove in Glasgow, it is light and airy. The main display area is based on a medieval hall with wood panelling, vaulted ceiling and windows showing heraldic motifs, but the building never swamps the exhibits. These are something of a mixed bunch: the new local history section works well but has to be set against the older collection of Victoriana. The building is an excellent setting for the stained glass, typified by a Dundee worthy as a medieval knight, holding an immense broadsword in one hand and patting little children on the head with the other. The art is very Highland Cattle.

The museum stands in Albert Square and looks across at the offices of D. C. Thomson, the principal J for journalism in Dundee. They produce many worthy publications, but are best known for *Beano* and *Dandy*. There is something appealing in a square of such patent respectability having been the birthplace of such anarchic characters as Dennis the Menace and the Bash Street Kids.

The other major museum, Barrack Street, is just down the road, but to get to it you have to pass the Howff. This is an odd spot: a graveyard apparently doubling as a public park in the very centre of the city. Inevitably, it has a complex history. It was originally the garden of a Greyfriars monastery, but was later given to the people by Mary Queen of Scots. It was used as a meeting-place for the town guilds, and guild symbols can be seen on many of the tombstones. After that the museum is something of an anticlimax, especially if you find little joy in the sight of stuffed animals.

But it is home to one splendid exhibit: the skeleton of the great Tay whale. How did it come to be here? Let Mr McGonagall explain in his inimitable way:

Twas in the month of December, and in the year of 1883
That a Monster Whale came to Dundee,
Resolved for a few days to sport and play,
And devour the small fishes in the silvery Tay.

The creature made an unfortunate choice, for Dundee was the principal whaling port in Scotland. It was hunted down and the body displayed before it found a skeletal resting place in the museum.

By this time, I had begun to appreciate that Dundee was a city of character, with a rich diversity of themes, but its attractions not limited to its centre. Dominating it to the north is Law Hill, the remains of a volcanic plug, a neat cone from which to view the city. One looks down on Dudhope Park, with the castle which was home to the Constables of

The telescope of the Mills Observatory

Dundee in the thirteenth century. It is due for restoration, but it has not been decided what use will be found for the ancient fort. With so much of the more distant past obliterated, perhaps some way will be found to bring it back into the life of the city. The visit to Law Hill gives you a sense of scale, and Dundee is revealed as a major city and port. At the same time, the panorama shows how closely it is bounded by fine countryside.

I visited more of the outlying areas and was delighted by the Mills Observatory on Balgay Hill, which has a ten-inch refracting telescope. Anyone can wander up in the evening to view the night sky – no credentials needed, no astronomical entry cards. But even if the sky is overcast, the observatory is worth seeing for its own sake. The mechanisms are beautifully simple: the dome is hand cranked open and little effort is required since it is made of papier-mâché. To keep the telescope fixed on the sky, the dome has to rotate in time with the rotating earth, achieved here by beautiful clockwork mechanisms made (I could not resist xenophobically noting) in Yorkshire.

The city also spreads eastwards, where it has swallowed up the old village of Broughty Ferry with its splendid castle. This might be called Dundee-on-Sea, because it is a self-contained spot with its own harbour and character. It is also very much Dundee Posh. The jute magnates made their fortunes in the city, but they celebrated their wealth and built their grand mansions here. For an Englishman it had one special charm: a pub, not a bar or a lounge but a real pub, which sold, among others, the pride of Keighley: Timothy Taylor's bitter. But it was in a way an alien presence, as out of place as on a Parisian boulevard. After a brief visit I was taken to a bar which looked as if it had scarcely changed since the Forties. This was a pint-of-heavy-with-a-Scotch-on-the-side es-tablishment which, to put it at its mildest, had not moved with the times. I should not care to try to buy a drink for a woman in the public bar of that establishment.

Often one receives immediate impressions of a city which are perhaps modified but not fundamentally changed. Dundee is not like that. It displays its qualities only gradually, and the casual visitor could miss them altogether. The longer I stayed the more I enjoyed it. The mistakes of the past are obvious, but they are matched by a determination to rectify them.

I can think of more than one town in Britain where the delights of the past are clearly on view, but one goes away horrified by the deeds of the present and fearful for the future. How very much better to leave wanting to return to see if the dreams of the builders and planners are realised. Dundee provided a splendid exit. The return journey took me across the bridge over the Tay. On this occasion it stood solidly against the waves.

CARDIFF

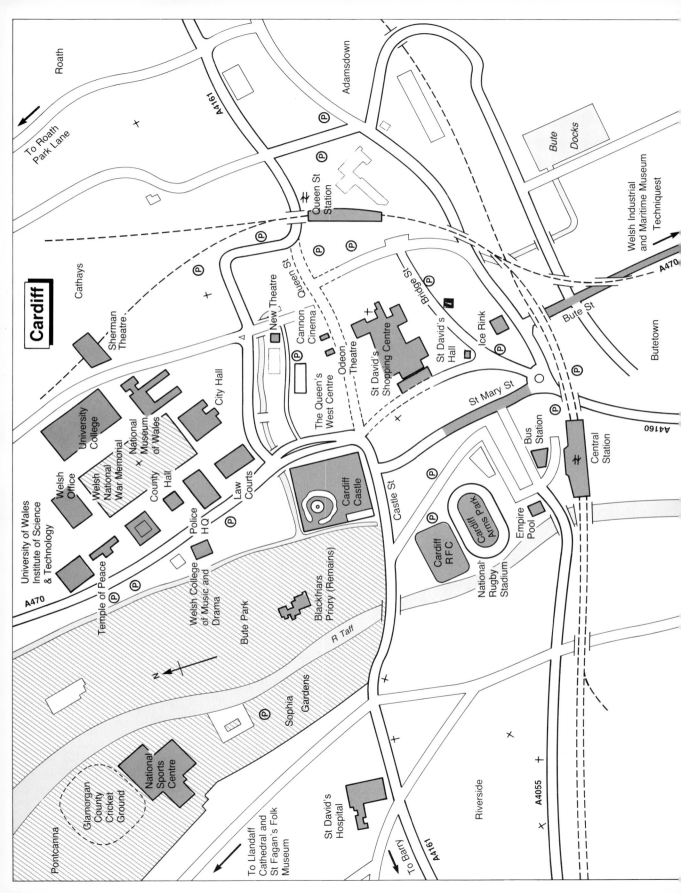

17
CARDIFF

Crossing into Wales is a slight disappoint-ment. Going by train to Scotland, the border country looks like border country; there is the sense of visiting a different land. On the Welsh trip, you disappear into the darkness of the Severn Tunnel and emerge into what looks indistinguishable from the opposite bank of the river. Cardiff soon makes it clear that it is certainly not in England, for almost the first thing to catch the eye is a water-tower decorated with daffodils. Yet going out into the city, even the bilingual street signs are not enough to create a sense of difference. Entering Glasgow, one was immediately con-scious of being in a Scottish city, with its spe-cial building types in the tenements, the liberal spattering of baronial-style decoration and the ubiquitous red sandstone of the region.

Cardiff does not produce the same immedi-ate effect. The major public buildings are very fine, but the stone was brought from Portland. One expects the capital city of Wales to have more of distinctive character than is at once apparent. But I had forgotten what a recent elevation this was: Cardiff achieved city status only at the beginning of this century and was not made the capital until 1955. There was some opposition to the choice, precisely on the grounds that it lacked some essential Welsh elements: the language is not as strong here as in some other parts of the country. But as I made my way to the hotel to drop off my bags, I looked down a side street and saw a building as Welsh as the leek and the daffodil – that great temple of Welshness, Cardiff Arms Park. If you doubt that England and Wales are two nations, I recommend an afternoon on the terraces when the white shirts take the field against the red.

It is interesting to compare Cardiff with Dundee. Where the latter is a great mix-up of a city, with its elements arranged in no logical order, Cardiff is a place of clearly defined zones: the city centre with its shops and offices, the docks and a formal civic area of public buildings. The city centre might seem indistinguishable from other modern shop-ping centres were it not for the dominance of the castle, whose battlements and towers are a backdrop to so many of the streets. Appropriately enough, the huge stands of the Arms Park are the only other structures with the dominating effect of the ancient ramparts. Cardiff is a city which, more than most, still shows clearly the effect of history on its development. So it seemed to be no bad idea to start with the most prominent symbol of the past, the castle itself – and what a good choice it turned out to be. The history of Cardiff can be read in good measure in its castle.

The frontage along Castle Street is somewhat bizarre: the approach is lined by a wall topped with a variety of stone animals, not sitting placidly on the parapet but peering over it, with what looks like aggressive intent.

A lioness peers over the wall of Cardiff Castle

The towers beyond, especially the colourful clock tower, seem to belong to some Bavarian fantasy. There is a romantic dream embodied here, but there is historic fact as well. As soon as you walk through the main gate you are confronted by the great Norman motte or mount topped by a stone keep; but even that does not represent the start of the story. Turning right inside the entrance brings you to the considerable remains of a Roman fortress. The legions came to this strategic site beside the river Taff in the first century AD. At first it had an important role in the conquest of Wales. Then, as more peaceful days followed, the fort became the centre of a settlement.

In the third century it had once again to look to its defences when the barbarian raiders began crossing the channel. Around AD250 a new fort with ten-foot thick stone walls was built, and a 270-foot long stretch of those defences survives under the great bank thrown up by the Norman invaders eight centuries later. The eleventh-century Normans saw the virtues of their predecessors' work and incorporated it into their defences. The castle witnessed dynastic change, battles and sieges

as any other great castle has done, until the time came when castles all over Britain lost their strategic importance. Many of the great fortresses fell into decay, as the keep has done at Cardiff. Some were given a new life, and this happened when the Earl of Bute was created Baron Cardiff of Cardiff Castle in 1776.

At that time Cardiff scarcely qualified as a town, with a population of no more than a thousand. But the Butes were to bring huge wealth to the area, based on the riches of the Industrial Revolution, and the ancient castle was the spectacular expression of their power and position. For a time strenuous efforts were made to turn the castle into a picturesque eighteenth-century house, with grounds landscaped by Capability Brown. Much of the medieval past was removed; buildings were knocked down and the moat filled in.

Then in 1865 the third Marquess of Bute took matters in hand. He had a Victorian and romantic view of the medieval past and, with the enthusiastic help of architect William Burges, set about restoring the castle to a grandeur it had probably never known before. The phrase 'no expense spared' is something of a cliché, but here it has literal truth. There is scarcely a square foot of unadorned surface to be seen: everywhere is decorated in brilliant colours and encased in exotic materials. From the outside, who would expect to find an Arabian fantasy with a splendid stalactite ceiling lurking in Herbert Tower? or anticipate discovering an ornate roof garden on the Bute Tower? There is no pretence of uniformity – anything owner and architect found pleasing was indulged. Medievalism gets its fair share, especially in the chimneypieces. The Earl of Gloucester rides out from a castle above the fireplace in the banqueting hall, waved on his way by the ladies in the battlements, while heralds sound their trumpets; Chaucer presides over his own room in the octagon tower. It is all so extravagant and outrageous as to be endearing.

Having transformed a genuine castle for the Marquess, Burges went on to design an even more elaborate and bizarre imitation for him on the outskirts of the city – Castell Coch. It is so obviously unreal that it is often chosen by film producers as what a genuine medieval castle should be. But the real importance of Castell Coch and the restored Cardiff Castle apartments is in the symbolism of a new Cardiff being born during the time of the Butes. Just outside Cardiff Castle, in Queen Street, is a more modest but telling reminder of this stage in the city's history.

Queen Street is a busy spot, so it is not surprising to find an underpass. What is surprising is to find it arched, with a built-up walkway down one side and, at the end, a metal plate cut with deep grooves. I have seen similar structures many times, but filled with boats floating on water and not pedestrians; the walkway was once a towpath and the grooves were cut by passing towropes. The underpass started life as a canal tunnel. The Glamorgan Canal linked a great new port complex built in the early nineteenth century to the burgeoning industrial centres of South Wales – the coalfields and the ironworks.

Cardiff has been called a port waiting for a city to happen: the Industrial Revolution finally gave the port the cargoes it needed and the city duly followed. From a population of just over a thousand at the start of the nineteenth century it grew to nearly 200,000 by 1914. And there is no escaping the Butes in this time of great change. Bute Street leads down to Butetown and the Bute docks, but like so many cities, Cardiff's old source of prosperity has gone; the days when ships crowded the docks, loading coal and iron, are ended. The old community known romantically as Tiger Bay (though there was little romance about the reality of the area) is little more than a memory. It is an area with a past which is looking for a new future, but has not much to show for the present.

Some aspects of the past are examined in the Welsh Industrial and Maritime Museum, with its array of old steam engines inside and a transport collection ranging from locomotives to canal boats outside. Among them is one special exhibit: a replica of the Trevithick locomotive, the first in the world to haul a train on iron rails. It did so on the old horsedrawn railway which linked the ironworks of Merthyr Tydfil to the Glamorgan Canal at Abercynon. South Wales was not just one of the great industrial regions, it was one of the great innovative regions, and Cardiff is the end product of the wealth created in the valleys.

Now the life has gone from the docks and the once busy piers are rotting islands. Cargo boats have been replaced by a smattering of small yachts and dinghies. Cardiff has realised that a waterfront has its own attractions and developments are well advanced, even if it is too early to see where they will lead. One side of the new thinking can be seen in the other 'museum' across the road from the industrial museum – Techniquest, a place to do things. This is 'hands on', with everything to be touched and used, a place to experiment and a place of oddities, which start with the entrance. You appear to enter through solid wooden beams which form a triangle. It is, of course, a clever three-dimensional optical illusion, a realisation of the so-called impossible triangle. Like everything else, it is there to teach a lesson while being good fun. So on one side of the road there is a monument to past technology, and on the other a glimpse into the scientific basis of future technologies. That seems about the right mix for a city which passed through the Industrial Revolution and

The Queen's West shopping centre

is now facing the post-industrial revolution. In a sense too they neatly round off this quick gallop through Cardiff's history. So what of the city as it is now?

The shopping and commercial centre has many of the already familiar elements. Like Leeds, it boasts some fine, ornate Edwardian shopping arcades. As in Leicester, it generally pays to raise your eyes above the shopfronts, because the upper storeys are a parade of architectural styles and it is clear that many streets were not planned, but simply happened. Buildings were slipped into whatever space was available and built to whatever style the newcomer fancied, with scant regard for the neighbours.

St Mary Street is an excellent example, with shaped gables butting on to classical pediments; stone mixing in with brick and plaster and styles ranging from Dutch to Italianate. The street is also memorable for its special and unmistakable aroma – the scent of brewing. Brain make their beer here (and very good it is too) and Cardiff has enjoyable pubs to drink it in. The Cardiff town pub is very much like its English equivalent; there is none of the cultural shock one finds in Scottish taverns.

Inevitably, Cardiff has its new shopping centres, as typical of their time as St Mary Street and the arcades are of theirs. St David's Centre is the big one, stretching across and engulfing the old street pattern. It has all the multiples under one roof for traffic-free shopping, but is dull as dull can be. No Eighties' centre can be built without an atrium – a device already becoming an architectural cliché, but the Queen's West centre is bolder than most. It is based on a criss-crossing grid which is on display as the main feature, supporting a wall of glass. The result is literally bright, and the atrium is a practical area housing

the escalators and enlivened by trees. It is unashamedly high-tech and has the courage of its convictions.

Cardiff is a good place to compare the architectural thinking of today and that of the recent past. The National Westminster Bank have new offices in the popular neo-vernacular; bricks instead of concrete and a façade enlivened by contrasting vertical bands of yellow and red brick. Not as bold as Queen's West, it might not even be worth mentioning were it not that it stands next to an earlier office development, Caerwys House. This looks Sixties but is early Seventies, and is the worst sort of system building. A series of concrete panels with standardised openings were stuck together like so many Lego blocks. Just around the corner, however, is Windsor Place, which demonstrates how the builders of one period can borrow successfully from an earlier age. This is a dignified Victorian terrace, based on Georgian notions of what a city street should be. The move from Windsor Place to Caerwys House is entirely retrograde: the NatWest moves back to some sort of sanity.

Cardiff has one of the major attributes I look for in a city. You can wander aimlessly and come up with views which surprise and delight. With so much of the city being Victorian or later, it is a joy to find the old parish church lifting its tower 130 feet above the surrounding streets. It is on a Norman foundation, but most of the present building is fifteenth century. It is attractive and unusual. The Herbert Chapel of the early seventeenth century is a real treasure, not just for its elaborate memorial to the Herberts but for its superb carved wooden screens. The tower is unusual in having a raised platform with seats looking down over the aisles. It was all restored in the 1880s but not, for once, out of all recognition.

The church is a private, secluded spot, but

The civic buildings of Cathays Park

cities have their public gestures too. I am always intrigued to see whom a city chooses to honour in bronze or stone, and here is Nye Bevan in pugnacious mood, emphasising a point with a stabbing forefinger. This at least is evidence of Welshness, for few politicians so completely belonged to their constituencies as did Bevan to the valleys of south Wales. Other public gestures can be seen in the formal cultural life of the city. Cardiff has in St David's Hall one of Britain's finest concert halls – most would demur only at the suggestion that there might be any better or as good. Like Scotland, Wales has its own opera company, which is one of the most exciting in the land. But where most cities look for bravura displays is in their municipal buildings, and here Cardiff is unique.

The Cathays Park area is laid out on a street grid in which imposing buildings front formal parks. It has no echoes of other British civic centres, but seems to stand in the tradition one sees in Washington or New Delhi. To build like this you need space and self-confidence, and at the end of the nineteenth century Cardiff had an abundance of both. The land was bought up in readiness for the time when it would achieve city status, and in 1901 the foundations were laid for a new City Hall. When it was completed in 1905, the city was officially born. By now, Victorian gothic was out and Edwardian baroque was in. The dominant features are the dome and the tall clock tower topped by a Welsh dragon. The outside is restrained, clean cut in dazzling white stone; the interior is a richer mix. A wide staircase leads up from the entrance to the Marble Hall, where columns of Siena marble provide an imposing setting for the white marble statues – the Heroes of Wales. They are a mixed lot, presided over by Wales' own patron saint. There are warriors and poets, Methodist ministers and kings, and I confess to knowing nothing whatsoever about most of them. Geraldus Cambrensis and Hywel Dda were as foreign to me as the ancient heroes of Peru, which is perhaps a comment on the narrowness of English history teaching.

The new City Hall set a standard and a pattern which was followed in the other major buildings – the Law Courts, the University, the County Hall and, most especially, the National Museum of Wales. Although the museum is neo-classical rather than baroque (still considered *de rigueur* for a museum), it was designed to match its neighbour. It is similar in size and its entrance is also topped by a dome. Its collection is worthy of a national museum, but it was not the famous works of art which held my attention. I was really impressed with the imaginative way archaeological finds are displayed and explained. Cases full of flints or Bronze Age axes can be less than enthralling: but did you ever wonder how such artefacts were made? Here there are push-button videos to show you. Experts of today, using the tools and techniques of the ancients, were filmed trying to make them. Unlike their predecessors of, say, the Bronze Age, they had a good knowledge of metallurgical theory, but their efforts were nowhere near as good as those of 3000 years ago. It was charming to find that the experts allowed their mistakes to go on public view, and it gave a new perspective to the skills of the ancient craftsmen. It also gave the National Museum a rather homely feel amid the strict formality of this city centre.

There comes a time when the needs of the stomach seem infinitely more important than those of the mind. I have always kept my eyes open for local food, but seldom find it. In Cardiff I found a true champion of Welsh cooking, or rather two champions – Patricia and Meirion Dally who run the Blas ar Gymru restaurant. The name, like the menu, may be in Welsh but there are translations for foreigners from across the Severn. Two things are soon apparent: Welsh food has its own distinctive dishes and the Dallys are not devotees of the daintily-arranged-minute-morsels-on-an-octagonal-plate school of cooking. They expect their customers to go away replete. So what was particularly Welsh? I had heard of *Bara Lawr â chig moch*, or laver bread with bacon, and laver bread is seaweed. I liked it very much, but I was told by a Welshman that it was real laver bread only if it still had sand stuck to it. I hope he was joking.

I followed that with Lady Llanover's salt duck, one of those dishes the cook cannot rush. The duck is covered in salt for three days, turned and salted again and then cooked in a double pan with frequent basting. The recipe was in Lady Llanover's *The First Principles of Good Cooking*, published in 1867. She was married to Benjamin Llanover who, as Commissioner of Works for the House of Commons, had his name immortalised in Big Ben. I was talked into trying Welsh wine, which was actually very good, but refused a Welsh whisky on the grounds that I had tried it once and had no intention of repeating the experiment. But it was pleasing to find such passionate enthusiasm for local dishes made from local produce.

The next day was set aside for wandering to the outskirts of the city. Such excursions sometimes involve long walks through dreary suburbs, but the inhabitants of Cardiff have their own escape routes. Bute Park – yet another gift of the Butes to the city – stretches for over two miles along the banks of the Taff. It is a mixture of natural riverside and formal parkland, and it is a lovely place to stroll. If you look ahead to the hills, it is not difficult to believe that you are on a genuine country walk. I was, however, distracted by shouts and cries and the sight of familiar dark and light blue shirts. It was not Cardiff rugby team strayed from the Arms Park, but the police playing a neighbouring force. At least it was Cardiff and rugby.

If you follow the park and the river, you will reach Cardiff's village, Llandaff. It stands in relation to the city rather as 'villages' such as Hampstead or Dulwich do to London; part of the greater whole, yet separate from it. Its own distinctive atmosphere is centred on Llandaff Cathedral. The cathedral, surprisingly, hides away in a hollow, so that even the spire seems scarcely to rise much above road level. It is not a very old building, but it is a very ancient Christian site. The first community

Llandaff Cathedral

was established here in the sixth century, when the sea raiders against whom the Romans built their fortress were still active, even if they now came from Scandinavia. In these circumstances it was unwise to advertise one's presence, and a secluded hollow was far safer than a proud hill. The cathedral built by the shrine of the founder St Teilo was there to serve pilgrims not wealthy businessmen and traders, so when pilgrimages were stopped by Henry VIII it fell into decay. It nearly became a Georgian church, but nothing came of those

St Fagan's, home of the Welsh Folk Museum

plans and it was left to the Victorians to restore the old fabric.

Llandaff Cathedral has not been blessed with good fortune, for restoration was scarcely finished when the bombs of the twentieth century undid the work of the nineteenth. So it all had to be done again and in the new version it received its most striking feature. The nave is spanned by a concrete arch, above which stands Epstein's great statue of Christ in Majesty. It is as bold as the Sutherland tapestry at Coventry. Visitors who want to brush up on their royal history can tour the outside of the building, where they will find carved in stone the heads of all monarchs up to and including the present Queen.

Llandaff has a cosy Home Counties feel to it, and those who come down the main road from town find the effect even more marked. You pass rows of solidly respectable villas, with suitably gothic motifs in deference to the name Cathedral Road. One begins to see why fervent nationalists were not overjoyed at the thought of Cardiff as the capital city. It is possible that I was looking too assiduously for some indefinable thing called Welshness, something to distinguish this city conclusively from an English city. But if you turn the proposition round, what is there about a city across the Severn to distinguish it as essentially English? Of course there are differences, real differences, between the two countries, but they are more pronounced away from the city centre. This is not surprising. Cardiff Castle was built by invading Normans, and the city developed on the tide of industrialisation which spread from England. Even the individual who did more than anyone to shape the town held his title from an island off the Scottish coast. The buildings seldom reflect a local origin; the local atmosphere, the Welsh atmosphere, derives from the people not from brick and stone. Yet one can find buildings which do have distinctive characteristics and which one could not find anywhere else.

You have to go to St Fagan's (pronounced with a flat 'a' as in faggot) and the Welsh Folk Museum. The name seems a little unfortunate, for it tends to suggest country dancing and singing through the nose, whereas it is a fine open-air site where all kinds of vernacular buildings have been brought together and re-erected. Some were originally working buildings, and these have been returned to use: the Esgair Moel Woollen Mill still uses all the machinery needed to turn the fleece off the sheep's back into flannel, while the wheels of the watermill turn the grindstones to produce flour. Other buildings seem to carry even stronger associations: how easy it is to imagine Welsh hymns resounding round the chapel. But for me the domestic buildings carry the clearest message. A row of miners' cottages seem to take one straight back to visions of so many similar terraces lined up beneath the spoil heaps and whirring headstocks of the collieries of the valleys. There are oddities, such as the circular pigsty, but by far my favourite building was the simple cottage constructed from the massive boulders of Snowdonia. Here, at least, was a building which derives every scrap of character it possesses from having been built in that particular mountainside location. St Fagan's tells a social as well as an architectural story, and succeeds in putting Cardiff itself within the context of the country of which it is capital. It reminds the visitor that the wealth so ostentatiously on display in the castle was created among the filth and the smoke of the industries in the valleys.

SWANSEA

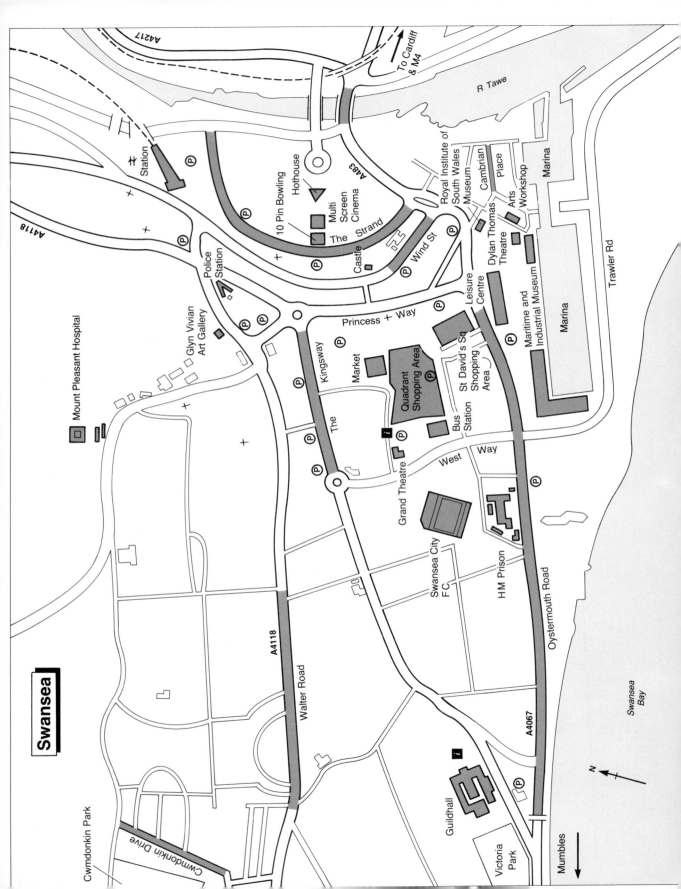

18
SWANSEA

Whatever I might have thought about a lack of contrast between the views on either side of the Severn, no such thought occurred on the journey between Cardiff and Swansea. Here was landscape which pronounced itself wholly and completely south Wales from the moment the train crossed the Taff, its bank dominated by the stands of the Arms Park.

To the north, hills covered with bracken reached down almost to the tracks, interrupted only by long, isolated terraces of houses. These were unmistakably part of the valley scene; what might have been dull, off-the-peg Victorian houses were prinked out in brilliant colours. In many, the stone of window surrounds and quoins were painted a different colour from the rest of the wall, so that the overall effect was of a brilliant patchwork. The houses sang out from the sombre colours of the bracken, which was turning an autumnal brown. To the south, the world of heavy industry still dominated the scene. There were memories of former days in the fortress-like stone blast furnaces of Neath, while their successors appeared in still more monumental proportions in the rolling mills and furnaces of Port Talbot. It is this conjunction of heavy industry and wild scenery which has always made this area special. In the past, Swansea partook of both worlds, but of all the cities I visited it is the one where continuity seemed at first sight to have been most decisively broken.

It was a coincidence that on successive trips I visited a pair of cities: one big with the legacies of history over it; the second quite small and with an apparently nondescript city centre. Swansea has an excuse for its centre – the old was flattened by bombs in three nights of raids during February 1941. There was an urgent need to rebuild and no one pretends that what was put up had any great merit. If that were all there was to Swansea, I would have been on the platform waiting for the first train home. This is not the case, and even as the train eased its way down the bank of the Tawe towards the station there were hints of better things.

The tidal river still has remnants of wharves and the outline of old industrial buildings and spoil heaps: the world of my south-facing train window. But the other world was here as well. Look down almost any street in the city centre and there is a glimpse of countryside at its end. And Swansea has something extra: the sea. What was by no means obvious on that first inspection was any sense of a historic city. As with Dundee, you have to hunt it down.

Swansea has a long and interesting history starting with its establishment as a Viking trading port. Its fine position made it equally attractive to the Normans and it developed slowly through the centuries. But no part of south Wales was to escape the effects of the Industrial Revolution. The surrounding countryside was rich in coal, while across the Bristol Channel were the copper mines of Devon and Cornwall. To get the metal from the ore you have to heat it in a furnace: Cornwall had the ore but no coal; Swansea the coal but no ore. As you need more coal for the smelting process than ore, the sensible answer was to bring the ore to Swansea, where copper works were established as early as 1717. The metal was so abundant that for the first time British coins could be struck from British metal. It is hard now to imagine the works with their belching chimneys which once lined the Tawe, the mountains of black slag and the harbour crammed with trading ships.

I got an inkling of Swansea's former impor-tance on a visit to the other side of the world. I had gone to look at the wrecks and hulks of the Falkland Islands and was amazed to find how many of the ships which ended their days there had been engaged in taking copper ore not from Cornwall but all the way from South America to the smelters of Swansea. It was not a romantic trade: the smelters were filthy and the whole town must have lain under a permanent pall, but a Swansea man expressed this view in the nineteenth century: 'One must not think of the beautiful, but of the useful with a capital U. Nobody talks of sea views or mountains here, but of how many ships were cleared last week.'

A new housing development between the sea and the marina

The days of the smelters are ended, and you hear a good deal of talk about mountains and sea views. Old Swansea would not have considered the possibility of tourism playing more than a minor role in its economy, and the rebuilt centre might lead a modern visitor to concur. There are, however, more appealing views. North of the shopping area, streets climb vertiginously up to terraces of neat villas. Many of the houses show the same love of colour and the technique of contrasting paintwork as in the terraces of the valleys.

It seemed worth exploring, and at least offered good exercise. The streets are so steep that paving stones are not set straight but angled against each other. This is not uncommon in city streets, but here it is done deliberately to provide ridges which stop people going downhill as impromptu skiers. The first terrace is backed by a cliff, above which sits another layer; then from the top the whole of Swansea is spread out like a map. Few buildings stand out – there is not much in the way of tower blocks in Swansea – but what one sees is the overall pattern along the great sweep of Swansea Bay. In the east are the distant smoking towers of Port Talbot; closer, the Tawe winds down to the docks; while to the west the curve ends at the Mumbles, beyond which the Gower Peninsula stretches. Looking down on the beaches of Swansea, you could as easily believe you are viewing Torbay in Devon as the old industrial heartland of South Wales. This is one of the secrets of Swansea's appeal: the second largest city in Wales is also in part a pleasant seaside town.

One route down from the high terraces takes you along a steep suburban street, much like others, of pleasant semis. But a little plaque on No 5 Cwmdonkin Drive announces itself as the birthplace and early home of Dylan Thomas. He looked out on the 'world within a world' of 'miniature woods and jungles' of Cwmdonkin Park and took in the wider views of his home town, which he described in words which would not be used in a promotional brochure: 'An ugly, lovely town (or so it was, and is, to me) crawling, sprawling, slummed, unplanned, jerry-villa'd, and smug-suburbed by the side of a long and splendid curving shore.'

It is hard to shake off the Thomas images: was it one of these 'trig and trim' villas which he saw as Bay View, home to Mrs Ogmore-Pritchard? Trudging up and down the hills, one can readily agree on the need to be a sherpa to live here. But there is one phrase that stays in the mind: the ugly, lovely town. That is precisely what Swansea is, and it will probably be the saving of the place, for it seems unlikely to become merely a picturesque spot to gawp at. I sherpa'd my way back down and set off to see what the centre had to offer.

There is something of a problem in getting to grips with old Swansea. It obviously grew up around the castle built to protect the river approaches. No problem there, because at the far eastern end of the town are the scant remains of the old fortress overlooking The Strand, a likely name except that there is no river in view. The answer lies in the New Cut; the old winding river was unsuitable for the increased trade and was diverted into a new straight channel. The area around the castle was quite literally left high and dry. It is a great area to poke around for traces of the Swansea that escaped the bombs. Here are remains of old quays and warehouses whose working lives have long since ended and which have gone through many uses since the last sailing ship tied up beneath the castle wall.

Wind Street, one of the main thoroughfares of the ancient city, is full of interest. One very old building has survived, but again in altered form. There was once a church of St

The castle

Mary beside the castle wall, and in the 1330s the Bishop of Gower decreed that a hospital should be built for the care of priests. At the Dissolution of the monasteries, the hospital became an inn, but kept its link with its Catholic past in its name, the Cross Keys – and the Cross Keys it remains.

This end of the city has changed and is changing. The surviving warehouses look out on a rash of new developments which include a tropical hothouse, like an overgrown transparent wedge of cheese. A barrage is now under construction across the river, so the Tawe will be altered yet again, its waters controlled for new projects along its banks. I looked in on the Glynn Vivian Art Gallery, which is no doubt an excellent place but was taken up with a special exhibition mounted as part of the Swansea Festival. One of the disadvantages of travel is that when exhibitions travel as well, you are likely to meet them more than once: Swansea had the show which I saw in Leeds.

The pattern of streets in the old part of the city runs north to south, following the line of the river. The post-war builders set down a basic east-west pattern, following wide boulevards of respectable Victorian villas, such as Walter Road. The Kingsway was built with the new demands of traffic in mind, but the buildings have dull, slab-faced façades. Only rarely does a note of excitement creep in, as with the dejected but intrinsically interesting art deco Union of Shop, Distributive and Allied Workers (USDAW) headquarters in Mansel Street, a splendid Baptist chapel and an even grander bingo hall. But things are changing here as well.

The new Quadrant Shopping Centre would be indistinguishable from a dozen others were it not for its clock, which is not, in any way, a static exhibit. Every so often one clock goes and another appears, but they are all lively affairs. I found the current incumbent charming: it was built as a model watermill and as the hour strikes everything moves. The waterwheel turns the grindstone, the sack goes up on the hoist and the miller gets to work. Alongside the new shops is the covered market. Swansea has a long market tradition, starting with a street market of eight centuries ago. What makes this covered market special is not the building but the produce on sale. Cardiff gave me a taste of Wales in a restaurant; here it was on display: local specialities galore and none more typical than cockles. If you want a snack, just pop into the market and pick up a pot of cockles. Having been cockling, admittedly in an inefficient, amateurish way, I have some idea of the effort involved in collecting these little beasts. But out on Gower this is still a regular trade, and you can still see the cockle carts going out over the sands as they have for generations. You can also see where they are boiled up, easily identified by the huge heaps of discarded shells. Incidentally, cockle shells make a good 'gravel' drive.

Next door to the market is the Grand Theatre. If the cities on my tour had one thing in common, it was an enthusiasm for restoring their Victorian theatres. The Grand can stand comparison with the best: its auditorium has the rich splendour of plush and gilt one expects of an interior designed in the 1890s, but new stage facilities have been provided. Theatres such as this have a mixed repertoire: they mount their own productions, take in touring companies such as Welsh National Opera and even lavish musicals. The Grand is able to take them all. Their scenery dock is huge: pantechnicons back straight in, and the stage machinery handles whatever they bring. The theatre also extends an invitation to the community as a whole by opening up its bar and restaurant and mounting exhibitions.

The extension to the old Grand marks

Sculpture at the marina

the start of a new development centred on the Quadrant which will take the centre southwards towards what is already a major redevelopment centre, cut off by the busy Oystermouth Road. It is similar to the Dundee problem, and the solutions too are similar. The Quadrant is to be extended at first-floor level so that the road will simply not exist so far as shoppers are concerned. And, as at Dundee, the new system will reunite the city with its waterfront. Unlike Dundee, however, the waterfront development is well advanced.

The area known as the Maritime Quarter is centred on what was the old South Dock, which connects through the Tawe basin to the river. It comes as no surprise to find a marina development, but what is remarkable about Swansea is the extraordinary mixture of elements which come together here – some, it must be said, more comfortably than others. To start with the most important element, houses and the people who live in them: whatever form the marina took it was going to be an attractive focal point. A lot of people would fancy a house with the bay on one side and a marina of cheerful boats on the other. There is the added attraction of a number of historic craft, from a steam tug and a light vessel to a beautiful old pilot cutter. I am not quite so sure about a replica eighteenth-century three-master, used as floating bars and restaurant. Given the overall attractions, here was a situation ripe for high-cost development. But what happened instead is that priority has been given to rehousing the occupants of the rundown terraces of dockland, and there is also an element of sheltered housing. Swansea is creating a village which, like all the best villages, will house a mixture of people. There are council houses and luxury houses, one-room studio flats and town houses, not to mention a floating, if temporary, population living on boats.

In the enthusiasm to build anew, the old has not been forgotten. Cambrian Place was, and indeed still is, the finest street in Swansea, built between 1812 and 1825 with all the elegant refinement one expects of that period. The Assembly Rooms, with an array of Doric columns, adds to its attraction. Old dock offices, the hydraulic pump-house and ware-houses have been retained and put to new uses. Not all the conversions are equally successful, but there is certainly an interesting variety.

The Maritime and Industrial Museum has its ships on the water and other exhibits in a former transit shed. They are cramped for space, which is not surprising when you consider that the building includes a working woollen mill. This is no handicraft exhibit, but a genuine industrial unit with all its machinery, including my favourites – the spinning mules. Other buildings have equally interesting uses: an arts workshop, where potters produce some of the most exciting work I have seen for a long time; and a splendid little theatre named,

Dylan Thomas looking at the marina

inevitably, after Swansea's most famous artistic citizen. Dylan Thomas sits stonily nearby listening, no doubt, to one of the regular performances of *Under Milk Wood*. Sculpture enlivens the scene – and lively is the word for it – while stone plaques set all around the basin depict different aspects of the city's maritime history. The objective which has been kept in view in the Maritime Quarter was to maintain a rich variety of both buildings and use: old sits next to new; workspace exists beside the leisure activities. A trawler disguised as a frigate and a slot machine amusement arcade would not have been my first choice of amenities, but accepting variety means accepting elements which appeal to a wide range of people. It would not be hard to find locals who would rather listen to the one-armed bandits than to Thomas's verse. Diversity brings vitality and there is nothing precious or exclusive about this development.

North of the Maritime Quarter is the leisure centre which offers a hydro slide, where bathers zoom down a transparent tube which takes them outside the walls and brings them back to the splashdown in the pool. Between the centre and the marina is a high embankment, a reminder of an important and historic feature of the city. In the early days of industrialisation, canals were the rage and there was a suggestion that one be dug out towards the quarries of Oystermouth. The idea was rejected and in 1804 work began on a railway along which trucks could be hauled by horses. The local citizens were as interested in moving themselves to the beaches of Mumbles as they were in moving goods, so in 1807 a passenger service was started on the Swansea and Mumbles Railway. It was the first of its kind in the world. Some passengers loved it: Miss Spence, travelling in 1808, declared that she 'never spent an afternoon with more delight', but travel writer Richard Ayton was less enthusiastic in 1813 about the shake, rattle and roll railway. The noise of the carriages was like 'twenty sledge hammers in full play', while the poor passenger was so hurled about and reduced to a state of dizziness 'that it is well if he recovers in a week'. By the end of the nineteenth century steam trains had joined horse trams on the line, which was extended to Mumbles Head. On public holidays as many as 40,000 passengers travelled. It was electrified in 1929 and closed in 1960. As is so often the way, Swansea at once began missing its little seaside line and regretting its departure. There are many voices saying that it should be brought back again. If you travel out along its route, you will see why.

Travelling west nowadays means following the Oystermouth Road, which runs between the prison and county hall: architecturally, the prison is the slightly more attractive of the two. Beyond that is the Guildhall. The old Guildhall was a modest affair, built at the same time as Cambrian Place and using a Doric style similar to the Assembly Rooms. It was extended and redesigned in the more florid Corinthian style in 1848. It is still there, but empty and more than a little woebegone. The new building was begun in the 1930s and is as good an example of the period as Cambrian Place is of the Regency.

A competition was held for the best design and won by Percy Thomas. His scheme had all the different elements of the new public buildings organised around a central courtyard: council chambers, administration, law courts and an area for the general public. It must have been beautifully light and airy, but increased demand for offices has resulted in the courtyard's being filled. At least the original exterior design was retained and the individual elements inside preserved, even if the view from the corridors has been lost. There is a monumentalism about the building, derived partly from its main entrance with its massive arched doorway, above which rises a slender tower.

The main entrance hall is on an equally large scale, but vaulted corridors leading from it ensure that the working spaces are not too daunting. Motifs are Viking, commemorating the Norse foundation of 'Sweyn's Ey', the island of Sweyn. Sweyn was a common Norse name; no records exist to contradict the theory, so the citizens of Swansea have assumed that their Sweyn was Sweyn Forkbeard, king of Denmark and briefly king of England in the early eleventh century. It is, after all, much better to have a genuine king as founder rather than just any old passing Sweyn.

The interior matches the exterior in typifying its period. One room, which borrowed its style not from Scandinavia but from Pompeii, still has its original furnishings and even its Thirties' carpet. But far and away the grandest part is Brangwyn Hall. In 1924, the artist Frank Brangwyn was commissioned to paint a series of panels for the House of Lords,

The water slide wriggling in and out of the swimming pool

and showed the huge diversity of people, plants and animals to be found in the old British Empire. There were seventeen panels in all, each on a scale to match the setting and breadth of the subject matter. Then the Lords decided that worthy portraits of themselves were more in keeping with the dignity of the House than colourful pictures of foliage, peacocks and bare-breasted African women. The Lords rejects became Swansea's gain – a bold decision for a local authority to take. Brangwyn was an artist of such influence that he got the ceiling of the hall raised to give better proportions, and there they hang today. I went to a concert in Brangwyn Hall and discovered that it is acoustically quite superb. Swansea did not become a city until 1969, but there was no need to worry about providing public buildings. They were there, ready and waiting.

Beyond the Guildhall, Oystermouth Road becomes Mumbles Road and Swansea shows its other face. More and more it takes on the attributes of a seaside town. A little 1920s' pavilion in Victoria Park is another good example of this period, and was donated to the city by the famous singer, Adelina Patti. Beyond that the bay with its beaches and golf course reaches around to Mumbles. Officially Swansea is not just the built-up centre but Mumbles and most of the Gower Peninsula. So all this is the city, even if there is precious little city life about it.

With its pier and its cottages clambering the steep hillside, Mumbles is everyone's idea of what a little seaside town should be, and the Gower is incomparable. It was the first designated area of outstanding natural beauty in Britain and there is no disputing the description. There are busy beaches and secluded coves; little narrow lanes and bracken-covered hills. On one side are tall cliffs and a sea which pounds the beaches with long, curling waves; on the other a mysterious land of marshes, creeks and reeds and the flat, muddy beaches where the cocklers work beneath the circling, titbit-hunting gulls. This is Swansea's back garden; it is where the citizens come out to play, and there could be no better garden than this.

The new city is both town and country. The growing tourist industry needs them both: Swansea for wet days, Gower for the dry. But the real city will survive and prosper only if it is something more than a jumping-off place for sea and scenery, however splendid they might be. There is every sign that it is building towards a more exciting future. I kept comparing it with Dundee, partly because I had come almost straight from one to the other, but mainly because they have similar problems. In each case there was a sense of moving in new and often exciting directions while still keeping in touch with the past. In both, the first glance was a little dismaying; from both I came away cheered and heartened and wanting to return.

I set out on my travels uncertain about what I should find. It is so easy to pass through a city and see no more than the anonymous accretions of the twentieth century. Was it going to be a waste of time? Had distinctive character been swamped in an orgy of redevelopment? At the end I could say: not yet. It was depressing to see how dull so much post-war building was, and how far the needs of the cities had been made subservient to the convenience of the motorist. The good news was that they still have immense vitality, and there is a new powerful movement to assert the need for individuality, the sense each city has of its distinctive personality. No one can avoid seeing the problems, but I was struck by the optimism and energy with which they are being tackled. I turned for home with the happy feeling that time has not yet eroded the personalities of these cities. They are still unique and strong.